THE GURDWARA REFORM MOVEMENT AND THE SIKH AWAKENING

THE GURDWARA REFORM MOVEMENT

AND

THE SIKH AWAKENING

TEJA SINGH

GYAN

Published by

GYAN

Gyan Publishing House
5, Ansari Road
Daryaganj, New Delhi-110002
Phone: 011-47034999, 9811692060
E-mail: books@gyanbooks.com

Distribution Network
gyanbooks.com
India, USA, Canada, UK, Australia

ISBN: 978-93-7014-449-1 (PB)

First Published, 1922

2nd Impression 2025

Printed at: Gyan Press, Delhi.

THE GURDWARA REFORM MOVEMENT AND THE SIKH AWAKENING
Author: TEJA SINGH

SAT SRI AKAL

THE

Gurdwara Reform Movement

AND

THE SIKH AWAKENING.

1922

FOREWORD.

I consider it an honour to be asked to introduce this book to the public with a few words of my own. In the rapid march of events all over the country during the past two years, nowhere has Mahatma Gandhi's non-violent non-co-operation been so completely vindicated as at Tarn Taran, Nankana Sahib and Guru-ka-bagh by the calm and cool courage, and the patient, and even cheerful, sufferings of the Akalis in the face of cruelties, inhumanities and death. The story of the recent remarkable awakening among the Sikhs, their struggles for the freedom and purification of their historical places of worship, their disappointments and triumphs, will, I am sure, be read everywhere with absorbing interest. As an eye-witness of some of the thrilling, if tragic, incidents narrated by the author, I cannot help remarking that the simple rustics, who mainly composed the Akali Jathas, appeared to us as the heroes of a twentieth century Epic which was being enacted before our very eyes. I hope it will not be long before the story of their heroism, inspired by a sublime idealism, is immortalised in verse by a poet of eminence. It certainly deserves to be enshrined in our memories with the same love, regard and admiration as the ancient Epics are treasured to-day.

In understanding the Akali movement, three facts, all connected with the early Sikh history, should clearly be borne in mind—

(1). *The democratic character of the Sikh faith.*

I doubt very much if any other religion enjoins upon its adherents equality between man and man more persistently and with greater strictness than Sikhism. It is well known that Maharaja Ranjit Singh was once arraigned before the Akal Takht on a charge of 'associating with an evil woman' and, as the author mentions, Guru Gobind Singh himself was, on a certain occasion, fined for a slight deviation from the rules of conduct laid down by himself. The Panth is considered to be supreme in all matters and none may defy its behests with impunity, whatever his rank and position in life may be.

Sacrifice and service are the sole tests for the faithful. The first five men who came forward to offer themselves, one after the other, to be literally sacrificed, as they believed, for the sake of the Panth, are the 'Beloved Ones' (*Panj Piyare*) of the community for all time to come. In the daily prayer of the

Sikhs, they are remembered along with the name of the last Guru. They were the first men to be initiated into the *Panth* by Guru Gobind Singh, and it was they who, in their turn, were considered fit to initiate the Guru himself. The initiation ceremony requires the Sikhs to consider themselves as belonging to the same race (Sodhbans) as the Guru himself. And, as some of the Beloved Ones happened to belong to low castes, all distinctions arising from caste, rank and profession are completely obliterated.

(2). *The Gurdwaras as centres of the religious, social and political life of the Panth.*

In the mind of the Sikhs, the question of the purification and freedom of the Gurdwaras has always been associated with their national destiny, and no sacrifices have been considered too great to make for bringing them under the control of the Panth. The fact is that the important Gurdwaras are either connected with one or another striking incident in the lives of the Gurus themselves, or they have been erected in memory of the numerous martyrs who gave up their lives, under very trying circumstances, in defence of their faith, during the long period of persecution to which the Sikhs were subjected. Many of these martyrs are also remembered in the daily prayer of the Sikhs along with the ten Gurus. All religious and social ceremonies of the Sikhs, from birth to death, must be performed in the presence of the Holy Book and often within the precincts of the Gurdwaras. Wherever the Sikhs have gone, they have carried with them a passionate longing for the freedom of their Gurdwaras, and, it is no exaggeration to say that, the control of the Golden Temple and other principal places of worship by the Panth as a whole has always been looked upon as a measure of their religious, social and even political liberties.

(3). *The Gurdwaras as Seats of Authority.*

Four Gurdwaras, namely, the Akal Takht, Anandpur Sahib, Patna Sahib and Hazoor Sahib (Nander in Hyderabad Deccan) are looked as the "Four Thrones" of authority, from which commandments for the guidance of the community are issued every now and again. Of these, the authority of the Akal Takht, which is situated opposite the entrance to the Golden Temple at Amritsar, is regarded as supreme, and all orders issued therefrom are considered as binding upon the whole Panth. The Akal Takht was founded by the sixth Guru, Guru Har Gobind, in 1609. It was here that he put on the sword which marked an important point in the development of the Sikhs as a martial race. All classes of men and women have, from time to time, approached those in charge of the Akal Takht to seek for help and protection against the tyranny of the strong and the wicked. On the other hand, the award of a robe of honour by the authorities of the Golden Temple or the Akal Takht has ever been regarded as a mark of very special favour, which is only conferred on those who may have rendered distinguished services either to the Panth or the public at large. The possession of these two historical places of worship obviously means, for the Sikhs, vastly more than their care-taking. Those entrusted with the sacred charge are regarded as the Interpreters of the inner-most longings and aspirations of the Panth. But in the hands of men unacceptable to the community, the control may degenerate into tyranny over the mind and conscience of the worshippers. A couple of illustrations will make this clear. The story of Baba Gurdit Singh's patriotic enterprise in chartering the 'Komagata Maru' and its aftermath is well known. A commandment issuing from the Akal Takht in 1915 condemned the Komagata Maru Sikhs. This gave rise to widespread indignation among the Sikhs. It was felt that the authority of the Akal Takht had been used for purposes for which it was never intended. Again, in 1919, immediately after the Jallianwala Bagh massacre, General Dyer had the audacity to present himself before the Golden Temple and was actually awarded a robe of honour by the Government-appointed Manager of the Gurdwara. It was on the strength of this mark of favour that General Dyer and his friends in the House of Lords boasted that the Sikhs had not only placed their seal of approval on his exploits, but that they had gone to the length of admitting him to their fraternity. The whole Khalsa Panth was scandalised and numerous meetings were held to condemn the action of the Golden Temple authorities.

It was in circumstances like these that the Gurdwara Reform Movement entered on its latest phase a couple of years back. A representative committee, now well known all over the country as the Shromani Gurdwara Prabandhak Committee, was formed. An active and well organised propaganda for securing the control of all the historical Gurdwaras was started. For a detailed account of the struggles, sufferings and achievements of the Committee, I cannot do better than refer the reader to the pages of this book.

LAHORE: } RUCHI RAM SAHNI
15th December 1922.

TABLE OF CONTENTS.

ERRATA.

Page.	Line.	
1	2	Read *his* for *this.*
,,	12	Read *Bedar* for *Behar.*
57	24	Read *agricultural* for *agriculture.*
69	16	Read *requested* for *request.*
72	3 of the footnote	After *arrested* add: *on 7th March, when he came to Amritsar to pay his respects.*
73	4	Read *on* for *upon.*
79	20	Read *provided* for *provide.*
81	1	Read *intelligentsia* for *intelligentia.*
134	5	Read *pick* for *pick up.*
170	32	Insert *of* after *Committee.*
192	24	Read *remains* for *remained.*
195	1	Read *15th* for *17th.*
254	last	Insert *are* after *Sikhs.*
261	21	After *up* insert: *the grave or pull it down. Near by we found some of the mud graves pressed low.*
342	7	Before *Akal Takht* insert: *and took away the bunch of 53 keys belonging to the Golden Temple,*
450	23	*Co-operat* should be *co-operate.*

CHAPTER I.

SIKHS AND ORGANIZATION.

When Yogis asked Guru Nanak to work a miracle, he replied that in carrying on this mission he relied on nothing but the Word and the Assembly.* Wherever he went, he left behind him a *sangat* or association of his followers, with an injunction to build a Gurdwara or temple for the purpose of meeting and singing his hymns together. So that in a short while there sprang up a network of Sikh temples all over the country. There were centres of his mission in Junagarh, Kamrup, Surat, Cuttack, Behar, Johar (Sbathu), Nanakmata (Kumaon Hills), Khatmandu, Persian Gulf,† Kabul, Jalalabad and other places. Many of these temples, such as the Nanakbara at Surat, Nanakmata in Kumaon, inspite of long isolation, are

---

*Bhai Gurdas, Var 1. 42.

†While returning from Arabia Guru Nanak left a sangat of Mohamedan converts to Sikhism in Mesopotamia. Descendants of these people, more or less still retaining some traces of conversion, were found by the Sikh regiments that went to fight in the last Great War. One of the Sikh commanders, writing to the "Loyal Gazette" of Lahore in January 1918 says that he saw the place commemorating the visit of Guru Nanak to Baghdad. Outside the city to the

still intact, although most of the incumbents of these places are not conversant with the Sikh scriptures or Sikh thought. Remnants of old sangats still exist in Colombo, Madras, Satur Kanjliban, Adilabad in Hyderabad Deccan, Mirzapur Deccan, Chittagong, Dhubri in Assam, and other places in the East founded by Guru Teg Bahadur or Diwan Mahan Singh of Patna. Very old copies of Guru Granth Sahib and autograph letters of Guru Tegh Bahadur and Guru Gobind Singh, addressed to different sangats, are found in the latter places. From the Var XI of Bhai Gurdas we get a list of prominent Sikhs who lived in Kabul, Kashmir, Sarhind, Thanesar, Delhi, Fatehpur Sikri, Agra, Gwalior, Ujjain,

---

south-west, beside a grave-yard, there is an open room situated within an enclosure wall. In one corner of the room is a platform on which Guru Nanak is said to have sat, while he was conversing with Shah Bahlol who sat on another platform in the opposite corner.

The present priest named Sayad Usaf, who is in charge of the place, described himself as the tenth in succession to the first incumbent of the place. The following words in Turkish dated 927 A. H. are inscribed on the wall behind the platform :—

گورو مراد ایلدی حضرت رب المجید بابا نانک فقیر

اوله تاکه عمارت جدیدن بدیدامداد ایدوب کلدی که تاریخنه

یاپدی ثواب اجرائیده انی مرید سعید ۹۲۷ سنه ه

The same account was sent to the Khalsa Advocate, Amritsar, by Subedar Major, Sardar Fateh Singh Assistant Censor in Baghdad in May 1918.

Burhanpur, Gujrat, Suhand, Lucknow, Piragraj, Jaunpur, Patna, Rajmahal, Dacca and other places. In an old manuscript copy of Guru Granth Sahib, written in 1675, is found the story of a Sikh's travels in the Deccan, called Hakikat Rah Mukam, from which we gather something about the Sikh sangats and temples scattered over Southern India and Ceylon.

Each sangat was in charge of a leader appointed by the Guru. The position of this leader, as we learn from the Life of Guru Nanak written by Sewa Das in about 1588, was called *manji*, as he sat on a manji or cot when preaching to the people. Bhai Lallo was preaching in the North and Sheikh Sajjan in the South-west of the Punjab. Gopal Das was in Benares, Jhanda Badi in Bushair, Budhan Shah in Kiratpur, Mahi in Mahisar, Kaljug priest's son in Jaggannath, Devlut in Lushai (Tibet), Salis Rai in Patna and Behar, Raja Shivnabh in Ceylon, and a host of other workers were scattered over the whole territory visited by Guru Nanak. Connection with the centre was kept up by the constant visits of Sikhs to the Guru.

After Guru Nanak, through the creation of twenty-two *manjis* or diocese and fifty-two *pirahs* or parishes, the mission work became more regular, but the sphere of its activity became narrow, as the forces it had created in the Punjab required the constant presence of the Guru there. The organization of the Sikhs had gradually progressed unmarked, until under Guru Arjan it became a power to be counted with.* Each district was under a masand,† whose duty was to preach religion and be responsible to the Guru for the Sikh organizations in his diocese. At the end of the year, on the Baisakhi day, he was to come to the Guru with a company of Sikhs to render account of the offerings received and to report on the progress of Sikhism. Amritsar, with the Golden Temple and the sacred Book installed in it, became the central place for the Sikhs. The Guru was the central unifying personality and, in spite of the changes in succession, was held to be one and the

*The Sikhs in those days used to pray: "May there be hundreds and thousands of Sikhs in every city and hundreds of thousands in every country." "May the Guru's Sikhs become hundreds of thousands, yea, countless in the world, and may a Sikh temple decorate every place."—*Bhai Gurdas*: Vars XIII. 19. and XXIII. 2. Khafi Khan says about the Sikhs: "Their Guru lived like a faqir near Lahore. Even from the beginning he had established sangats and temples in every city and town of note under a saint."

†That these masands were not tax-gatherers, as is often alleged, will appear from the *Dabtstan-i-Mazahib*, which says that they propagated religion, and the money they brought yearly to the Guru was a voluntary offering of the Sikhs who brought it themselves to a masand according to their means.

same as his predecessors.* The love existing between the Guru and the Sikhs was more

---

*From the beginning it was held as a patent fact that each succeeding Guru had the same spirit as his predecessor. In the Coronation Ode written by Satta and Balwand, two bards who lived from the Second Guru's time upto the time of the Fifth Guru, the following verses occur :

"Guru Nanak proclaimed the accession of Lehna as the reward of service.

He had the same light, the same method : the Master merely changed his body."

"A scion of Guru Nanak exchanged bodies with him and took possession of his throne."

"The wise being, Guru Nanak, descended in the form of Amardas."

"Guru Amardas obtained the same mark, the same throne and the same court."

"Thou, Ramdas, art Nanak ; thou art Lehna ; thou art Amardas ; so I deem thee."

"The human race comes and goes ; but thou, O Arjan, art ever new and whole."

Sundar, the great-grandson of Guru Amar Das, while describing the death-scene of the 3rd Guru, says :

"All fell at the feet of the true Guru, into whom Guru Amar Das had infused his spirit."

Mohsin Fani in his *Dabistan* says about the Sikhs :

"Their belief is that all the Gurus are identical with Nanak."

Guru Gobind Singh says about the Gurus in his *Vachittra Natak* :

"All take them as different from one another ; very few recognise them as one in spirit. But only those realise perfection who do recognise them as one."

intense than has ever existed between most romantic lovers of the world.* But the homage paid to the Guru was made impersonal by creating a mystic unity between the Sikh and the Guru on the one hand and the Guru and the Word on the other†. Greatest respect began to be paid to the incorporated Word, even the Guru choosing for himself a seat lower than that of the Scripture‡. The Sikh Assemblies also acquired great sanctity,§ owing to the

---

See Bhai Gurdas : Vars 1. 45, III. 12, XX 1, XXVI. 31, and 34.

See also the Swayyas at the end of the Adi Granth.

The Gurus always signed themselves as Nanak.

* Bhai Gurdas, Var XXVII. Sujan Rai of Batala in his *Khulasatul-Tawarikh* says about the Sikhs : "The faith that these people have in their Guru is not to be met with among any other people."

† "The Guru lives within his Sikhs and is pleased with whatever they like."—*Gauri Ki Var*, IV.

"Guru is the Word and the Word is Guru."—*Kanra* IV.

‡ E.g., Guru Arjan in the Golden Temple Amritsar. Guru Har Rai was once lying on his couch, when somebody began to recite hymns from the Holy Granth. The Guru at once fell down from his couch in his anxiety to avoid irreverence. See *Suraj Prakash*, X. 21.

§ Bhai Gurdas says: "One disciple is a single Sikh ; two form a holy gathering; but where there are five, there is God Himself" Guru Arjan was never tired of praising the manifold spiritual

belief that the spirit of the Guru lived and moved in them. They began to assume higher and higher authority, until collectively the whole body called the Panth came to be considered as an embodiment of the Guru. Guru Gobind Singh himself received baptism from the Sikhs initiated by himself. After him the Sikhs ceased to have any personal Guru. They could name Guru Nanak and Guru Panth in the same breath. The 'Sarbat Khalsa' or the whole Sikh people met once at least at Amritsar on the occasion of the Diwali and felt that they were one. All questions of public interest were determined by the resolutions or gurmattas of assemblies which existed everywhere; and these gurmattas, when passed, were supposed to have received Guru's sanction. Even ordinary breaches of the rules of conduct were punished in such representative meetings and no person, however high-placed, was above the jurisdiction of such conclaves. Even Guru Gobind Singh was once fined Rs. 125.

---

advantages of attending the congregational meetings, and the people, too, resorted to them as well for the sake of getting their wishes granted as for getting devotional merit. (See *Dabistan-i-Mazahib* and Bhai Gurdas, Var V). Guru Gobind Singh also enjoined upon his followers to elect five *Beloved Ones* from among themselves for any executive work, and he promised that he would be present in them (See *Suraj Prakash*: VI, 41).

It was the organization of the Sikhs that turned the Mogul Government against them, and it was their organization that saved them in times of persecution, when prices were laid on their heads, when to grow long hair was held a crime their* presence in cities was banned and they had to roam about in jathas in the deserts of Rajputana or in the forests of Northern Punjab. The daily Prayer of the Sikhs with the words, "May God's protection and grace extend to all the bodies of the Khalsa, wherever they are," still pathetically reminds them of the time when their sacred places were in the hands of others or were desecrated by the foreigner, and their associations were cut off from the centre with no link of union except this Prayer.

It was their peculiar democratic organization that in the days of the missals developed a federal form of government among them. Every Sikh was free and was a substantive member of the Khalsa. But their positions and their abilities were

---

* See Malcolm's *A Sketch of the Sikhs.* An army was sent round the country to hunt out the Sikhs who wore long hair. It was at that time that some people, who believed inSikhism but had not the courage to face the troubles consequent on the adoption of Sikhism, began to go about without *keshas* as a disguise. Such people were called *Sahjdharis.*

different and unequal. Therefore, feeling that all could not lead, they unconsciously developed a confederate system in which different groups of people elected willingly to serve under a leader.

It was the destruction of this democratic spirit under the imperialistic Maharaja Ranjit Singh that undermined the Panthic strength and missionary activity of the Sikhs. It was there, and not during Farrukh Siyer's days of wholesale persecution, that Sikhism suffered the greatest harm. For Sikhism can work best through associations, when different equal individualities are gathered up into one. Even the Sikh prayer is not individualistic. It is from all and for all. There is no word for which other communities can rally themselves as a whole. The Catholics have got the word 'Church,' but it cannot include all the functions of a nation, its history, its military, worldly and religious units into one. But the word 'Khalsa' includes all the institutions and activities of the Sikhs into one whole. There are all possibilities for the Sikhs as long as they can feel that they are the Khalsa. Even Maharaja Ranjit Singh, in order to succeed with the Sikhs, had to keep up the forms and conventions of the Khalsa. When after him there came confusion and no stable head was allowed to rule for a long time, it was the regimental *puncha-*

yats, formed of country representatives, that maintained some form of government.*

Look at the activities of the Sikhs even outside India, in Malaya, China, or Canada, and you will find an ample proof of the Sikhs' love for organization. They are a meeting people; and even when they are only two or three individuals, they will seek occasion to meet and please themselves by singing a few hymns together. If they find themselves larger in number, they will surely found a temple and an association to meet therein. With this instinct in them and the tradition behind them, whenever they have found freedom to think about themselves, they have sought to form themselves into jathas or diwans in order to carry out the required propaganda.

* Cunningham's *History of the Sikhs, p. 239.*

CHAPTER II.

SIKHS AND TEMPLES.

To Sikhs even more important than the asscoiations are their temples, which have played a great part in their history. So much of their history is taken up with either founding of temples or their protection against different kinds of aggressors. The Sikh Prayer, in which the most stirring events of Sikh history are daily recounted, grows most eloquent when reference is made to the brave heroes who suffered martyrdom for the sake of the temples. Much of the daily religious discourse turns on the labours of the devout Sikhs, like Bhai Buddha, Bhai Bhagtu, Bhai Bahlo, Bhai Kalyana and thousands of others, in connection with the excavation of sacred tanks or the collection of material for the raising of temples; or it expatiates on the sufferings borne by the Sikhs, like Bhai Mehtab Singh* and

---

* After the martyrdom of Bhai Mani Singh, Granthi of the Golden Temple in 1738, the temple was turned into a nautch-house and its precincts into a stable by Massa Ranghar, the Mohammedan taluqdar. The Sikhs, who had been declared outlaws,

Baba Dip Singh† in their attempts to rescue their temples from the rulers or the immoral priests. Sometimes it is a Massa Rangarh and sometimes a Sarbrah, but the story is always the same. To tell the truth, the freedom of their temples has always been the measure of the Sikhs' freedom or prosperity.

During the days of persecution when the Sikhs were living in a forced exile outside the Punjab, their temples had oome into the charge of certain monastic orders or those who professed Sikhism but did not conform to its outward symbols. The prominent Gurdwaras were made the chief mark of hostility by the enemy. When Taimur, the son of Ahmad Shah Abdali, took charge of

---

were passing their days and biding their time in the desert of Bikaner. They heard of the desecration in 1740 and sent Bhai Mehtab Singh of Mirankot, a village near Amritsar, to free the temple. He came with only one companion and, killing the taluqdar and his party, cleared away in a few minutes. Afterwards he himself was martyred.

† Hearing at Damdama Sahib near Bathinda that the Amritsar temple was being desecrated by Ahmad Shah Abdali, he vowed to go and save the temple or give up his life there. He came fighting, until at a short distance from Amritsar his head received a mortal cut. But it is said that he did not mind it, and supporting his head with one hand he fought on with the other, until he fell down in the precincts of the temple, where his cenotaph stands.

the Punjab in 1757, the first thing he did was to destroy the Amritsar temple and fill up the sacred tank. This enraged the Sikhs as nothing else had enraged them before, and when in 1758 under two Jassa Singhs they won complete victory over the Afghans, the first thing they did was to restore the temple and the tank. When the Durrani came again in 1762, in his zeal to root out the Sikhs he again demolished the temple, polluted the sacred tanks with the blood of cows, and took away the Holy Book to Kabul. But the Sikhs rose again strong as ever and restored the temple in 1763. Similarly in Delhi a mosque had been erected on the spot where the body of Guru Tegh Bahadur, executed by the orders of Aurangzeb, was burnt. When, however, Sardar Baghel Singh of the Karor-singhia Missal got control over Delhi, he used his authority only to raise temples over the places sacred to the memory of Guru Tegh Bahadur, Guru Harkishan, Mata Sahib Kaur and Mata Sundri, and then he retired.

With the establishment of a centralised Sikh Government the security and splendour of the temples was ensured. Munificent jagirs were added to them. All the wealth of art was lavished on their buildings and their equipments, and richest offerings suited to the taste of a ruling people began to pour in from all directions. Once a beautiful canopy decked with gems and jewels, was presented to Maharaja Ranjit Singh. When he stepped towards the royal chair placed underneath it, he was so greatly impressed by the beauty of the workmanship that he exclaimed: "Oh! take it away to the Golden Temple. The Guru alone deserves such a precious thing." That canopy is still preserved in the Golden Temple treasury, although many of the precious stones have since been removed by somebody. There is another story showing how the most valuable things were considered worthy of the Sacred Temple only. At the marriage of Prince Nau Nihal Singh, the grandson of Maharaja Ranjit Singh, when a garland of pearls worth lakhs was brought to him to wear, he said that it was too good for him and at once sent it away to the Golden Temple, where it is still exhibited in *jalau* on certain ceremonial occasions. All this interest, however, was shown on the ornamental side of Sikhism, and no intelligent attempt was made to preserve the purity of the ritual, which was likely to grow corrupt as soon as the Sikh influence was lifted off.

In the days of the Gurus the temples were supervised by the local sangats in the Guru's name, or by masands, who were appointed by the Guru himself and who, according to the *Dabistan*, worked for their living and did not receive any pecuniary help unless they happened to be very poor or were found incapable of helping themselves. They were punished and their order was abolished by the Tenth Guru, when they became corrupt. This wholesome tradition was kept up even after the Tenth Guru, when the Panth itself as the Guru-incorporate became self-governing and continued to govern the temples through local congregations. The income of the temples was not permanent and being very small, hardly sufficient to maintain the incumbents, there was no temptation for them to grow corrupt or defy the congregations. Besides, the offering of money was looked upon by the incumbents as poisonous* and was spent on the free kitchens invariably attached to the temples or in some other way beneficial to the sangat †.

There are many examples of Sikh preachers, who refused to accept jagirs. Bhai Lakha Singh refused to accept the *patta* of the pargana of Sujanpur granted to him by Sardar Amar Singh Bapa in 1764. Bhai Bhagat Singh refused to accept the grant of seven villages made by Sardar Sada Singh Bahrwalia

---

* See Macauliffe : Vol. I, p. 45 and Vol. III, p. 8 ; Bhai Gurdas : Var XXXV. 12 ; and Rattan Singh's *Panth Prakash* prepared at the desire of Sir David Ochterloney.

† See *Suraj Prakash* : instructions of Guru Gobind Singh to one Santokh Singh.

Nakai in 1766. Bhai Suba Singh refused the pargana of Mirpur granted to him by Sardar Gujar Singh of Gujrat. Maharaja Ranjit Singh, in recognition of his service to the Panth, made a grant of land near the Akhara of Santokh Das to Pundit Nihal Singh who had translated the Japji into Sanscrit. The Pundit tore up the *patta* in the presence of the Maharaja and refused to see him in future. The names of Bhais Dargah Singh, Jai Singh Thakur Dayal Singh, etc., are worthy of mention in the same category*.

Even when they accepted any permanent source of income as a charitable endowment, the priests were kept straight in their conduct by the influence of sangats. There are instances of changes made not only in the management but also in the control of Gurdwaras. The Golden Temple of Amritsar and the Gurdwaras of Anandpur, Gandiwind and Hafizabad were once in the hands of Udasis, but when the Sikh sangats thought it fit they removed the Udasi priests and appointed Singhs instead. Similar changes were made from time to time in other places also.

But with the establishment of the British Government the situation was entirely changed. The central Sikh temples

---

* See the *Nirmal Panth Pardipka.*

at Amritsar and Tarn Taran gradually passed into the hands of Government. The new law made the position of the Mahants or priests virtually as independent as that of persons owning private property. The law, as amended later, did provide in a case of the misuse of trust that any two or more persons interested in the affair, with the consent of the Advocate General (Section 92 of the C. P. C.) or the Collector (Section 93 of the C. P. C.) could bring the matter to a court. But this provision was hedged round with so many restrictions in favour of the incumbent who enjoyed great influence on account of his riches, and the whole procedure was so lengthy and expensive that it could be rarely availed of. The Mahants began with impunity to sell off the lands and property attached to the temples and to squander the income on drinking and loose-living. In many cases, with the connivance of authorities, they got the Gurdwara properties entered in their own names and became their masters.

They could defy the Sikh Sangats with impunity not only in the matter of disbursing the income of jagirs, but also in the observance of ceremony and ritual. Those who had no other source of income except the daily offerings could not dispense with the congregations, but here, too, the Sikh control being absent, they began to adapt the ritual to the inclination of the people who formed a majority in the congregation. The extent of this mischief may be measured from the fact that the Sikhs form a majority nowhere in cities. In the central Gurdwaras at Amritsar and Tarn Taran the Manager and the priests were secure against any check from the public and could introduce any changes they liked in those temples. Many superstitions and corrupt practices began to prevail, first unobserved and then in defiance of the Sikh sentiment. Idols were set up and openly worshipped in the precincts. Thieves and rogues began to haunt these places with impunity. The worst of it all was, that these places being the premier temples, their example came to be followed everywhere else.

CHAPTER III.

THE NEED OF REFORM.

Sikhism as a religious movement remained pure as long as the lust of worldly power did not contaminate it. The Gurus had been fighting against tyrants, but they always kept their hands clean. Although the Sixth Guru won all the battles he fought and the Tenth Guru was often victorious, they did not acquire even an inch of territory as a result of these victories, and whatever land they possessed was either bought with money or was accepted as an offering from devoted men. They were opposed to ruling over men against their wishes. "Only those like to rule over others, who are either stupid or uninstructed," says Guru Nanak. The ideal of simplicity was kept up even in the midst of the circumstances of comfort. The bards, whose compositions are included in the Holy Granth, are never tired of praising this balance of character, called *Raj Yog*, maintained between asceticism and prosperity. It is wrong to say that by the time of the

Fifth or the Sixth Guru the ideal of Sikhism was lowered and the Guru came to be called *Sacha Padshah*, his seat a *takht* or throne, and the assembly of his followers a *durbar* or court. It will appear from the writings of the early Gurus, and especially from those of the bards who began to write in the time of the Second Guru, that these terms were not later innovations, but had been used from the beginning*. They are eastern euphemisms used in respect of all revered faqirs. Guru Nanak himself was called Nanak *Shah*.

A change did come over the spirit of Sikhism, but it was after the last Guru had gone away from the Punjab and died in the Deccan. The chosen ones, who had been trained in the school of Guru Gobind Singh and whose presence could keep alive the spirit of truth among the masses, were called upon, soon after the death of the Guru, to fight for their lives or defend the weak from the oppressor. They were removed from amidst the common people, who were left to their own resources or had to depend upon the old professional teachers, who now got the chance of renewing their hereditary vocation of mercenary teaching. The Sikh temples fell into the hands of the monastic orders and the congregations, depleted of the initiat-

*See foot-note *on page 5.

ed Sikhs, came to give the rule to those who governed the temples.

There was another circumstance that checked the balanced growth of Sikhism. It was the fact that in later Sikh history conversions to Sikhism came to be confined to one community only. As this side of the question has been generally ignored we intend to study it in some detail.

Sikhism was meant for all castes and communities, and in the beginning converts were made from Mohammedans as well as Hindus. Guru Nanak left a host of converts in Mesopotamia*, Persia and other countries visited by him. Sewa Das in his Janam Sakhi mentions many places like the Kiri of Pathans where a large number of Mohammedans became Sikhs. From the list of Sikhs given by Bhai Gurdas in his eleventh Var we find among others such names as Mardana, the rebeck-player, who accompanied Guru Nanak in his journeys, Daulat Khan Pathan who became a Sikh Saint, Gujjar a blacksmith who was a Sikh of Guru Angad and preached Sikhism in his village, Hamza, and Mian Jamal the happy, who remained constantly in the presence of Guru Hargobind. From history we gather many names of Mohammedans who became admirers of Sikhism, like Rai Bular, the Mohammedan

---

*See foot-note † on p. 1.

Chief of Talwandi, who appreciated Guru Nanak better than his own parents did; Allah Yar and Hussaini Shah, who profited spiritually by Guru Amar Das and may be considered almost Sikhs; Akbar, who was influenced in his toleration policy and his abolition of Sati by Guru Amar Das; Mian Mir, who was so intimately connected with the work of Guru Arjan that the latter asked him to lay the foundation stone of the Golden Temple; Dara Shikoh, who was persecuted by his brother Aurangzeb for being a convert to Sikhism; Sayyed Budhu Shah of Sadhaura; Kale Khan and Sayyed Beg, who fought for Guru Gobind Singh. There were others who actually became Sikhs. A few of them may be named: Sajjan* who had been a robber but who became a Sikh of Guru Nanak and preached his religion; a Nawab's son† who was converted by Bhai Paro of Dalla in the Jullundur Doab; Wazir Khan‡ who was an assistant Minister of Akbar and who secretly followed the teachings of Guru Arjan; Budhan Shah § the Simeon of Sikh history, who was devoted to the memory of Guru Nanak and ultimately died a Sikh in the time of Guru Hargobind;

---

* Macauliffe: Vol. I. 45.

† Ibid, Vol. II. 66.

‡ Ibid, Vol. III. 17, 18; Vol. IV. 11, 26.

§ Ibid, Vol. IV. 140, 142, 213, 215.

Bibi Kaulan,* who was the daughter of the Qazi of Lahore and was converted to Sikhism by Guru Hargobind ; Saifuddin† of Saifabad in Patiala, who was converted by Guru Tegh Bahadur just before the latter's arrest; Sayyed Shah converted by Bhai Nand Lal ; and a faqir called Brahmi‡ or Ibrahim, who was the first Mohammedan who offered himself to Guru Gobind Singh to be baptised. The Guru when baptising this Mohammedan, who became Mahma Singh, issued orders that "if any Moslem, whether of high or low position, in good faith desire to join the Khalsa, it is proper that he should be baptised and received into our community." These are only a few names out of many who must have embraced Sikhism. From the study of these conversions, in the time of Guru Nanak and later, we find that the Pathans, Sayyeds and Shias, whose races had been defeated by the Moguls, were more prone to accept Sikhism than the Moguls, who had too much of the conqueror's pride to adopt the religion of the conquered. The chief complaint of Jehangir against Guru

---

* Macauliffe : Vol. IV. 43, The Guru in 1621 caused a tank to be dug near the Golden Temple to commemorate her virtuons life. This tank, called Kaulsar, is one of the holiest in Amritsar.

† Ibid, Vol. IV. 373.

‡ *Suraj Prakash*, Ayan I, Chap. XVIII.

Arjan, as recorded by the Emperor himself in his Tauzak, was that "so many of the simple-minded Hindus, nay many foolish Moslems too, had been fascinated by his ways and teachings." The Gurus also converted many outcastes and men of the lowest castes, such as Ramdasias or shoemakers. Guru Gobind Singh opened the door of pahul or equal baptism to all, even to sweepers, who, for their staunch faith, came to be called *mazhabis* or faithfuls. The Mazhabis are sometimes called Ranghrets, a term which may be due to the fact that some of them owe their origin to Mohammedans of the Rangarh clan. On their showing gallantry in rescuing the mutilated body of Guru Tegh Bahadur, Guru Gobind Singh called them *Ranghrete Guru ke bete*—the Ranghretas are the Guru's own sons.

Beside making impartial conversions, there were other ways, too, by which the spirit of Sikhism was kept balanced. In the free kitchen, established by the Gurus as a means of levelling down all social barriers based upon caste or other prejudices, it was made a rule that all who came to take food, whether Hindus or Mohammedans, must sit in a line and eat together.* Even Akbar

* "The whole congregation would come to the kitchen and, without considering any distinction of *Varna* or *Ashram*, were seated in a line. They

and the Raja of Haripur, when they came to see Guru Amar Das, had to do the same. In order to show that those who were born among Mohammedans or low-caste Sudras were as acceptable as high-class Hindus, Guru Arjan included in his Granth the compositions of Kabir, a weaver and Mohammedan by birth; Farid, a Mohmmedan saint; Bhikhan, a learned Mohammedan; Sain, a barber and sculptor; Namdev, a calico-printer and washerman; Ramdas, a shoemaker; Mardana, who had been a Mohammedan drummer; and so many bards some of whom were Mohammedans. The significance of this can be best realised, if we remember that the whole Book containing these compositions is considered by the Sikhs divine and is held in greatest veneration by them.

The effect of these arrangements was visible in the customs and habits of the Sikhs of those days. They considered Hindus and Mohammedans in the same light and did not identify themselves religiously with any party. The first utterance of Guru Nanak when he took up the work of preaching was: "There is no Hindu, no Moslem*, and when he died, both Hindus and Moslems claimed him

---

were treated as if they were all equally handsome and clean,"—*Suraj Prakash*, Ras I.

* *Janam Sakhi* by Sewa Das.

as theirs. Guru Arjan says boldly in his Book:—

I don't keep the Hindu fast, nor that observed by Mohammedans in Ramzan.
I serve Him, and Him alone, who is my ultimate refuge.
I believe in one Master, who is also Allah.
I have broken off with the Hindu and the Turk.
I won't go on Hajj to Mecca nor do worship at the Hindu places.
I shall serve only Him and no other.
I won't worship idols or read Nimaz.
I shall lay my heart at the feet of one Supreme Being.
We are neither Hindus nor Mussalmans:
We have dedicated our bodies and souls to Allah-Ram.*

The author of *Dabistan*, who visited the Punjab in the Sixth and Seventh Gurus' time, says about the Sikhs:—

"The Sikhs of Guru Nanak condemn idolatry and believe that all the Gurus are identical with Nanak. They do not read the Hindu Mantras, nor do they pay any regard to their shrines. They do not believe in the Hindu Avtars, and do not study Sanscrit,

* **Bhairo.**

which, according to Hindus, is the language of gods."

"The Sikhs do not have any faith in the ritual and ceremonies enjoined by the Hindu Shastras, nor do they observe any superstitious restrictions about dining. A learned Hindu named Partap Mal, seeing that his son was inclined towards Islam, said to him, 'There is no need for you to turn Mohammedan. If you want to get freedom in eating and drinking, you may better join Sikhism."

Beside opening free kitchens and distributing communion food in order to teach equality, the Sikhs in their temples observed no elaborate ceremonials, and therefore there was no cause of friction that could give rise to separate sects within Sikhism. The whole religious service inside the Golden Temple consisted of nothing else but the reading or singing of sacred hymns from the Holy Granth night and day. With the exception of a small interval of an hour or two at midnight, sacred music, performed by relays or singers, went on without break. There was no lecturing, no discussion allowed, and therefore there was no controversy. This simple and beautiful custom among the Sikhs was seen and remarked upon by Sujan Rai of Batala who wrote in 1697 in his *Khulasatul-Tawarikh*:

"The only way of worship with them is that they read the hymns composed by their Gurus and sing them sweetly in accompaniment with musical instruments."

Guru Gobind Singh has said quite clearly that the Sikhs, with all their sympathy and love for other communities, are not to confuse their ideals with those of others :—

"The Sikh is to keep his observances distinct from those of other people of all the four Varnas.

He should have dealings with everybody,

But his belief and programme of life should be different all the same."*

The Sikhs had for a long time been able to keep their doctrines distinct and, though

---

* *Suraj Prakash*, Rut 3, Adhya 50. One outward sign of distinction was the Keshas or the long hair, which every Sikh was enjoined to wear by Guru Gobind Singh. When this Guru entered on his mission he called upon the Sikhs to rally round him. But such was the fear of persecution by the Government that many of the Sikhs denied their Sikhism and declared that they had never departed from their old religion. The Guru, astonished at this illusiveness of the so called Sikhs said: "Now I shall create such Sikhs who, in spite of themselves, will not be able to hide themselves even in lakhs. He ordered that all Sikhs should wear long hair. This was the form most suitable to the Sikhs who were to be brave and at the same time saintly like the rishis of old. The stern discipline and bodily strength were combined with the saintliness of looks.

liberally benefitting by the Hindu and the Moslem association, had been able to maintain their growth free from any obsession from either side. But the opportunities for the display of this balanced spirit began to decrease, when the Sikhs began to fight against the tyranny of the Mogul Government. Guru Gobind Singh, out of his abundance of love, was able to inspire love even in the hearts of his enemies. Sayyed Beg, a commander of Aurangzeb, came to fight with the Guru, but on meeting the Guru was suddenly struck with remorse and turning away in shame vowed never to fight in aid of tyranny. It was Mohammedans, like Budhu Shah, Nabi Khan and Ghani Khan, who at most critical times came to the aid of the Guru. But the growing antipathy of the Moslems against the Sikhs began to tell on the work of Sikh mission among the Moslems, until, with the intense religious persecution started by the later Moguls against Hindus as well as Sikhs under Baba Banda, the scope of conversions to Sikhism came to be confined solely to the Hindu masses, who brought to the contemplation of the new moral forces revealed by Sikhism an imagination saturated with the spiritual convictions of the old era.

The same thing happened to Christianity in its early days, when most of the conversions were confined to the Jews. The proselytes were dealt with in the old Jewish manner, which was to make distinction between proselytes of the sanctuary and proselytes of the gate. The former, who went through the ceremony of circumcision and observed Mosaic ritual, were allowed to enter the innermost part of the temple; while the latter, who did not conform to these rules, were declared mere 'sympathisers' and were allowed to worship only at the gate. The Christians also made the same distinction between the Jews and the Gentiles. The full privileges of the Christian Church were granted only to the Jewish converts who would submit to circumcision.

Similarly, when the veteran Sikhs disciplined by Guru Gobind Singh himself had been martyred and their descendants forced to remain in exile, the rump congregations began to drift back to the old customs and beliefs. Those who came from low castes began to be distinguished from those who came from the so-called high castes. Even after receiving baptism, some were assigned positions at the gate, others in the sanctuary. Some, who in the days of persecution could not dare to confess Sikhism openly, were allowed to go about without the outward symbols. Such men were called *Sahjdharis* or slow-adopters. In those days, when to wear *keshas* was to invite death, nobody could have the heart to question the disguise adopted by the Sahjdharis, who believed in Sikhism but could not afford to die for it. The Sahjdharis who had adopted this apologetic attitude never pretended to be representative Sikhs. They always looked upto the spirit and form of their brethren in exile, whom they helped in every way.

The Sikh spirit and form were, however, kept intact in the ranks of the Khalsa even after it had been slackened in towns and cities. From the *Panth Prakash* of Sardar Rattan Singh, written in 1809 at the suggestion of Sir David Ochterlony, we can see that in spite of the hard times through which they had passed, the old spirit still burned clear and steady in the fighting Sikhs. They still kept aloof from idolatry, performed the Anand form of marriage, obeyed the Panth as the highest authority, conducted themselves by resolutions passed in their assemblies, did not believe in the sacred thread, incarnations, caste or the pollution of food* and freely reconverted those who had gone over to Islam. Many notable Sikhs married Mohammedan women converted to Sikhism. Some of them were: Anup Singh, who had been a Brahmin of Chanarthal; Takht Singh, who had been a

* There is a proverb coming down from those days: "The cooking square of the Khalsa extends within 12 miles round."

Khatri of Paijgarh; Nand Singh Bairar; Kehar Singh Randhawa; Karam Singh Man, etc. Bhai Gurmukh Singh, Reis of Bagrian, baptised a Mohammedan named Maula and renamed him Ram Singh. Ram Singh's grandson named Harcharn Singh was still living in 1906. Saunta, a Mohammaden, was converted and named Ram Singh, and his daughters were married to Ramgarhia Sirdars. Bhai Hari Singh of Bhadaur was by birth a Mohammedan, whom Bhai Ude Singh of Kainthal had converted to Sikhism. A Mohammedan, who was baptised and renamed Nihal Singh, became Mahant of the Gurdwara of Bhaliani. At the instance of Maharaja Narindar Singh of Patiala one Sadr-ud-Din was converted to Sikhism and named Fateh Singh by Mahant Haiba Singh. For 26 years he was Mahant of the Dharmsala of Phul and died in 1869. Raja Sarup Singh got one Allia converted into Gian Singh. This man became Mahant of a Gurdwara at Jind. A Mohammedan of Chugana, who was converted and renamed Massa Singh, became priest of a Sikh temple at Bhaliaiyna in Muktsar pargana. Thousands of Mohammedan men and women were brought into the fold of Sikhism in the time of Maharaja Ranjit Singh.

When, however, Maharaja Ranjit Singh came to rule, Sikhism received a rude shock even in the Khalsa ranks, where it had been preserved more or less in its pristine purity. He destroyed the simplicity and independence of the Sikhs by building his luxurious empire on the ruins of the democratic principles laid down by Guru Gobind Singh. In fact, Sikhism is a simple and stern religion and does not easily lend itself to luxury and ease. Most of the religious and even secular ceremonies of the Sikhs contain nothing but hymn-singing and prayer. How can a Maharaja keep his position among his brother-Maharajas, if he does not invite astrologers and pundits to help him in making his coronation or marriage imposing and circumstantial ? The Sikh monarchs and grandees have always found it difficult to break Sikhism to their taste. They are, therefore, often obliged to go out of the pale of Sikhism, when they want to indulge in mere ceremony and show.

After Maharaja Ranjit Singh, when kingship became a thing of jewels and clothes, Sikhism, too, with the higher classes, became a mere fashion of the turban and the beard, until a people with sterner ways and better discipline struck the sceptre from their hands. It was the people who retained some semblance of the old spirit; and they too, with the change coming over the temples along with the shock they had received on the battlefield, felt paralysed for the time being. They declined in numbers too. The English, however, forgot the late enmity in the admiration for the noble bravery of the Sikhs, which now began to be used on their side, and tried to befriend them. This friendship put the Sikhs again in some heart, and they began to enlist in the British Army, where they could keep their baptismal forms intact. But in all other ways the Sikhs showed no life, religious or national, in them. They worshipped the same old gods, indulged in the same old superstitious practices from which their Gurus had so heroically worked to extricate them. Their baptism and five symbols became a mere anomaly.

CHAPTER IV.

THE GENESIS OF REFORM.

A great upheaval, second only to Chilianwala, came to rouse the Sikhs from stupor, but, as it was not preceded by a general educational awakening, it was not felt by the whole Sikh nation. Attempts were made to restore Sikhism to its original position. But the circumstances had so changed and the progress of Sikhism had been so long neglected that to a great extent the battle had to be fought over again.

Two reform movements, the fore-runners of the Singh Sabha movement, began about the same time in the North-Western Punjab. One was the Nirankari and the other the Namdhari movement. The first originated with Baba Dyal of Peshawar, who came to settle in Rawalpindi and died there in 1870. He preached against idolatry and sought to restore the worship of one *Nirankar* or God in spirit. He inveighed against the fast-increasing evil of drink, which the military service had introduced. The purely Sikh forms of marriage and funeral services were revived, and widow marriage and other reforms were encouraged. But owing to the want of education the movement touched only a few business men of the locality, who came to believe in Baba Dyal as a successor of Guru Nanak and Guru Gobind Singh.

The Namdhari movement was started by Baba Balak Singh (1799—1861), a shop-keeper of Hazro, and his disciple Baba Ram Singh of Bhaini in the Ludhiana district. This puritan movement was a protest against the prevailing laxity of morals and sought to revive the old devotional spirit among the Sikhs. It was a vigorious campaign against the immoral and superstitious practices of the priests in charge of Gurdwaras. Baba Ram Singh, born in 1815 of a poor carpenter family, rose to be a great leader of men. He had learnt discipline in the Sikh army, which he left in 1841 at the bidding of his religious preceptor, and wonderfully organized his followers. He appointed a *Suba* in every district, two *jathadars* in every tehsil, and one Granthi in every village. He established elementary vernacular schools and free kitchens wherever he went, and exhorted the Sikhs to live simple lives and support these institutions. He saw that the Western culture was undermining the simplicity of life and the strength of character. He, therefore, banned the Western education and interdicted the Government service and courts.

His preaching made a great stir in the country. The priestly class, annoyed with his criticisms, shut the Gurdwaras against him and his followers; and the Government interpreted his attacks on Western civilization as due to racial hatred. Measures were adopted to restrain him and his followers' activities.

Strange as it may seem, the Baba's mission was specially marked by the teaching of righteousness, toleration and mercy. It is true, some of his followers got out of control and in a religious frenzy committed unpardonable excesses. But this evil is due to an intensity of feeling in ignorant men, aggravated by great provocation. The large majority of Namdharis disapproved of such actions* and the Baba's influence was always exerted on the side of moderation and kindness. A murderer, who had escaped conviction, came under the influence of Baba Ram Singh. He went at once to the Sessions Judge, confessed his guilt, and cheerfully accepted the punishment. In the summer of 1870 a few Namdharis happened to pass by the Lahori Gate of Amritsar, where, in spite of the long tradi-

*The *Ludhiana Gazetteer*.

tion and an order* of John Lawrence passed in 1847 against cow-killing in Amritsar, a slaughter-house had been established. There was a rumour in the city that four butcher shops were going to be opened in the sacred city. A great indignation prevailed among the Hindus and Sikhs. The Namdharis, who had a great hatred for cow-slaughter, came after some deliberation in the city, fell upon the butchers, and killing a few of them ran away. After a year Baba Ram Singh, who came to know of it, sent for those men and said to them: "You have committed murders, and innocent Nihangs have been arrested. Go to the court and confess your guilt so that the innocent may be saved." They went, cleared up the case before the authorities, and calmly resigned themselves to their fate.

In January 1872 a bullock was provokingly slaughtered by a police officer of Malerkotla before the very eyes of a Namdhari Sikh, who had remonstrated with the owner of the bullock for his cruelty to the animal. The news told in the yearly diwan at Bhaini stirred up wrath in the audience, and, in spite of the attempts of Baba Ram Singh to dissuade them, about 150 Sikhs got out of hand and

*This order inscribed on a wooden board was upto 1922 still hanging outside the north-western entrance of the Durbar Sahib, but it has now been taken down for safety.

marched towards Malerkotla to take vengeance. The Baba Sahib at once informed the police about it*. First Malaudh and then Malerkotla were attacked with sticks and axes, and 10 men were killed and 17 wounded, while the Namdharis got 9 killed and 38 wounded. They were ultimately surrounded by the army, and Mr. Cowan, the Deputy Commissioner of Ludhiana, without trying them ordered 49 of them to be immediately blown away from guns and the others were tried by the Commissioner, Mr. Forsyth, and executed on the following day. Baba Ram Singh, who was admittedly 'a thoroughly religious character' and who had helped the Government in this crisis, was deported with his Subas to Rangoon, where he remained prisoner upto 1885, when he died.

The Government of India recorded on these proceedings an elaborate resolution,

---

* For these and other facts mentioned before about the Namdharis the author is indebted to some Namdhari records and a history called *Panth Prakash* by Bhai Kala Singh. This book mentions among the Sikhs, who attacked Malerkotla, two women also who are said to have been let off when men were blown away from guns. For the remaining account the *Ludhiana Gazetteer* and some information supplied by Namdharis has been availed of.

which contained these words : "His Excellency in Council is under the painful necessity of affirming that the course followed by Mr. Cowan was illegal, that it was not palliated by any public necessity, and that it was characterised by incidents which gave it a complexion of barbarity. And so His Excellency was compelled with deep regret to direct that Mr. Cowan be removed from the service." Mr. Forsyth, too, though later recompensed in other ways, was removed from his appointment as Commissioner. Sir Henry Cotton says in his *Indian and Home Memories* : "For my part, I can recall nothing during my service in India more revolting and more shocking than these executions, and there were many who thought as I did, and still think that the final orders of the Government of India were lamentably inadequate."

The troubles of the Namdharis did not end with these executions or the deportation of their revered leader. A police guard was stationed at the door of their central temple at Bhaini, and all the Namdharis were interned in their villages and their movements restricted. Most of these restrictions, which involved unthinkable police harassment continued upto very recent time. It was only on 10th December, 1920, that the long-standing restrictive orders were cancelled and the police guard was changed into a police station*. For fear of harassment the Namdharis changed the peculiar mode of their turban and wore the woollen rosary under their clothes. They were left in isolation and in their agony they had nothing else to console them except the memory of Baba Ram Singh, whom they raised, unauthorised by him, to the position of a Guru or successor of Guru Nanak†.

This reform movement was successfully paralysed owing to the want of a common feeling among the Sikhs, which could be engendered only by education. It

---

* The Government communique announcing the removal of restrictions against the Namdharis begins thus :—

"In 1872 after the Kuka disturbances restrictions were placed by the Punjab Government ovar the movements of the leaders of the sect and a police post was established at Bhaini Ala, their head quarters in the Ludhiaha District. Those restrictions involved the reporting of their movements by the leaders, supervision over visitors to the shrine and prohibition of meetings without sanction from the authorities."

† Of course the setting up of a Guru after Guru Gobind Singh, except Guru Granth Sahib, was against the basic principles of Sikhism, and this was responsible for the growing isolation between the General Panth and the Namdharis, who fell away more and more from the high ideal of Baba Ram Singh until in the present movement of Gurdwara Reform they are doing nothing but playing into the hands of the enemies of Sikhism.

is a significant fact that, while all other communities at that time felt the inspiration for reform from the Western education, the Sikhs' first attempts at reform were the result of their own inherent genius. They realised, however, that their endeavours to rouse the whole community to feel the necessity of reform would be fruitless unless they first got themselves educated. The first and most urgent need was education.

A reform association called the Khalsa Diwan was founded at Lahore in 1888. It had a network of Singh Sabhas spread over the province, with the common object of restoring the purity of religion and making the Sikhs feel their lost individuality. A few English and Gurmukhi papers were started to help the movement. The Punjabi language also began to make a conscious advance. Modern poetry and especially prose owe their origin to the strong advocacy of religious reform by such writers as Bhai Dit Singh. They were later improved and their scope was enlarged by Bhai Vir Singh of Amritsar and his associates in the Khalsa Tract Society. Free-interdining, removal of untouchability, abolition of caste, performing of marriage, funeral and other ceremonies according to the Sikh rites—these were the main features of the reform propaganda.

Soon after the establishment of the Lahore Diwan an active campaign was started to found a central college for the Sikhs to be worked in connection with a system of schools in the outlying districts. The movement was due to such enthusiastic Sikhs as Sardar Gurmukh Singh, a teacher in the Oriental College of Lahore, and Sardar Jawahir Singh, a clerk in the N. W. R. Office, but they were whole-heartedly helped by the Government and the Sikh States. Those were the days when the Sikhs fully trusted the Government as their best friend ; and the Government, too, fully confided in the devotion and friendship of the Sikhs tested in many trying crises. That was the time when a Viceroy could say : "With this (educational) movement the Government of India is in hearty sympathy. We appreciate the many admirable qualities of the Sikh nation, and it is a pleasure to us to know that, while in days gone by we recognised in them a gallant and formidable foe, we are to-day able to give them a foremost place amongst the true and loyal subjects of Her Majesty the Queen Empress ; * and a Lieutenant Governor could feel "that the British Government owed the Sikhs a debt of gratitude for their large share of the credit

---

* Lord Lansdowne in his speech at Patiala on 23rd October, 1890.

for victories won by Punjabi Regiments in Hindustan and in China, and afterwards in Abyssinia, Egypt and Afghanistan."*

The Sikhs, too, appreciated this sympathy in such glowing terms: "They are actuated by no other motives than those of philanthropy, of friendliness towards the Sikhs, and we are very grateful to them."†

The College was founded in 1892. Col. W. R. M. Holroyd, Director of Public Instruction, Mr. J. Sime, another D. P. I., Sir W. H. Rattigan, Mr. W. Bell, Principal, Government College, and several other European gentlemen gave active assistance to the Sikhs in the work of founding and conducting the College. They were associated with the Sikhs with the latter's free consent and were elected as special members, simply to help them, and were not there to exercise official control.

When, owing to the deaths or abstention of its active members towards the end of the 19th century, the Lahore Diwan became

---

* Sir J. Lyall, while laying the foundation stone of the Khalsa College Main Building on 5th March, 1892.

† The Secretary of the Khalsa College Council, while referring to the European members of the Council in his speech at the opening ceremony of the Khalsa Collegiate School on 22nd October, 1893.

deteriorated, the College, too, was found verging towards bankruptcy, and it was seriously proposed by Sir Mackworth Young, the Lieutenant-Governor, that the College classes should be abandoned altogether. But fortunately the Chief Khalsa Diwan, another central body, came into existence at Amritsar just at the time when the Lahore Diwan became defunct, and Sardar Sundar Singh Majithia, the moving figure in the new dispensation, became Secretary of the College in 1902. To facilitate business the unwieldy College Council, under the advice of the Lieutenant-Governor, delegated all its governing powers to a small Managing Committee of thirteen members. With the return of public confidence and the patronage of princes, the financial condition of the College began to improve, and in 1904, as a result of a great Sikh Conference held at the College under the presidency of the venerable Maharaja Hira Singh of Nabha, the Endowment Fund, not including the promises, went up by a leap to Rs. 15,30,477, and the Main Building Fund stood at Rs. 3,28,480 including Rs. 50,000 granted by Government. Sir Charles Rivaz, the Lieutenant-Governor, exerted himself utmost in the interest of the College, and with his help ½ anna per rupee on the Government revenue was collected from the Sikh zamindars.

The policy of Government up to that time had been of trust, and in return for its help it did not require any official control to be introduced *. But after some time the vicious policy of Lord Curzon, inaugurated by the Universities Act of 1904, came to overtake the former policy of saympathy; and when the mistrust of the educated classes led the Government to take the Universities under a stricter State control, the Khalsa College, which was the fountain-head of Sikh education, also came in for its share. A little incident† in the College and the

* The European members did show anxiety in 1900 to reserve the Principalship for an European even when a Sikh at a great sacrifice was offering himself for the post, but on this point the Sikh members themselves were divided. Even the appointment of Sardar Sundar Singh as Secretary in March 1902 was strongly opposed by the European members, who wanted Mr. Cole, the Principal, to be also the Secretary, but they could not withstand the growing influence of the new Sikh party and, in spite of the threatened deadlock, Sardar Sundar Singh was confirmed in his position.

† The Sikh Engineer Sardar Dharam Singh, who was working honorarily and was against carrying on the building operations on the original extravagant scale, was replaced, at the suggestion of the Lieutenant-Governor, by a paid European Engineer. This appointment and specially Major Hill's remark about the honorary services of the Sikh Engineer, that 'the labour of love was nonsense,' created a great sensation in the community. About 75 Sikh

general unrest in the country in 1907 scared away the old trust which had always inspired the Government officials in their dealings with the College. After the Managing Committee had worked for six years, much to the advantage of the institution, it was discovered by Government and the Punjab University that the Committee had been illegally constituted in 1902 and that its funds were bogus*. The threat of disaffiliation was held out, unless the fundmental rules of the Society were changed, which meant that the Society should consent to the introduction of Government control. A sub-committee, appointed by the Punjab Government and consisting of the Commis-

---

associations sent resolutions of protest against the European member's remark, from which the Managing Committee were also obliged to record their dissociation. There was a strong agitation against Europeans or officials being present on the management. When the new engineer came to the College on the 10th February, 1907, some boys are said to have behaved rudely towards him. The whole students body put on black badges and held a fast. The Government was highly offended and the Phulkian States withheld payment of the interest on their endowed money.

* The reference was to the fact that the donations of the Sikh States, on which the College mainly depended, were deposited with the States themselves and were not placed in the hands of the College trustees. But this had been the case from the beginning and upto the present remains the same.

sioner of Lahore (Chairman), the Director of Public Instruction, a Sikh Sirdar who was a 'safe' man, and Sardar Sundar Singh Majithia who protested all along, proposed revision of the constitution of the College. The draft rules, approved by Government and passed by an Executive Committee suggested by Government, were placed before the old Council on 10th June, 1908, but without the requisite number of votes forthcoming the rules were declared passed, and the remaining votes were secured later on by July 3rd*. By the new arrangement the Commissioner became president, and the Deputy Commissioner, the Director of Public Instruction, the Political Agent, Phulkian States, and the Principal were appointed *ex-officio* by the Government to the College Council. With the Commissioner as Chairman, the Deputy Commissioner as Vice-Chairman of the Managing Committee, and the Secretary nominated and removed by Government, the effective control of the College may be said to have passed into the hands of Government.

The Principal, Mr. Cole, could say complacently that "the reconstitution of the College Managing Committee on the lines indicated by Government and the University

---

* See the Secretary's report for the year 1908-09.

has served to place matters on a more definite basis;" but the Sikhs thought otherwise. There was a great outcry in the community. The independent-minded member Sardar Harbans Singh of Atari resigned, and the position of Sardar Sundar Singh also became more and more difficult. The great influence he commanded in the management was too much for the Principal and the official members, and "the Government expressed a desire that the constitution should be changed as it did not work well."* It was proposed in September, 1912, that the number of members from the British districts should be reduced and the Secretary should not be an honorary but a paid officer to be appointed and removed by Government. He was not to have a seat on the Managing Committee, and his powers were further sought to be limited and placed at the mercy of the Principal. After a hard contest the Secretary's position was more or less maintained, but the proportion of the members from the British districts on the Committee was reduced, and the Lieutenant-Governor of the Punjab was given the power "to suspend the rules and to direct the Committee to take such action as the special circumstances may appear to demand, and it shall thereupon be binding upon the Committee to take such

* Secretary's report for the year 1912-13.

action." Sardar Sundar Singh had, of course, to resign his office in November 1912, and several 'strong' men on the staff were forced to retire soon after. To help the institution the Government consented to provide three English professors, including the Principal, to the College.

The College became very unpopular and, as admitted by the new Secretary, was openly cried down as a Government College. The Lieutenant-Governor, who came to distribute prizes in 1914, noted this change in the attitude of the Sikhs, but tried to justify the officialising of the College by referring to the happy results of the Sikhs being led by British officers in the army. The story of India in the leading strings was repeated here. The same efficiency and the same outward show of prosperity* was there, but it stunted the growth of the native genius.

Disgusted with this state of affairs the Sikhs left the College to its fate and began to concentrate their attention on the growth of school education, which had been one of the objects of the Lahore Diwan in founding the College. Ever since 1908, when the higher

---

* More than 15 lakhs have been spent on the buildings alone and the capital for the maintenance of the College exists mainly on paper. The Government and the States can stop the College any day by refusing their grants.

education began to slip away from the Sikh control, the Chief Khalsa Diwan, through its Educational Committee, had been holding an Educational Conference every year; and wherever it was held it left a school behind it, until in a few years it came to support a host of Primary, Middle and High Schools in the Province*. It heroically fought for the cause of the Punjabi language and its influence was felt by the Educational, Postal and Railway authorities, although the attitude of Hindus and Moslems, with the exception of a few like Professor Ruchi Ram, Choudhri Shahab-ud-din, Chaudhrani Sarla Devi, etc., became more stiffened against Punjabi as the mother tongue of the people †. The Educational

---

* At present the following number of educational institutions are affiliated to the Educational Committee of the Chief Khalsa Diwan:—

33 High Schools for boys; 37 Middle Schools for boys and 7 for girls; 4 Miscellaneous schools; 3 Lower Middle Schools; 5 Boarding Houses; 49 Primary Schools for boys and 70 for girls; 19 Mixed Schools; and 7 Night Schools.

The Committee spends on education about Rs. 40,400 annually out of which about Rs. 28,000 are given in grants. Beside those under the Educational Committee, there are scores of other privately managed Sikh institutions which are not affiliated to the Committee.

† The prejudice against Punjabi is so strong, that in the Reformed Council of the Punjab it is Urdu that is officially recognised as the Vernacular of the

Committee, as admitted by Government, became the most active educational body in the Punjab.

The Sikh schools were not only dispensers of education, but they also served as strongholds of Sikhism wherever they were established. Even the Singh Sabhas, which had been organized to propagate reform, could not compete in popularity with the schools. This spread of education created among the Sikhs a public spirit with which they came to feel for their religious and political disabilities. Just at that time occurred a few incidents which roused the Sikhs most and gave a point to their grievances.

---

speakers, and even in the national scheme of education promulgated by the Punjab Congress Committee no proper place is given to the mother tongue of the people.

CHAPTER V.

IRON ENTERS THE SOUL.

Gurdwara Rikab Ganj.

The first incident was the Rikab Ganj affair. Rikab Ganj is a Gurdwara in Delhi built on the site, where the body of Guru Tegh Bahadur, martyred by Aurangzeb, was cremated. With the transfer of the capital to Delhi in 1911 preparations began to be made to build the Viceregal Lodge opposite to the place where the Gurdwara is situated. The Government considered that the old six-cornered enclosure wall of the Gurdwara was too ugly to stand in front of the Viceroy's palace and proposed that it should be demolished. In 1912 under the Land Acquisition Act the Government acquired from an accommodating Mahant the whole land lying between the Gurdwara and the outer wall. Early in 1914 a part of the wall was pulled down. The Chief Khalsa Diwan, which was consulted as the only representative body of the Sikhs, seemed inclined to accept the Government's position, in view of the fact that the Government did not want to do it to injure the feelings of the Sikhs but simply to improve the outlook of the Gurdwara. There was, however, among the Sikhs a great agitation against the action of Government, and the Chief Khalsa Diwan also came in for its share in the unpopularity. A voice of protest was raised by Sardar Harchand Singh of Lyallpur even in the Educational Conference held in April 1914 at Jullundur, but it was immediately hushed up. The voice, however, could not be hushed outside, in the press and on the platform. A separate meeting was held on the same night after the Conference and strong exception taken to the proposal of the Government. The voice of opposition grew in volume, until the Chief Khalsa Diwan was constrained to call a general meeting of the Sikhs whom it considered representative. About 245 Sikhs, thus summoned, met in the Town Hall of Amritsar on the 3rd of May, 1914, and in the midst of great uproar passed six resolutions, one of which ran as follows :—

"That the Government be humbly requested to restore the land and enclosure wall of the Gurdwara garden to their original condition; but if for reasons of State it is considered essential to change their form, then in the opinion of this Committee it will be acceptable if, without reducing the total area of the land, the whole place is given a rectangular shape and the Gurdwara comes in the middle of it, with roads running on both sides. The entire work, however, should be entrusted to a Managing Committee of Sikhs who should be helped by Government financially for this purpose." In the other resolutions they requested that the Sikhs should be allowed complete liberty to visit or reside in the Gurdwara at all times in the day or night; that a Committee of 7 Sikhs be formed to control and manage the Rikab Ganj and other Gurdwaras situated in the new Delhi; and that for their maintenance sufficient canal land should be granted in compensation for the village of Raisina. The Government agreed to form a Committee and give full freedom of staying or worshipping in the Gurdwara. It also promised to grant 30 squares of land on the Lower Bari Doab Canal in compensation for the Gurdwara lands acquired by Government. It did not, however, accept the main demand that the garden land attached to the Rikab Ganj should be allowed to remain as it was. The Government expressed itself ready to give an equal area of land on the condition that it was made parallel to the roads on the two sides of it, and that before constructing any building in the compound or erecting any wall or railing round it, Government sanction must be secured.

The Chief Khalsa Diwan seemed to be satisfied with this offer, but the other Sikhs would have none of it. On 31st May a great meeting was held at Lahore to condemn this arrangement; and then meeting after meeting began to be held—at Patti, Khanna, Bhasaur and innumerable other places, until the Government was alarmed and it stopped a meeting that was going to be held at Gojra.

It was August, when people's minds were also greatly exercised over the Hansli question. Hansli is the water channel dug by the Sikhs long before the British rule to provide river water from the Ravi to the sacred tanks of Amritsar. Mr. King, the Deputy Commissioner, stopped this aqueduct and made insufficient arrangements for providing tube-well water to the tanks. There was great uproar, and in spite of his threatenings the people held huge meetings to protest against his arbitrary action. Just at that time Sikhs were going in large numbers to jail, where they were not allowed the use of the comb (which beside being a religious symbol is an absolute necessity for the Sikhs) and were forced to wear caps which are forbidden to them by their religion. The Kirpan question had also come to the fore. Through the efforts of the Khalsa Youngmen's Association, Rawalpindi, the Kirpan had been allowed to the Sikhs in the Punjab, but they were still suffering hardships in other provinces, where it was not allowed. This only aggravated the situation which was already becoming bad on account of the Komagata Maru affair.

Komagata Maru.

Sikhs like other Indians have gone abroad, but they prefer those countries where labour is free and respectable life possible. They have gone in very large numbers to the Malaya States, Burma, China (Hong Kong, Shanghai, etc.), Africa (Nairobi and South Africa mostly) and America. There are several thousands in the Malaya States, doing very great business and owning property worth lakhs. Like their brethren in Shanghai and elsewhere, they contributed very handsomely to the War funds, beside frequently sending princely donations to different Sikh institutions. There are thousands in Burma and China. There were in 1913 about eight thousand Sikhs in America. Their chief centre of business was Vancouver, where they had got their temple with a Khalsa Diwan, and very large trade and agriculture business. The Canadian Government, like many other Colonies, was bent upon keeping these 'Blacks' away.

In 1908 it was proposed to induce the Indian labourers to go to British Honduras. The Indians saw through the scheme, which, according to the memorial prepared in 1913 after the Bradlaugh Hall meeting in Lahore, was designed 'to effect the wholesale transportation of the Indian settlers to British Honduras ....by offering them plausible terms, which were not only to reduce them from free immigrants to the level of indentured coolies, but also to considerably reduce their earnings.' A commission appointed by the Government reported against the proposal, and in a large meeting the Indians unanimously resolved not to go to Honduras. The matter was dropped, but the Canadians began to put other difficulties in the way of the Indian immigrants. Sometimes they brought charges of the want of civilization and sometimes of polygamy. There was no great leader with the Sikhs as Mahatma Gandhi in Natal, and they suffered a great deal. They, however, proved in courts that they were Aryan by blood and were not polygamous. At least those who went there did not have more than one wife. They were not allowed to have their families with them. All appeals to the Candians' humanity, all appeals to them as British fellow-subjects proved futile. The Indian Government also did not fight for those Sikhs as zealously as it is now doing in defence of the Indians in Africa. The Sikhs were fighting their battle single-handed.

In May 1910 certain ordinances were passed in Canada, which prohibited immigration into the country of persons of every nationality except by a continuous journey on through tickets from their country of origin, and imposed on all Asiatics—other than those who were admissible under treaty or other restrictive terms—the necessity of being possessed of 200 dollars before being allowed to land. As there was no through shipping service plying between India and Canada, this ordinance appeared to be directed specially against Indian immigration.

In 1912 the families of Bhai Balwant Singh and Bhai Bhag Singh Granthi of the temple at Victoria came to Canada, but the Immigration authorities ordered their deportation. The case was taken to courts, but, before the case came on for hearing, a deputation attended by a Christian missionary went to Ottawa, and as a result of that the families were allowed to land.

The general prohibition, however, continued and there was great agitation over it. All representations to the Canadian Government having proved fruitless, a deputation composed of Bhais Balwant Singh Granthi, Nand Singh, B. A. and Narain Singh left Vancouver on 14th March 1913 to influence opinion in England and India and move the Governments of these countries to intercede with the Canadian Government. Leading Indians, like the late Mr. Gokhale, in England supported the deputation, and in India, too, the deputationists created a sensation by their revelations of the ill-treatment of Indian settlers in Canada. The meetings were attended by thousands. Never had Indians heard such a tale of woe, such a description given by Bhai Balwant Singh in their own tongue of their helplessness in the British Empire, for which they had shed their life's blood in the past and were still ready to do so. The Amritsar meeting was presided over by Sardar Sundar Singh Majithia and the Lahore meeting, held in the Bradlaugh Hall on 18th August, was presided over by Sardar Baghel Singh (who became President of the Chief Khalsa Diwan.) The most important resolution passed at the meeting was moved by Sir P. C. Chatterjee, the famous Chief Court Judge, and supported by Sardar Sewa Ram Singh, Vakil, now a Sessions Judge. Deputations were sent to the Lieutenant Governor and the Viceroy to secure help for getting the restrictive laws of Canada relaxed as regards their operation on Indians*.

---

* It was for such activities in India and elsewhere that Bhai Balwant Singh was charged three years after with waging war against the King 'in Lahore and India', Japan, Canada and other countries, and in spite of such defence witnesses as Sardar

Beside sending deputations, the Sikhs in Canada were also conducting an English-and-Gurmukhi paper called *Sansar*, in which they were airing their grievances.

Their activities were perfectly constitutional and, not to mar the justice of their cause, they were scrupulously keeping themselves aloof from the *Ghadar* party, whose centre was San Francisco and which, created by Hardial, was carried on by such non-Sikh revolutionaries as Ram Chand, Munsha Ram, Barkat Ullah, Guru Datt, etc. It appears from evidence recorded in British courts that when in 1913, in the absence of Bhai Balwant Singh, an attempt was made by Bela Singh, a secret agent of the Canadian Immigration Department, to smuggle in Bhagwan Singh, a man who later fell away from Sikhism and who at that time had taken to sedition preaching, the Sikhs of Vancouver led by Bhai Bhag Singh Granthi opposed the landing of such a mischievous man; and when in spite of their attempts he was allowed to land and began to preach sedition, they helped the Canadian Government in deporting him. They were well-organized and all their proceedings were carried on above-board. Therefore they were able to keep themselves free from in-

---

Sundar Singh Majithia, S. Mehr Singh Chawla, S. Sewa Ram Singh and S. Baghel Singh, was hanged.

fection, and even the Tribunal trying the first Lahore Conspiracy case had to record that "the prosecution has not considered it necessary to place before us much evidence in regard to Vancouver" as a centre of conspiracy. Indians in Canada were described in the memorial presented to the Viceroy after the Bradlaugh Hall meeting as "men of industrious, regular and steady habits, temperate and thrifty living, and pleasant and straight-forward manners."

On 17th October 1913 about 39 Sikhs, who went in a ship to Canada, were arrested by the Immigration Department and orders for their deportation were secured from the Ottawa Government. But the Canadian Sikhs, in behalf of their countrymen, appealed to the court of Chief Justice Hunter, who decided on 24th November, 1913, in their favour, declaring that restrictive notification issued in 1910 was invalid and *ultra vires*. The news of this decision were published far and wide in Canada, Japan, China and India. Wherever the Sikhs received the *Sansar* of Vancouver and the *Khalsa Sewak* of Amritsar, they hailed the news with joy. From letters and wires, too, received from Canada they felt sure that for six months at least, until the Candian parliament forged a new law for them, there would be no restriction on landing in Canada.

Baba Gurdit Singh, a Malaya merchant who had emigrated from India some 30 years before and was looked upto for his age and experience in the East, came to Hong Kong on 5th January 1914 and began to make arrangements for taking Indians to Canada. At first some shipping companies agreed to take Indians to Canada, but they soon withdrew their promises, and the Sikhs in the East were left the only alternative of chartering their own vessel at any cost and settling the immigration question once for all. They expressed their readiness to subscribe freely to start a navigation company, and for this venture the Sikhs in Canada also held out large promises. But for the present they confined themselves to chartering a vessel. Baba Gurdit Singh wanted to leave nothing to chance and proposed to start direct from Calcutta after a ship was chartered. But in negotiating with different companies in Singapore he had to spend about a month and the intending immigrants wanted to be quick and reach Canada before the Dominion Parliament met. Therefore they had wired to him at Singapore on the 29th January, urging him not to go to Calcutta but to come and start a vessel direct from Hong Kong to Vancouver. They must have heard by this time that the Governor-General of Canada had re-issued an order in Council on 7th January, 1914, identical with the one already declared invalid in the court of Justice Hunter, but they trusted on the judgment of the court and believed that there would be no difficulty about getting admission into the country, or hoped to win their cause legally as their brethren had done before.

After trying many Chinese Companies, a ship called the *s.s. Komagata Maru* was chartered for six months from a Japanese Company for 11,000 dollars per month, and was renamed the *Guru Nanak Jehaz*. The hire was to be paid in instalments, the last one being due after two months from commencement of the charter. It was clearly stated in the charter that the ship would be taken to Canada. Baba Gurdit Singh issued tickets to a large number of the intending emigrants but many of them were not able to pay their fares, as is evident from the fact that notes for nearly 24,000 dollars executed by various passengers on this account were found afterwards in the ship. "Majority of them were poor men who had saved but little and many had sacrificed all they had in the way of savings to pay the expenditure incurred by this voyage. There is also evidence to prove that many gave up regular service and appointments in which they were receiving good pay in Hong Kong, Shanghai, and elsewhere to embark on this disastrous voyage."*

* The Report of the Enquiry Committee appointed by Government.

The ship was to start on 27th March, but on 25th March Baba Gurdit Singh was arrested by the Hong Kong Police, and most of the intending passengers were scared away. Only 165 out of 500 or more were ready to start. When after a great deal of trouble the case was withdrawn, the Governor refused to sign the clearance certificate. The Baba Sahib strongly protested to the Governor against this illegal detention and represented that he was being put to a great loss. The acting Governor, who turned out to be an old friend of Baba Gurdit Singh, admitted in an interview that he had detained the ship because he was expecting a reply from the Ottawa Government and the Indian authorities in London, whom he had wired six days before for instructions. After waiting uselessly for a reply, the Governor allowed the ship to start on the 4th of April. He also promised to move the Governments of Canada and India to help the Baba Sahib.

The ship proceeded to Shanghai where it took in 111 new passengers, and then to Moji and Yokohama where more passengers were taken on board, until there were 376 men in all, of whom only 25 were Mohammedans and the rest Sikhs. At Moji it was discovered that the ship-doctor Raghunath, a renegade from Sikhism, was an informer and was trying to create parties among the passengers. His offer for service in the ship had been accepted on his promising that he would give up smoking and become a Sikh in earnest. But now that he was found out to be a secret agent, he was asked to go. The Baba Sahib was, however, persuaded to forgive the man and re-employ him. This leniency cost the Sikhs a great deal afterwards.

On 21st May the s. s. Komagata Maru anchored off Victoria, where the authorities of the port demanded the clearance certificate from Yokohama. On the ship-captain's saying that the paper was missing, the authorities at once wired to the Ottawa Government for an order to send back the ship. The situation was, however, saved by Baba Gurdit Singh's secretary who went to the captain's cabin and found out the paper hidden there. Two days later the ship reached Vancouver.

Here the tussle began. The Immigration authorities held up the ship at some distance from the coast and placed it under a strong guard in launch boats. Dr. Raghunath with his family was, of course, admitted and so was the Japanese Captain of the ship, who, according to the Charter, was under orders of the charterer, but became a ready tool in the hands of the coast officers. Other passengers, in spite of their repeated protests, were not allowed to land. If the coastal authorities had been minded to proceed strictly according to law, they should have allowed Baba Gurdit Singh and his personal staff to disembark as non-immigrants, for he was a merchant come with his ship to touch the coast temporarily. Then they should have put the remaining passengers in the Immigration Shed and held a regular enquiry into each individual case. The ship should have been released. But nothing of the sort was done. The attitude of the Immigration officers of Canada may be gathered from the following recorded words of one of them: "The Hindus on board the ship came to this country deliberately intending to force their presence upon a people *who do not wish them.*" From 1st June onwards they began to take one passenger after another to the coast and leisurely examine each case before a Board of Enquiry, simply to cause delay. The authorities were informed by the Captain that Baba Gurdit Singh had to pay the last instalment of his ship-rent by the 4th June, failing which he would lose his ship and incur enormous loss. They, therefore, would not allow him to sell his coal and realise money or to see or correspond with his countrymen on the coast, who had formed a committee to help him. Even his legal adviser was not permitted to go on board the ship.

By 2nd June provisions ran dry and the passengers began to starve, but in spite of protests from Baba Gurdit Singh the Immigration Department would not help him nor allow him to go to the shore and make his own arrangements. The Baba Sahib had to wire to the King Emperor in London and to the Governor General at Ottawa before he was allowed relief on that score. He also wired to the Chief Khalsa Diwan at Amritsar to move the Indian Government for aid. But beyond acknowledging the receipt of the Diwan's representation, the Government of India seems to have given no assurance of help. The Baba Sahib in despair had to transfer the ship's charter to Bhai Bhag Singh and Mr. Rahim, the representatives of the Shore Committee. But even these assignees of the charter were not allowed to have control of the ship.

About 20th June, at the suggestion of the legal advisers of the Immigration Department Baba Gurdit Singh consented to take a case to the Board of Enquiry, which would test the validity of the Order in Council without prejudicing the other cases. But, as confessed by Messrs. Macrossan and Harper, who were asked by the Hindustani Association to take up the Komagata Maru case, the matter had gone quite out of the legal sphere and had become political. They wrote on 24th June: "We feel that the matter has become of such great moment that it has got beyond the realm of mere legal proceedings, and has become largely, if not entirely, a question of national policy of vital importance to not only the Government of this country but also involves conflicting Imperial interests. In the face of this, it seems to us, *it is a question for diplomacy rather than law*, and we do not feel that we could conscientiously enter upon a legal fight under these circumstances, notwithstanding the fact that you have offered a very generous retainer." The case was, of course, doomed.

Now the Shore Committee, which claimed the ship, request the Immigration Department to allow the cargo to be loaded and also to provide passage money for the passengers, who were now ready to go back, or to take them off to some other ship. But the Department would not allow any man of the Shore Committee to go to the ship nor send any relief to the passengers who were clamouring for food. When they were sick and starving, an attack was made by the police on the night of July 20 to force away the ship, but it would have been death for them to go away in that impoverished and unprovided condition, and they resisted the cruel attempt. The authorities then provided food and, bringing an armed force in a vessel, ordered them to return to the ports from which they had come.

They started on 23rd July. A few disembarked in Japan, but after that none of the passengers was allowed to land either in Hong Kong, Shanghai, or any other place on the way. Baba Gurdit Singh had now no authority over the Captain or the ship, but he asked the Captain many times during the voyage to satisfy himself that there were no arms kept by the passengers. The Baba Sahib had been very scrupulous on this point and had always been on the alert against the smuggling of arms or undesirable literature. When staying off Vancouver, an attempt was made by the Immigration agents to discredit the Baba's cause by throwing in seditious literature, but as soon as he found a bundle of such papers he sent them at once to the authorities, protesting against such tactics.

On 27th September the ship, with 321 men on it, arrived at Budge-Budge, some 14 miles south of Calcutta. By the Ingress into India Act of 1914 the Bengal Government, in consultation with the Government of the Punjab, had decided that the returned Punjabis on landing at Budge-Budge should be put into a special train and conveyed to their homes in the Punjab. All were searched three times upto the time of their landing, but no arms were found on them. 17 Mohammedan passengers consented to obey the orders, and went into the train, but the others represented that they had got nothing left in the Punjab to call their own and that they should be allowed to seek their fortune in Calcutta. They began to move towards Calcutta in a procession with their Holy Book before them. They were shown a military force which brought them back to the railway station. On the way, as it appears from evidence, some of the European police sergeants roughly handled the Sikhs. When they came back to the station a bloody scene ensued in darkness. Twenty of the passengers and four on the Government side were killed. Beside these two Indian residents of Budge-Budge also fell, one of whom at least is admitted by the Government report to have been killed by the British troops. A constable killed on the Government side had also received a gun-shot wound from some of the troops. Those Sikhs who escaped were arrested. They were brought to the Punjab and interned or thrown into jails. Baba Gurdit Singh had escaped*. A large sum of money belong-

* After seven years' wanderings, during which he suffered terrible difficulties, the old Baba suddenly appeared in a big national assembly held at Nankana Sahib on 16th November. 1921. The whole concourse of people numbering lakhs, accompanied him peacefully to the Dak Bungalow, where he offered himself for

ing to Baba Gurdit Singh was left at the place of occurrence, and the Baba's complaint is that no account of it has been published so far.

The story of the Komagata Maru men is strange. Even now you might come upon a straight-walking, pathetic-looking man, who would, like the Ancient Mariner, hold you with his eye, and not let you go until you

---

arrest. After some months' detention he was released on 28th February, 1922, as there was no case against him. He was, however, again arrested at the Golden Temple.

He was originally charged under the Seditious Meetings Act for the speeches made about his own sufferings and in reply to the welcome addresses presented to him by the Congress and the Khilafat Committees ; but about a month later the Government thought it fit to prosecute him for the much graver offence of sedition for the same speeches. The Government did not provide him with his private papers which had been seized at Budge-Budge in 1914, and which he required in preparation of his defence. The Court, too, disallowed, as irrelevant as many as 19 witnesses out of 21, whom Baba Gurdit Singh wanted to produce to clear up certain allegations that had been made against him in connection with the Komagata Maru and the Budge-Budge affairs ; and this in spite of the fact that the judge himself devoted about one half of his lengthy judgment to the same affairs. The Baba Sahib, therefore, gave up his defence in protest. He was convicted on July 26, 1922, under Section 124A of the Penal Code and sentenced to five years' transportation.

have heard his rueful tale and assured him that the Ship would sail again.

After the departure of the Komagata Maru men, upon account of the scarcity of business consequent on the War and the increase of prejudice against them, the Sikhs found it more and more difficult to remain in America. Some of them, especially those coming under the influence of the Frisco revolutionaries, out of bitterness did take to anarchical methods and deserved punishment. But many innocent men, like Bhai Balwant Singh, also suffered with them. Their lives were sworn away before Special Tribunals by such men as the notorious Bela Singh of the Immigration Department of Canada, who had murdered with impunity Bhai Bhag Singh Granthi in broad daylight in the Vancouver temple. Under Sir M. O'Dwyer an America-returned Sikh ran a perilous chance of being taken as a seditious man, and to get such a Sikh interned or arrested on some charge was considered the height of loyalty. If any paper like the *Loyal Gazette* of Lahore expressed the panthic grief over it, it was at once punished. It was war time, and the Sikhs did not want to embarrass the Government by making any strong agitation. But iron had entered into their spirit.

CHAPTER VI.

POLITICAL AWAKENING AMONG THE SIKHS.

The War and the democratic principles for which it was waged by the Allies created a passion for democracy everywhere and the Sikhs had their share. When the great announcement of August 1917 was made and Mr. Montagu came to hear evidence, the Sikhs felt hopeful and free to express their views before the Secretary of State. The Chief Khalsa Diwan gave expression to these views and demanded that the Sikhs should be given 1/3 of the seats in the Provincial Council. In 1909, in spite of representations made in behalf of Sikhs by the present Maharaja of Nabha, who was then a member of the Imperial Legislative Council, and Bhai Sahib Arjan Singh of Bagarian, the Sikh claims had been quietly passed over in the Minto-Morley Seheme. By a compact made at the Lucknow Congress in 1916, Hindus and Mohammedans also had divided the seats in the Punjab Council equally among themselves ignoring the share of the Sikhs. In the Montagu-Chelmsford Report, however, the Sikhs' claim to separate representation was recognised ; but when the franchise rules were framed, out of 54 seats the Sikhs were recommended for

8 seats only. This was quite inadequate, as this number was fixed on the numerical strength of the Sikh community, and not on their special qualifications. The words in the Report were: "To the Sikhs, therefore, and to them alone, we propose to extend the system already adopted in the case of Mohammedans." This system according to the Minto-Morley Reforms had based the scheme of Mohammedan representation on the principle that a community in minority cannot allow itself to be swayed by the majority vote purely on a numerical basis. Therefore, in those Provinces where they were in minority, they were allowed seats far in excess of their numerical strength. Why not in the case of Sikhs? The Punjab Government had written about them to the Government of India on 23rd November, 1918: "But their (Sikhs') influential position in the Province, which is based partly on historical and political factors, partly on their military prestige, and partly on their comparatively high educational level and economic importance in the Central and Colony districts, entitles them to a considerably greater degree of representation than is indicated by numbers alone."

The Sikhs themselves emphasised the following points in support of their claims:—

(1) They have a large stake in the country, comprising as they do among them-

selves, besides the ruling princes, no less than half of the aristocracy and the greater part of the landed gentry and peasantry of the Punjab.

(2) They pay at least 40 per cent. of the land revenue and canal charges of the Province.

(3) The number of voters among the Sikhs is 93,725, while that of Hindus and others 92,450, and of Mohammedans 1,37,989.

(4) Their services in the Mutiny, in the Afghan Wars and other wars, were out of all proportion to their numerical strength.

(5) In the Great War, so wrote the Punjab Government, " the number of Sikhs in the Army is now believed to exceed 80,000, a proportion far higher than in the case of any other community." Being about 11 per cent. of the population of the Punjab, their strength in the entire Indian Army was 20 per cent, and they supplied not less than one-third of the total number of men recruited from the Punjab. The awards made for distinguished services on the battle-field were won by the Sikhs to the extent of one-third of the total won by the Punjabis.

After all the efforts of the Chief Khalsa Diwan and the Sikh League, two more seats were given ; but the total number of the non-special elected seats was also increased, so that the Sikhs had now 10 out of 58 seats.

Even their deputations to Simla and to London were not able to effect a further change. When Sardar Sundar Singh Majithia expressed his disappointment at the result of the Diwan's humble representations, Mr. Hallifax, who represented the Punjab Government, said to the Sardar Sahib tauntingly: "Will you now go and join the Congress party?" The difficulty with the Government was that it wanted to keep the number of the Mohammedan seats intact and let the Sikhs divide seats with the Hindus. This greatly disappointed the Sikhs. If the Government had altogether abolished the system of separate representation based on religion, the Sikhs would have gladly agreed to it. It was, however, not possible for them to accept a status proportionately inferior to that accorded to a sister community in other Provinces.

Over and above this came the Jallianwala Bagh Massacre. The Sikhs lost at least one-third of the whole number. It was the Baisakhi Day in Amritsar, the day on which the Sikhs had been baptised as the Khalsa by the Tenth Guru. On the same day again, they received the baptism of fire in the city of their Gurus. General Dyer, instead of expressing regret, vaunted of his deed and called himself a Sikh. Lord Finlay repeated this absurdity in the House of Lords. Many non-Sikhs were calling themselves Sikhs in order to swamp our interests, and here was another addition to our ranks! After this who would not call himself a Sikh? And yet the Government would not change the definition of a Sikh. It defined a Sikh to be a person who simply declared that he followed the Ten Gurus and their teachings. In this way even those who were condemned by the Sikhs as apostates were declared Sikhs by Government, *e. g.*, Harnami Shah in Amritsar and Ganda Sinh in Sialkot.

Thoughtful Sikhs were gradually coming to the conclusion that they must organize themselves, if they wanted to save themselves in the rush of events. Sardar Jogendra Singh, in his speech at the Educational Conference of April, 1917, had exhorted the Sikhs to organize; and again while writing in his *East and West* about the Sikhs and the Reforms he said: "They must organize their villages, towns, districts and the central representative assembly." But as long as there was war, the Sikhs chose to remain mute on all questions of political reform, believing that the supreme necessity of the hour was the successful prosecution of the war. When the war was over, the Sikhs saw nothing but complete disillusionment of their long-cherished hopes.

Their other grievances apart, they were at the mercy of the Government even in regard to the wearing of religious symbols. A police officer in the Jhelum district removed the comb and the iron bracelet from the persons of three Sikhs who were committed to the judicial lock-up. Sardar Gajjan Singh put a question about it in the Council and asked if the Government would instruct the Police Department not to interfere with the religious possessions of the Sikhs. Mr. French, Chief Secretary, on behalf of Government, admitted the fact, but relying on the police rules, which did not allow any articles to be taken into a lock-up by an accused person, he did not give any assurance against the repetition of the wrong, 'for in the hands of a dangerous or desperate criminal these symbols could be used to attempt suicide, or possible escape, or to cause self-inflicted injuries'! We must remember that the jail regulations provide the compulsory wearing of an iron bracelet by habitual offenders.

Circumstances were forcing the conviction on the minds of Sikhs that their public voice was everywhere disregarded because of their political backwardness. In the autumn session of the Punjab Council in 1918, while refusing to accept the amendment of Sardar Gajjan Singh to his resolution recommending the Congress division of the seats between Hindus and Muhammedans in the Punjab, Mian Fazl-i-Hussain told the Sardar that as his community had kept aloof from the Congress it had no ground to complain afterwards and amend its decisions.

At Amritsar, when the Congress held its sittings in 1919, the Sikhs also held the first session of their political body called the Sikh League. The big-wigs or title-holders did not join it. But all the middle class people were with it. It had a host of district leagues scattered over the Province. A vernacular paper, the *Akali*, was started at Lahore in May, 1920. It roused the people to respond to the national call. It influenced the common people in the villages. A fund was started for the relief of the families of those Sikhs who had gone to jail for their religion and country, among whom were many who, in spite of the King-Emperor's Amnesty Proclamation, were not released. Harrowing stories were told by the Sikhs who went in disguise to distant jails to see how their brethren incarcerated there suffered for not wearing topees or not salaaming proud jailors.

There were going on political meetings in the villages at the same time. The educated people had been taunted by the bureaucrats that they were mere agitators, that the masses were contented and undisturbed by the passing political storms. Mahatma

Gandhi threw a challenge to the intelligentia of India by demanding suspension of legal practice and studies in colleges. The talking politicians retired from the field, and only those remained who could make some sacrifice. The appeal, therefore, began to have greater effect on the masses who could make sacrifice. The political meetings in the villages began to produce great effect on the people. In October, 1920, the Sikh League passed the full Non-Co-operation programme.

The practical effect of this resolution on pleaders and title-holders was next to nothing. But it gave a great shaking to the inner spirit of the people, many of whom had fought for liberty in the West. They began to recognize what was their own, and felt it keenly when it was not given to them. While other communities were preparing themselves in other ways, the Sikhs were thinking of righting the long-standing wrongs and acquiring by the way a discipline and experience which could be useful in the struggle for Swaraj also. They wanted to do something practical. They found that in spite of their humble but urgent requests their Golden Temple and their Khalsa College were still in the hands of the Government.

We shall see in another place how the Golden Temple was taken. Here we may note in passing how the Khalsa College was freed. Long before the political movement had begun, the Sikhs had been talking and writing about nationalising the management of the Khalsa College. They had requested the Government in their Educational Conference of April, 1920, to hand over the control of the College to the community. Resolutions to the same effect were passed by associations all over the Province, even in Basra and Baghdad. The professors of the College also had, a year before, drafted a few essential changes to be made in the constitution of the College, and the Principal had sent the draft to the Commissioner-Chairman. But nothing substantial had come out of it. Now seeing that the storm of Non-Co-operation was coming and fearing that it would destroy their beloved College, they wanted to be beforehand with it by proposing changes themselves and getting the indefensible weakness removed. They decided to take strong action, so that their earnestness might not be doubted. They sent a letter to the Government asking it to withdraw its control from the management of the College before 5th November, 1920, or they would resign. After much haggling for a month, during which the College remained closed and the Professors had to resign, the thing was done and the College saved. By that time the first wave of educational Non-Co-operation had spent itself.

At the same time agitation about the Rikab Ganj wall began again. To satisfy the public it was announced that by an agreement between the Government and the Khalsa Diwan Delhi the old contested wall was not to be touched. The Committee of the Diwan welcomed the suggestion of an extra grant of land to the Gurdwara. The whole compound was to be squared by building a new wall enclosing the whole area on a pattern to be approved by the Chief Engineer. The Committee further agreed not to make any buildings inside the enclosure without the permission of the Imperial Delhi Committee or its successors. The land inside the enclosure wall was to be in the perpetual possession and control of the Khalsa Diwan. If the Diwan wished to rebuild the Gurdwara and the residential quarters attached thereto, the Imperial Delhi Committee would welcome the proposal. A contribution towards the building of the Gurdwara wall was promised from the New Capital estimates. Thirty squares of land on the Lower Bari Doab Canal were to be given as compensatory grant.

As far as the site was concerned, this arrangement was fairly satisfactory, but the Sikhs still insisted that the demolished portion of the old wall should be rebuilt at the Government expense. H. H. the Maharaja of Nabha is also said to have moved in the matter. Sardar Sardul Singh Caveessieur proposed in September a band of 100 volunteers who would go to Delhi and restore the wall with their own hands. There was great enthusiasm shown by Sikhs in giving their names for this work, and in a short while about a thousand men and women offered themselves. Most of these volunteers met at Lahore on the occasion of the Sikh League session in October 1920 and resolved to go to Delhi on the 1st of December and rebuild the wall. Before they went, however, the Government got the work done and peace was restored.

CHAPTER VII.

GURDWARA REFORM.

PRELIMINARY STAGE.

While the struggle was going on for getting control of the Khalsa College, the Sikhs were also getting control of their temples. For, the control of the temples to them is as important as the Khilafat is to Mohammedans; and Swaraj, too, means nothing to them, if it does not mean this. The freedom of their temples is also the measure of their religious purity. They live their religion in their temples, which are not only places of worship, but training grounds of social service, public deliberation and other kinds of practical religion as well.

After carrying on for some years the reform propaganda through Singh Sabhas and schools, the Sikhs found that their work was seriously hampered by the corrupt condition of their temples*. All efforts of the reforming Sikhs were practically undone when, opposed to their solitary temple in a city, there were hundreds of other temples made

---

* "The world is on the way to ruin when the sacred places become corrupt." *Dhanasari I.*

proof against all reform by wealth and the absence of popular control.

There were three ways open to Sikhs to carry out reform in their temples : boycott, pressure of public opinion, and litigation. Boycott could never be effective against priests, who possessed enormous wealth and could easily dispense with the offerings made at the temples. With the existing law litigation, too, without the conscientious support of the Government, could be of no avail, as the priests could afford to weary out the poor congregations in this expensive game. Some of the priests had an income of Rs. 200 a day, others had a yearly income of Rs. 200,000 or Rs. 300,000 from land alone, beside what was got from cash offerings every day. The Sikhs, therefore, in the beginning relied chiefly on the pressure of public opinion and went to law-courts whenever they hoped for Government support.

The Singh Sabha, helped by such newspapers as the *Khalsa* of Lahore, was the only movement by which their public opinion was formed and exerted, and there being no political movement among the Sikhs their public voice did not carry as much weight as it deserved. Beside the fear of Government always kept the leaders in check. They would push their claims so far as they safely could, but never beyond the point where official displeasure began.

Wherever reform was needed, Sikhs would go in large numbers and hold a diwan. Thousands of people would thus see with their own eyes the things that required reform, and the custodians of the place, too, would see for themselves the awakening among the Sikhs and the Panthic power this awakening brought with it. The Mahant would accept reform forthwith, or weigh the influence he could exert with the officials and challenge the whole community in the courts of law. From about 1895 a jatha of Lahore Sikhs under the leadership of Sardar Mehr Singh Chawla would go yearly on foot to Nankana Sahib and hold a diwan there. Public subscriptions were raised for extending the building and gold-plating the central dome of the Janam Asthan, providing certain rooms to the Baradari and a well to the Bal Lila. After some time it was proposed that a representative committee should be appointed to control all the Gurdwaras at Nankana Sahib. On a fixed day a meeting was held, which was attended by many Sikh leaders and Mahants of the local Gurdwaras. The Deputy Commissioner of Lahore, Mr. Hallifax, was also present. After some discussion the Mahants, who were present, agreed that the Gurdwaras were the property of the Panth and that they would serve under a Committee of Control. They signed a document to this effect, which document and a lengthy report by Mr. Hallifax must still be found in the District Office of Gujranwala. Soon after this agreement was signed, the Mahants, it is said, acting on the advice of a Hindu Tehsildar, changed their minds, and as the Deputy Commissioder came away the matter was left where it was. Mr. Hallifax went again to Nankana Sahib some months after, but was not successful in settling the affair. The Sikhs, however, went on struggling until about 1905 the lands attached to the Nankana Sahib temples were entered in the name of the temples instead of their Mahants.

The case of Babe-di-Ber, Sialkot, is much older. But in 1895 definite complaints were made against the Mahant that he was misappropriating the Gurdwara money. We will deal with this case separately. The case of Bawli Sahib was started about 1904. Although two courts had found that the misconduct of the Mahants was proved beyond doubt, the Chief Court set aside the decision on merely technical grounds. In 1913 again it was found established by a District Judge that the temple was in the hands of a Mistress of the Mahant who was dead, and an appeal about it is still pending before the High Court.

In 1905 a very interesting case occurred in Kabul. There is a Gurdwara there, sacred to the memory of Guru Har Rai. A Brahmin priest had quietly put up an idol in the temple. The Sikhs protested, but did not do anything beyond that. After some time, when the Brahmin died, the Sikhs requested the relations of the Brahmin to remove the idol. They refused. The matter went to court. A commission was appointed to enquire into the case. There was a great excitement among the Hindus and the commission decided in their favour. But the Amir himself looked into the file and gave the following interesting judgment :—

" I, Abdur Rahman, Amir of Kabul, am King of Afghanistan. In our reign has occurred a suit between certain men who worship God and others who worship idols.

There is a temple called the Dharamsala of Guru Har Rai in this city. The idol-worshippers claim that in that Dharamsala they possess a room in which they worship idols.

The God-worshippers contend that the old servant who was a Brahmin used to keep idols in the Dharamsala secretly in a niche. After the Brahmin's death the Sikhs handed over the images to another Brahmin. The contention of the God-worshippers is reasonable and is supported by evidence.

In our view idol-worshippers have got nothing to do with a place called Dharamsala. This Dharamsala is named after Guru Har Rai, the seventh successor of Baba Nanak Sahib, who was the greatest Unitarian and was opposed to idol worship. Similarly Sikhs have got no concern with a place called Thakurdwara or Shivdwara, which must belong to Hindus. As this particular place is a Dharamsala, the only people interested in it are the God-worshippers.

I, as King, order that the suit of the idol-worshippers be dismissed."

In the summer of 1905 idols were removed from the precincts of the Golden Temple, Amritsar. Those who disliked this action tried to influence powerful parties among the Sikhs against the reforming party. The venerable Maharaja Sir Hira Singh of Nabha, who was the most respected Sikh Ruler of the time, was asked to interfere, but he refused. Then the priests of Hazur Sahib (Nader) in the Deccan, which is one of the Four Thrones, or places of highest authority for the Sikhs, were moved to condemn the Singh Sabha movement. These priests issued a bull, addressed to the other three Thrones at the Akal Takht, Patna and Kesgarh (Anandpur), forbidding Sikhs to associate with the Singh Sabha people, who were converting Mohammedans and men of low castes and were giving the same baptism of the double-edged sword to women as to men. They forgot that in 1879 (on 12th Kartik 1936 Vik.) the priests of the Akal Takht and Darbar Sahib had issued a joint Hukamnama welcoming the Singh Sabha movement as the restorer of the original form of Sikhism, and calling upon all Sikhs to join the movement. The Sarbrah or Manager of Hazur Sahib itself had issued, some time before, a letter to the press contradicting a rumour that the Singh Sabha people were not welcome at the Takht Hazur Sahib. As to the conversion of Mohammedans, it is interesting to find that on August 11, 1906, one Sheikh Ahmed Din of Sialkot, with his whole family, was converted to Sikhism by the Akal Takht priests and was renamed Jiwan Singh. The priests issued a Hukamnama proclaiming the fact and ordering all Sikhs on peril of their souls not to have any scruple in eating and drinking with the newly-converted family. It was signed by the following priests :—Bhais Arjan Singh, Sundar Singh, Teja Singh, Bur Singh, Multana Singh, Partab Singh, Dial Singh and Narain Singh. But in 1905 they acted against their convictions, as they did again in 1920, and openly condemned the reform movement. There was great indignation expressed at the conduct of the priests. They were reminded that "the

Gurdwaras belong to the Community and not to the priests, who were mere servants of the Panth."* They were told that the Gurdwaras were no hereditary possessions of the priests, but were given to them for the performance of service, and that those who did not perform their duties well could be ousted by the Panth. An example was given of Babu Gopal Singh, Mahant of the Akal Takht, who had recently been dismissed on account of his non-Sikh character. The removal of Udasis from the control of Darbar Sahib and the appointment of Sikh Granthis was also quoted to shew that the Panth could exert its right of effecting changes in the administration of temples.

From that time onward, as the rest of India was slowly awakening to the consciousness of its lost liberties, the Sikhs began to agitate for the freedom of their temples. The abuses prevailing in the sacred places were mercilessly exposed and were rightly ascribed to the want of Panthic control. The *Khalsa Advocate*, the *Khalsa Samachar*, the *Khalsa Sewak*, the *Punjab*, and other newspapers were most active in advocating the temple reform. Beside airing grievances about the central temples at Amritsar, it was complained that the Gurdwaras in Majha and Malwa were being converted into

* The *Punjab* of Amritsar : October, 1905.

private houses by Udasis and other sadhus.* In August, 1906, certain visitors found the priests of Muktsar drunk and holding a music party within the temple. About the same time a complaint was made that the Udasi custodians of the Dharamsala of Saidoke in the Ferozepore District were wasting their income on drinking and loose-living. Seeing that no reform was possible there, the people erected a new temple, where the morals of their women would be safer. Some Christians took possession of a Bungah belonging to the temple of Tarn Taran. A hard struggle led by one Sardar Sant Singh followed. The case went to court and on 5th January, 1907, it was decided in favour of Sikhs. We read in newspapers about that time that the management of Hazur Sahib had recently been put in the hands of a committee, a great majority of whom were non-Sikhs and the Sarbrah was only a Secretary. Mahant Mitha Singh of Panja Sahib got the land attached to the Gurdwara entered in his own name. Several Sikh associations, led by the Singh Sabha of Abbottabad, passed resolutions condemning the action of the Mahant and calling upon him to render accounts of his income and expenditure to the public.

In 1906, when there was a rumour about the change of the Sarbrah of the Golden

* The *Punjab* : October 15, 1906.

Temple, the Singh Sabhas and the Sikh press urged on the Government to allow the Sikhs to appoint the Sarbrah themselves in future, and called upon the Chief Khalsa Diwan to move in the matter. This agitation continued, and in the Chief Khalsa Diwan itself a resolution was passed that in consultation with the Panth the Dastur-al-Aml, by which the Golden Temple was governed, should be changed. But nothing came out of it.

The Chief Khalsa Diwan had formed a Sub-Committee for the reform of Gurdwaras, but the position of the Diwan was not strong enough to enable it to effect reform in the teeth of all the opposition that was daily gathering strength. People, although admiring the work of the Diwan, had in fact begun to take less and less part in the performance of the work, and even in 1906 it was complained that the members did not care to attend the Diwan's meetings. The whole burden of the work fell on the shoulders of a few veteran workers, who could not, therefore, feel strong enough to face the difficulties involved in the struggle for releasing the Gurdwaras. In 1915 a pamphlet was written in English, advocating the freedom of temples as the basis of all reform. It was printed at the expense of the Chief Khalsa Diwan, which circulated it among prominent Sikhs for opinions and suggestions. The few gentlemen who cared to give opinions were not very hopeful about success in reclaiming the Gurdwaras, and the matter was dropped as impracticable.

The most serious attention of the Sikhs was, however, drawn to the necessity of reform in temples by the irresponsible conduct of the Rikab Ganj Mahant, who had sold the land belonging to the Gurdwara into the hands of Government without letting the public know anything about it. In view of the strong agitation described before the Government suspended its action in regard to the wall, but the grievance still remained there.

In the same year it was found that Mahant Harnam Singh of Akali Phula Singh's Samadh at Nowshera had sold a great portion of the endowment land and was wasting the remainder in riotous living. The Samadh was the monument erected by Maharaja Ranjit Singh in honour of Baba Phula Singh, his captain, who had fallen on the spot while fighting against the border tribes in 1823. The Maharaja had also assigned two-thirds of the land of Pir Sabak for the up-keep of the shrine. Hearing that the Mahant had alienated so much of the land, the Sikhs of Peshawar, especially Military Sikhs residing in the cantonment, held a great meeting under the auspices of the local Singh Sabha and resolved to rescue the shrine from the profligate Mahant. In October, 1914, permission to sue the Mahant was obtained from the Collector. Subedar-Major Bhagwan Singh, Jamadar Thamman Singh and Bhai Bhag Singh, who were the leaders in the movement, had to struggle hard for two years in collecting funds for the expenses of the suit, which was filed on 13th April, 1916. The claim under Section 92/93, C.P.C., was that the Mahant be dismissed and a Committee be appointed for management and control. The case went on in the court of the District Judge, who accepted the plea of the defendant that he held the land in his own right and dismissed the suit with costs. The Sikhs appealed to the court of the Judicial Commissioner, who set aside the decision of the District Judge on 5th March, 1917, and ordered the case to be tried anew on its merits, provided the Sikhs secured from the Collector a certificate permitting them to sue the Mahant as Jagirdar. The Mahant in the meanwhile had sold another portion of the land for Rs. 8,000. An order was issued by the District Judge on 27th July, 1917, forbidding the Mahant to sell any land belonging to the Gurdwara. The case lingered on for another year and the conductors of the case had a great deal to do to collect subscriptions to meet the expenses. In the beginning the response was very meagre and the failure of the Sikhs of Rawalpindi to carry on a similar suit against the Mahant of Panja Sahib for want of funds was a discouraging example. But Bhai Bagh Singh and his colleagues went on heroically, until with constant appeals in the press and on the platform they were able to create a sufficient interest not only among the Sikhs but among the lovers of reform in other communities also. The following letter from Rai Thakur Datt, an Arya Samaj leader, will speak for itself: "Will you kindly remit the enclosed Rs. 15 to the gentleman who is conducting the case about the Samadh of Akali Phula Singh. I would have sent this small contribution to him direct, if I had known his name and address. I sympathise with his laudable object of trying to regulate and purify the management of a religious endowment." An attempt was made by the counsel for defence to prove that as Akali Phula Singh was a Nihang, the trust was of a private nature, concerning the Nihang Sikhs alone, and that Sikhs of the Singh Sabha persuasion could have no interest themselves and absolutely no status to interfere in the management. But the evidence of the *Four Takhts*, or the highest places of Sikh authority, and the opinions of some eminent Nihangs and other Sikhs were accepted by the Judge as supporting the contention of the plaintiffs that the place, with the property, was a public religious trust and that the Singh Sabha people had full interest in it. The case was decided on 18th July, 1918. The Mahant was removed on account of his "mismanagement and frailty of character" and was further called upon to render an account of the income and expenditure of the shrine for the past ten years. The court also directed that for the management and control of the institution a Committee of three members be appointed in consultation with the plaintiffs or their representatives and the representatives of Akali Phula Singh's family. The Committee was empowered to appoint, subject to the approval of the court, a Mahant who was to be an Akali Sikh. The Mahant preferred an appeal to the Judicial Commissioner, but it was rejected. The counter appeal which the Peshawar Singh Sabha had filed to enlarge the Trust Committee under new arrangements, was accepted.

It was reported in June, 1915, that the Gurdwara of Nanheri Sahib in Patiala, erected in honour of the 9th and 10th Gurus, was in a deplorable condition. There had been 350 bighas of land originally attached to the temple, which came to be administered by the Mahant of Bhai Bir Singh's Dharmsala in Patiala City. This land had been alienated. One Bhai Nidhan Singh set up a movement in the locality to reform the Gurdwara and held diwans for the purpose. Information was received about the same time that Bhai Mukand Singh, Mahant of Takht Patna Sahib, where Guru Gobind Singh was born, was putting a ban on progressive Sikhism and would not allow any Singh Sabha man to enter the Takht. While giving evidence in a case in April, 1915, he admitted that like his predecessors on the gaddi he had been selected by the Sikh public out of many candidates for the Mahantship of the Takht and had been made to sign an agreement about his appointment. In the same year it was reported in the *Panth Sewak* of Lahore, which was becoming an energetic advocate of Gurdwara Reform, that Mahant Mitha Singh had got the Gurdwara of Panja Sahib as well as the land attached to it entered in his own name. In June, 1916, in response to a general commotion in the community, the Singh Sabha of Rawalpindi called a meeting of representative Sikhs and decided to sue the Mahant in the court. For want of funds, however, the case was not long pursued.

In Chittagong there is a Gurdwara, of which possession had been taken from the old idolatrous priests and given to an Udasi, Bawa Kirpal Das. The rejected priests attacked the new Mahant and were punished each with a fine of Rs.25. That was in July,

1916. Their appeal was rejected by the Collector. After some time when Bawa Kahan Singh, a railway overseer, with whom Bawa Kirpal Das had left the keys, was also absent, the old priests came in a force and, breaking the locks of the Gurdwara, took its possession. They removed the Holy Granth to an almirah and put idols in its place. Bawa Kahan Singh went to the police and then to the Collector, who sent him to a First Class Magistrate, who ordered that the Sikhs should have the control. The Sikhs went with a police constable to the temple, but the priests refused to give access. Bawa Kahan Singh with Bawa Arjan Singh went again to the Magistrate and got an order, but the priests again refused to comply with the orders. On this the police broke open the locks and gave possession to the Sikhs, who removed the idols and re-established the Sikh form of worship.

Bawa Kirpal Das brought to light many similar cases in the east, where non-Sikhs were insinuating themselves into the management of Gurdwaras, sacred to the memory of Guru Nanak and Guru Tegh Bahadur, and were substituting idols for the Holy Granth. In 1921 he invoked the help of the Shromani Gurdwara Parbandhak Committee to aid him in rescuing a Gurdwara in Dacca. In October, 1921, news was received that this energetic Mahant, who kept the flag of Guru Nanak flying in the east, had been asked to furnish a security for good behaviour! On refusing to give security he was sentenced to one year's rigorous imprisonment.

One of the most important Gurdwara cases, over which the minds of Sikhs were exercised for long, was that of Hafizabad temple, which is sacred to the memory of Guru Har Gobind. There is some land attached to the Gurdwara. Once the Gurdwara was in the hands of an Udasi Mahant, who died without appointing a chela. The Sikh sangat of the city appointed a baptized Sikh in his place. After some time, when the descendents of this Sikh Mahant increased, they began to shift the burden of their duties on one another's shoulders. Seeing the service of the temple suffering from neglect, the Sikh leaders of the city again made a selection and appointed out of the same family one named Bhai Dyal Singh to carry on the duties of collecting the income and keeping the establishment in good order. After him the sangat gave the charge of the place to his son, named Bur Singh. The man began to adopt strange ways and, in spite of remonstrances from the sangat, would not improve his character. One day in the winter of 1915-16 he was caught in the act of misbehaving with a woman of a respectable family. The sangat condemned the Mahant in an open meeting and unanimously resolved to remove him. They went in a body to the Deputy Commissioner, Mr. S. W. Hamilton, and gave an account of the whole affair. The Deputy Commissioner asked the people to nominate another Mahant. The sangat again held a meeting and resolved that the new Mahant should be a married man. They unanimously elected Bhai Fateh Singh to be Mahant, and reported their decision to the Deputy Commissioner the next day. The Deputy Commissioner approved of the nomination and ordered that the name of Bur Singh as Mahant be removed from the records and that of Bhai Fateh Singh substituted. The change was duly made in the Government records by the officials concerned. The Deputy Commissioner having refused to listen to the protestations of Bur Singh, the latter in August, 1916, filed a civil suit against the following five gentlemen : Bhai Fateh Singh, Sardar Sohan Singh, Pensioner Postmaster, Sardar Bhagwan Singh, Reis, Sardar Gurdial Singh, Reis, and Bhai Ladha Singh. The case went on for several years until finally in an appeal against the order of the District Judge of Gujranwala, Messrs. Broadway and Abdul Qadir decided on 22nd November, 1921, that " a self-constituted sangat, not proved to have any customary right to interfere in the control of the Gurdwara or removal of its Mahant whose succession is quite independent of any action on their part, cannot remove a Mahant without having recourse to law."

In August, 1916, it was learnt that the Gurdwara of Balia in U. P. was in danger of passing completely into the hands of non-Sikhs. The Gurdwara, situated in a beautiful place on the Ganges, is sacred to the memory of Guru Tegh Bahadur, who had visited the place when on his way to the east. There being no source of maintenance for the Gurdwara, which was in constant need of repairs, a few Sikhs of the locality approached the Collector, who moved the Government to grant 10 Viswas of land for the temple. Sometimes a Sikh from Moghal Serai and sometimes Bhai Lachhmi Singh of Balia would come to sweep the place and open the Holy Book. There being no regular Granthi there, and the place being isolated from the home influences, non-Sikh influences began to prevail, until Bhai Lachhmi Singh was obliged to ask Bhai Mukand Singh of Patna to rescue the temple. The latter. who was already falling out with the Panth, came and gave the control of the Gurdwara to those very people from whom Bhai Lachhmi Singh had in vain tried to save it. In a few days the Holy Granth was removed and images of Shiva and Ganesh were installed in its place. The Sikhs from different centres sent resolutions of protest to the Collector of Balia and a case was started.

After two weeks more another case of corruption was brought to light. In a village named Bodal, in Hoshiarpur District, there is a Gurdwara called Garhna Sahib, founded by Guru Har Gobind, who had stayed there while going from Hargobindpur to Kiratpur. The temple has got one ghumaon of land and a fine new building erected at the expense of the Doaba Sangat. With the increase of income and influence the Mahant of the Gurdwara, Bhai Lachman Singh, came to fall into questionable ways. He got the land entered in his own name, and began to practise magic on women. The Khalsa Diwan of Jhingar Khurd tried to reform the Mahant, but he persisted. A great agitation was the result. In the end a big meeting of the local Sikhs was held, and the Mahant was called upon to mend his ways or quit his post. The Mahant came and expressed his readiness to follow the orders of the Panth. The sangat asked him to act on the true principles of Sikhism and not to associate with certain loose women. The Mahant submitted and said that if ever again they saw him in the company of those women or any men of evil repute, the sangat would be free to oust him and to appoint another in his place. An agreement to this effect was drawn up and signed then and there. Bhai Pala Singh Granthi of the place, against whom were proved graver charges, was dismissed at once. There was great satisfaction expressed at this amicable settlement.*

In September, 1916, measures were taken by the Managing Committee of Gurdwara Diwan Khana in Chuni Mandi, Lahore, to improve the condition of its buildings, etc. This is the place where Guru Arjan as a boy had spent his time in preaching Sikhism while attending the marriage-party of Bhai Sahari Ram's son. The revenue of village Qadian near Shahdara had been granted for the upkeep of the place, but some time after the advent of the British rule the grant was confiscated. Since then the Gurdwara had been lying in a neglected state.

In October, 1916, a case of usurpation of waqf property came to light. There is a Dharamsala of Baba Daraz near the Old Kotwali in Lahore. Beside the Sikh temple, it also contains Baba Daraz's tomb, a Hindu temple and a well. From fifty years the whole place had been a waqf property. Lala Mohan Lal, a Hindu Goldsmith, wanted to appropriate the place and began to build a private house there for himself. At this,

---

* The Mahant willingly accepted the control of the Gurdwara Parbandhak Committee of Hoshiarpur on February 10, 1922.

two public-spirited Hindu gentlemen, Pandit Girdhari Lal and Lala Gurditta, filed a complaint in the court, and as a result the tomb, the Hindu temple and the well were spared. Seeing this the Sikhs of Lahore also bestirred themselves, and Bhai Lal Singh, timber merchant, who was their leader, filed a suit. The building was stopped.

The *Panth Sewak* of Lahore exposed the deplorable condition of the Gurdwaras at Kurchhetra, Thaneswar, Sultanpur, Dalla and many other places.

Complaints continued all along about corruption and mismanagement in the Darbar Sahib, Amritsar. The Sikhs said that the temples belonged to the Panth. But Bhai Partap Sfngh, Granthi of the Darbar Sahib, who had already made himself notorious for opposing the passage of the Anand Marriage Act, openly defied the community by declaring that the Gurdwaras were the property of Granthis.* At Campbellpur certain non-Sikhs, basing their claim on the offerings made by them, demanded the local Gurdwara for themselves. The case was decided in favour of Sikhs. The decision was upheld by the Chief Court. There arose a dispute between Sikhs and certain followers of Yogis about a Gurdwara at Dhamtaur in Abbottabad District. This, too, was won by Sikhs in July, 1917. At the same time the Hindus

* The *Khalsa Advocate*, June 9, 1917.

of Hazro claimed the right of placing idols in the local Sikh temple. The Sahjdharis contested this claim. A Hindu Sub-Judge of Cambellpur decided the case in favour of Hindus. But the Sahjdharis took the case to the High Court, where it is said to be still pending.

In October, 1917, a report reached the Punjab that the land attached to the Gurdwara in Dhubri (Assam) was acquired by the Government for the erection of water works. Dhubri, which is situated on the right bank of the Brahmaputra, was a place visited by Guru Nanak when he was proceeding to Kamrup. Guru Tegh Bahadur had erected a temple on the beautiful spot, where Guru Nanak had sat meditating with the forest-clad Garo hills to the south and the snow-clad Himalayas to the north. When Guru Tegh Bahadur made peace between the Moghal invader and the Raja of Kamrup, he asked the soldiers of both armies to join together and, filling their shields with earth, to raise a huge mound, on which a tempfe was built in honour of Guru Nanak the Prince of Peace. The revenue of the whole place was conferred on the temple. In the course of time, due to isolation from the Panth, the land was gradually appropriated by the people, until the Gurdwara was left with seven houses only. These, too, were measured, and an order was given to vacate them. The Mahant Bachitter Singh protested and wrote to all the Four Takhts and the different leading societies in the Punjab. Hundreds of resolutions were sent to the Chief Commissioner protesting against the action of the authorities.

The Chief Commissioner many months later informed the Chief Khalsa Diwan that, though he believed the land under dispute was the personal property of Mahant Mukand Singh in whose name it was registered, yet in view of the feelings of the loyal Sikh nation he had abandoned the idea of erecting an engine there. S. Gurbakhsh Singh, Superintendent, Telegraphs, brought to light the neglected and corrupt condition of many Gurdwaras in Assam, Bengal, Behar and U. P.

In January, 1918, the whole Sikh community was shocked to hear that, in spite of warnings giveu beforehand, the Government had appointed a non-Sikh retired Tehsildar as Manager of the Kartarpur State, which includes the sacred Gurdwara where the original manuscript copy of Guru Granth Sahib is kept. He was also to be in charge of two Sikh minors, who, when grown up and educated, would come to administer the religious place.

The Municipal Committee of Amritsar passed a resolution on 4th February, 1918, proposing, on sanitary grounds, the filling up of Santokhsar, the oldest sacred tank in the city. It was, however, saved by a strong agitation carried on by the Gurdwara Service Union. To remove the complaint of insanitation, the Sikhs undertook voluntarily to clean the tank. In 1905, when Babeksar was cleaned, attempts had also been made to pump out water from Santokhsar and remove the silt, but with no great success. Now Bhai Sham Singh, the oldest saint alive among the Sikhs, with Bhai Gurmukh Singh, led the Sikh sangats from the city and outside to take out mud with their own hands. The tank was cleaned, and the situation was so improved, that some gentlemen in the Municipal Committee proposed to float a pleasure boat on the sacred water. The Sikhs had again to agitate to prevent this desecration.

In the summer of 1918 the case of the Gurdwara near the railway station of Lahore, which had been lingering in the court, ended successfully. The Gurdwara had got 4 kanals of the adjoining land for its maintenance. Its management was now handed over to a Committee.

Another successful case was reported about that time. There is in Benares a Gurdwara of Guru Tegh Bahadur, to which some house property was attached by the Patiala State. Many years ago a man, named Munnoo, took possession of this property and, in spite of all efforts on the part of the Sikhs, would not vacate it. After his death his widow, Anandi, continued the legal fight about possession. After her the Sikhs pursued the case for seven years against one Bachu, who claimed to be her successor. In the end the case was decided in favour of Sikhs.

In 1919-20 the opportunity given to Sikhs to exert themselves for the safety of the Gurdwara of Kartarpur roused in them their old love for the service of Gurdwaras. This Gurdwara is the place where Guru Nanak had spent the last sixteen years of his life as a preacher and farmer. Some years ago, as a result of some operations by the Government Engineers, the river Ravi had turned away from the side of Dehra Baba Nanak and had come to attack Kartarpur. A local Committee, with the advice of Baba Shiv Singh Bedi, took the work of defence in hand. In the rainy season of 1919 the floods washed away the defences and the water came to flow within barely 9 feet of the temple. Hearing of the danger thousands of Sikhs gathered on the spot, and with their impromptu labour—throwing in of trees and stones—some temporary safety was secured. The expenses, about Rs. 1,500, were met by the Sikhs. Then came some respite with the winter. The Sikhs wanted to do something before summer set in with the rise of water consequent on the melting of snow in the upper streams. The Chief Khalsa Diwan took up the work. The Government also sent its engineer, who reported that at least Rs. 35,000 were required for temporary defences and about four lakhs for a permanent bund. Government lent the services of two Sikh engineers, Baba Shiv Singh Bedi and Sardar Mangal Singh, and promised financial help. The Diwan also approached the Maharaja of Patiala who sent Rs. 35,000 at once and promised to give two lakhs more when the permanent scheme was ready. The people's enthusiasm in working with their own hands knew no bounds. Men and women, rich and poor, from all directions went to the place, and thought it a privilege to carry stones and baskets of mud on their heads. The work is not yet complete.

After the terrible year of 1919, when the whole of India went through an unprecedented crisis, the agitation about reform assumed a new shape. The Sikhs could not remain content any longer with the piecemeal reform of their temples. They had tried the courts for a sufficiently long time, and except in a few minor cases, had found them quite unavailing.

The process of law was dilatory and the expenses almost prohibitive. The Court fee of Rs. 10 on the plaint was only a small fraction of the enormous expenses that the reformers going to court had to incur. Even this fee became too much for the poor enthusiasts, when the courts insisted that it should be levied on the full value of a property attached. The plaint of Sialkot Sikhs in the case of Babe-di-Ber was rejected on the ground that the plaintiffs had failed to pay the Ccurt-fee on Rs. 50,000. The Sikhs had to depend on public subscriptions, while the Mahants had at their disposal the vast revenues of the Gurdwaras. The few successes of the Sikhs rather worsened the situation. The Mahants were put on their guard, and they found out the weakness of the law and the strength of their own position.

They began openly to defy the Panth by selling the property of the Gurdwaras and recklessly wasting the money on wine and mistresses. One of them was carrying on his love affair with his own aunt. His love letters in which he admits his wine drinking are filed in the court. Another Mahant, whose love letters have also been captured and whose photo drawn with a loose woman is on the court file, boasted in another court that he had got more than 300 Gurdwaras under him. The existing law had proved a veritable boon to him. He said in the court that he was the Shri Mahant or the acknowledged head of all the Sikh temples in northern India; and the sign of his Shri Mahantship, he said, was that he received from Government two boat-loads of *bhang*, which he supplied to all the Gurdwaras under him. Another Mahant, that of Nankana Sahib, who had taken the vow of celibacy, was openly living with a low class Mohammedan woman and had children by her, whom he was providing with property worth lakhs out of Gurdwara funds. What could the Sikhs do to reform them?

They had tried the experiment of litigation in many cases, but after some time they began to despair. They could not free the temple of Sialkot from an apostate, who openly flouted Sikh religion. What was this law that allowed a man, even whose company was forbidden to Sikhs, to give the rule in their temple. In the past they had resorted to law in the hope that the Government would realise their position and help them. But the Government failed to realize their position. When in those days a bill* to secure

* Act XIV of 1920. It authorised any person interested in a religious or charitable trust to apply to a competent Court for the examination of accounts or for any information about the object, value or condition of the trust. No application, however, could be made in respect of accounts relating to a period more than three years prior to the date of petition. It also provided that the trying Court, i

a little more effective control of religious and charitable endowments was introduced in the Imperial Legislative Council, it was the Punjab Government that heroically stood up against it, saying " the bill is in advance of the public opinion ! " Which public opinion? The question of Sikh temples had just at that time become most serious, and if there was any province in which the particular reform was needed, it was the Punjab. Sardar Sundar Singh Majithia from his seat in the Imperial Council had expressed his profound regret at the strange attitude of the Punjab Government, and the Home Member had said that if so be thought (that the Bill was in advance of public opinion), then the Punjab should be excluded from the area to be provided under the Act. The Sikh press and certain associations like the Reform Committee of Sialkot protested against this indifference of the Government to the question of temple reform.

What to say of Government helping the Sikhs in their attempt to get control of other Gurdwaras, it would not withdraw its own control from the premier temples at Amritsar and Tarn Taran. Sardar Gajjan Singh who presided over the first meeting

---

it thought "necessary in the public interest," might direct the defendant to deposit a sum to meet the expenses of the plaintiff in whole or in part.

of the Sikh League at Amritsar in 1919 asked for this control. The League itself in a resolution referred to "the sore and long-standing grievance of the Sikh community" that the administration of the Golden Temple was still in the hands of a Government nominee, and demanded that it should be placed in the hands of a representative body of Sikhs, constituted on an elective basis and responsible to the Panth. It also asked that "the management and control of Sikh temples and endowments should no longer be withheld from the community."

Finding the existing law of no avail and the Government indifferent, the Sikhs, in the words of a memorandum by the Chief Khalsa Diwan, began to rely mainly on the ancient right of reform by the assertion of public opinion. It meant that the Sikhs in their usual daily or extraordinary meetings held in the temples would exercise the right of gurmatta which had been granted to them by Guru Gobind Singh. By this constitution the Sikh community assumed the position and authority of the Guru. Wherever there were Sikhs, they were to organize themselves into sangats or congregations, and whenever there arose an important question, affecting the whole community or any part of it, the sangat was to elect from among its members five *piaras* or Loved-Ones and submit to them the execution of all the work in hand according to the spirit of Guru Granth Sahib and the rules laid down by Guru Gobind Singh. When a Sikh committed some fault against Sikhism, he was expected to present himself before the nearest sangat and, standing in the lowest place with folded hands, he was to make an open confession of his fault. Or if he did not confess himself, he would be publicly arraigned by somebody else. The congregation would refer the question to a duly elected Commission of Five, who would consider the case among themselves and report their decision to the Assembly. The Assembly would then confirm the decision by a hearty shout of Sat Sri Akal. The punishment meted out was willingly received and was humorously called *Tankhah*, a reward or salary. There was no rancour left in the heart of the man punished, for the punishment came from the whole sangat represented by five Loved Ones. The resolutions passed in such assemblies were called gurmattas. When the gurmatta was carried unanimously, it was supposed to have received the sanction of the Guru, and any attempt made afterwards to subvert it was taken as a sacrilegious act. If a man would not submit, he was called a *tankhahia*, and no Sikh would have anything to do with him.

In actual practice in the present movement it worked in this way. Whenever grave complaints were received about a Mahant or custodian of a Gurdwara, some representative Sikhs would approach him with a request to remove the grievances and to come to an understanding about the management. Sometimes an agreement was reached. But if the Mahant refused to reform, and inspite of warnings continued in his perverse course, he would be called upon by a gurmatta in a public meeting to explain himself. If his faults were proved, he would be asked to submit to a religious form of punishment, which usually consisted of cleaning the shoes of the congregation, bringing water to the temple, or completing the reading of the Sacred Book once or twice. That the man of sin trembles before his pure accusers has been often examplified during this movement. He not only trembles, but sometimes actually runs away, leaving the temple into the hands of the reformers, who are obliged to make a temporary arrangement for the continuation of service. This temporary arrangement often becomes permanent, when the runaway priests, inspite of invitations to come back, do not consent to resume their duties. This happened actually in many cases, as at the Akal Takht. It is true that in this method there is a danger of violence. Only in two cases, however, actual violence with loss of life occurred, and in both cases, it is important to observe, the reform party scrupulously refrained from raisig even the little finger to defend themselves against violence and suffered terribly. In all other cases the Mahants submitted and often saw prudence in applying to the reform committee to take charge of the Gurdwaras. The trouble arose only when the Government gave up its policy of non-intervention, which it had followed since the successful termination of the Sialkot broil, and the Mahants began to feel that the Government, as well as the law, would support them in resisting the reform activities of the Sikhs.

Some people are of opinion that the Sikhs should have waited and postponed the movement until the coming of Swaraj in India. But the Sikhs could not wait upto the advent of Swaraj, because the property attached to the temples was being sold or alienated everywhere, and immoral practices could not be tolerated. Besides no Swaraj is successful without religious reform, as Russia and China have learnt to their cost. More than half of what Swaraj meant to Sikhs was the emancipation of their religious and educational institutions and their management by themselves. When others were thinking of building a new heaven and a new earth of national freedom, the Sikhs had still to struggle hard to get rid of the foreign control even from their central Temples and their central College. Could they wait ?

They had tried many times before but had failed, simply for want of a strong public spirit. Now that with the coming of national feeling they gained a sufficient amount of enthusiasm, they did not want to miss the opportunity. People called them impatient. But reformers have always been so. They are compelled to move fast, because bigots or their supporters will not move early. Reformers are compelled to do their work in times of excitement, because bigots will not do the needful in times of peace.

CHAPTER VIII.

GURDWARA BABE DI BER.

When Guru Nanak visited Sialkot he sat under a Ber tree, which exists upto this time and has given its name to the Gurdwara, which was built on the spot. Sardar Natha Singh Shahid, a Sikh Chief, endowed the shrine with a jagir, which was increased by Maharaja Ranjit Singh. At the time of the annexation of the Punjab by the British Government the jagir was continued partly for the life of the priests and partly in prepetuity for the maintenance of the shrine. The value of the jagir for the shrine was Rs. 3680 in 1855, and the condition of its grant, as laid down by the Government of India, was the good behaviour of the Manager. According to an agreement, signed by all the priests and the sangat before Raja Tej Singh in 1853, the whole income of the shrine, which amounted to about Rs. 5000, was to be spent under the following heads :—

(1) Free Kitchen Rs. 1,800 per annum.
(2) Food to servants
(3) Karah parshad, lighting, festivals 174/8 „

(4) Gurmukhi School
(5) Establishment
(6) Cold drinks for the public
(7) Building Repairs

In 1861 Baba Mehtab Singh of Kotli Faqir Chand decided a dispute about certain disbursements between the Manager and the priests and made both the parties sign an agreement, according to which the income of the jagir was to be spent in the following ways :—

			Rs.
(1)	Public Kitchen	....	1440/-
(2)	Establishment	....	404/-
(3)	Zari Tax	....	200/-
(4)	Repairs, etc.	....	932/2.
	Total	....	2976/2

The free kitchen was a great feature of the shrine. Mr. Bunbury, A. C., Sialkot, reported in 1891 : ' In the Baba Ki Ber Sahib itself there is a langar (Kitchen) kept up, from which food is dispensed twice a day to any one who may come and ask for it. This is one of the best features of the institution, and in the distribution of food no distinction is made of class or tribe or caste. Sikhs, Hindus and Mohammedans are all treated alike '. The report also mentions a regular expenditure on repairs, alms and clothing to the poor. The grants worth

Rs. 1,047, sanctioned for the lives of Bhais Nihal Singh and Gulab Singh priests, were resumed by Government in 1891. In 1900, however, the Government granted ten squares of land on the Chenab Canal to the shrine. Among other terms clause 5 of the lease lays down as follows:—"The tenant shall duly and regularly apply the whole and every part of the produce, rents, profits and all other income whatsoever of the land to the maintenance, support and service of the aforesaid Ber Baba Nanak's institution."

In the beginning there were priests with a manager at their head. The manager used to receive a fixed salary, as did the rest of the establishment. Bhais Gulab Singh and Nihal Singh did not call themselves Mahants, and were paid Rs. 400 and Rs. 375 per annum respectively.

The appointment of the Mahant was always subject to the sanction of the Sikh public.

In 1885 when Mahant Nihal Singh wanted to appoint Bhai Prem Singh to officiate for him temporarily in his absence, he stated in his application that all the residents of Sialkot approved of this appointment. The Tehsildar, too, recorded the opinions of the leading Sikh citizens.

In 1887 Bhai Nihal Singh convened a meeting of the citizens of Sialkot and with the approval of the Sikhs Bhai Prem Singh was appointed his successor. When a rival claimant to the Mahantship filed a suit against Mahant Prem Singh in 1890, the latter stated in his defence that the office of the Mahant was not in his power, nor could it be regarded as a hereditary post, that the appointment was in the hands of the Sikhs, who had faith in the shrine. About his own appointment he said that he was appointed by all the leaders of the town of Sialkot in the presence of the Deputy Commissioner, Cantonment Magistrate and Amla, with the consent of Mahant Nihal Singh and all the priests of the temple. In a civil suit decided in 1886 Mahant Nihal Singh, too, had pleaded that the office of the Mahant was not hereditary. When Prem Singh appointed Harnam Singh, his grandson, as his successor in 1901, he sought the approval of the residents of Sialkot.

Mahant Harnam Singh died on 26th September, 1918. Four days later Prem Singh wrote to the Deputy Commissioner that he had appointed Gurcharan Singh, his grandson, as Mahant, and requested that the Deputy Commissioner might kindly grace the occasion of the installation, which was to take place on 8th November, 1918. As the Sikhs objected to the appointment of Gurcharan Singh, a minor, as Mahant, the Deputy Commissioner refused to attend or send any officer to represent him. A reference to the statement of Hazura Singh, brother of Prem Singh, made before Bawa Kanshi Ram, E. A. C., shows that Gurcharan Singh was in the presence of D. Charan Das, Pleader, P. Todar Mal and Mr. Ganda Sinh appointed Mahant by Prem Singh, who himself was not Mahant at the time. No leading Sikh joined the ceremony. The Collector, however, held that he was only concerned with the mutation side of the case, which he thought advisable to carry out in favour of the deceased's lawful heir, leaving the contending parties to go to the civil courts. He sanctioned the mutation of the jagir in favour of Gurcharan Singh on 6th May, 1919.

The story of abuses prevailing in the management is long. They entered when the Mahants began to take the Gurdwara property as their own. Soon after his succession Mahant Prem Singh began to transform from a priest to a layman. The Settlement Collector, Sir James Dunlop Smith, wrote on 25th May, 1891 :—" I agree with what Mr. Bunbury says about Prem Singh. I would only add that he keeps up a certain amount of state in the world and interests himself a good deal more in lay matters than has been the custom of his predecessors. He never loses a chance of improving his social position and, as is inevitable, finds that the possession of money smooths his way." He succeeded in gagging the mouths of the complainants and getting the files of complaints consigned to the record room.

It was complained against Mahant Prem Singh in 1895 that he did not pay the priests and was misappropriating the Gurdwara property, and that he should be called upon to render accounts. The Mahant admitted that a garden near the Aik Bridge was in his name because he was the Mahant, but that in the past it was the property of the temple. He also admitted that he had purchased some land in his own name with the money belonging to the temple, and that the building in which a press was located was built with the temple funds. After some enquiry the Collector said that he could not interfere in the internal management of the shrine, nor could he call on the Mahant for accounts. He, therefore, referred the petitioners to the civil court.

In the same year another case was filed against Mahant Prem Singh for the examination of accounts under Section I8 of Act XX of 1863. The Mahant stated before the District Judge that he had full authority to dispose of the income in any way he pleased. The judge ordered that the sanction of the

Collector should be obtained under Section 539 of the C. P. C. The required sanction was obtained and a civil suit was filed in June, 1896. The relief prayed for was :—

(1) That a new trustee should be appointed under the trust ;

(2) That an Executive Committee be appointed to administer the funds of the trust, or that a scheme of management might be framed ;

(3) That the past accounts should be audited and rules for the audit should be framed for the future.

On 31st August, 1897, the District Judge passed a decree, by which the Mahant was not removed from the office, but was required to render accounts to the District Judge. It was also directed that on the death of Mahant Prem Singh a Committee of management should be appointed. The plaintiff appealed against this order to the Sessions Judge, who on 18th April, 1898 held it proved that the Mahant was unfit for the post he held as a trustee, and directed his removal from the post. The rest of the District Judge's decree was confirmed with certain modifications necessitated by the Mahant's dismissal. The Mahant appealed to the Chief Court, which set aside the decrees of both the original and appellate courts.

The next Mahant Harnam Singh proved worse than his predecessor. He felt emboldened by the fact that none of the complaints made against him even upto the Local Government could harm him in any way. It was complained in July, 1907, that Mahant Harnam Singh was neglecting to maintain the Shahid Bungah or the tomb of Sardar Natha Singh Shahid, who had endowed the shrine with a jagir and had been its first manager. After enquiry the Tehsildar fixed the responsibility on him, and reported that the Mahant was not maintaining the free kitchen, nor was he keeping any regular accounts, but was wasting the temple funds in luxury, as if it were his private property. The Revenue Assistant practically supported the Tehsildar. The Deputy Commissioner however, on 29th May, 1908, filed the case with the remark that he had explained to the Mahant that he should pay attention towards the buildings and repairs of the Shahid Bungah. There had another petition been filed in September, 1907, complaining against the personal character of Mahant Harnam Singh and his lack of interest in the maintenance of the central shrine, the out-houses of which were badly falling out of repair. It was also pointed out that the money of the jagir was not being spent for the purpose for which it had been granted. The Deputy

Commissioner consigned the petition to the record room with the illuminating remark " Seen " on 4th October, 1907.

In March, 1909, S. Hazura Singh Pleader, S. Kapur Singh, B. A. and several others petitioned the Lieutenant Governor, saying that Mahant Harnam Singh was addicted to drink and did not properly take care of the institution, and that the jagir income was not being utilized for the purpose for which it was granted. They prayed that a portion of the money be entrusted to a committee for the upkeep of the shrine. The matter came to the Deputy Commissioner for disposal.

There was another petition signed by a very large number of citizens, including Mr. Ganda Sinh, praying for a committee of management. It was stated therein that the income of the institution was being spent by the Mahant for his own personal and unlawful purposes and the requirements of the temple were being met from private subscriptions. The Tehsildar reported in March, 1910, that the Mahant was wasting the money in luxury and for private purposes. The Revenue Assistant, however, put a white-wash on it, saying that the kitchen was not expressly maintained in the terms of the grant, but that the character of the Mahant was not very objectionable, as he only drank and was not a drunkard! He suggested a warning to the Mahant. The Deputy Commissioner on this passed the following order: "I agree generally, and the Mahant may be informed accordingly and advised to give up drink. He bears the marks of heavy drinking."

Mahant Harnam Singh died in September, 1918, and Prem Singh also died some months later. We have seen how Gurcharan Singh was made Mahant in spite of the local Sikhs, without whose consent the appointment could not be valid.

The Singh Sabha (now Khalsa Diwan) of Sialkot petitioned the Deputy Commissioner and the Collector, requesting that as the Mahant had died and there was no regularly-elected Mahant, the management of the shrine should be handed over to a committee of management to be constituted in the following manner:—

Five members to be nominated by the Khalsa Diwan, Sialkot.

Five members to be nominated or elected by the Singh Sabhas of the district, one from each tehsil.

Two members to be elected by Sialkot City who are not members of the Diwan.

Two members to be nominated by the Sikh jagirdars of the district.

One member to be elected by the priests.

The Mahant should also be a member. He should be appointed by the Committee and should work under it.

While this matter was pending before a local E. A. C. who was ordered by the Collector to make an enquiry and report, the widow of the late Mahant appointed by a registered deed Mr. Ganda Sinh, an apostate from Sikhism, as the guardian of her son and the Manager of the shrine. A very strong voice of opposition was raised by the whole Panth against this outrage. Telegrams from almost all the important Sabhas were sent to the Lieutenant Governor, the Commissioner and the Deputy Commissioner. After the submission of the report by the specially deputed E.A.C. the Collector sanctioned the mutation in favour of the minor son of the late Mahant. Application was then submitted that the Jagir should not be paid to Mr. Ganda Sinh till the matter was decided by the civil court, but the Collector rejected this petition also.

Then after having obtained the sanction of the Collector under Section 92, C. P. C., a civil suit was filed in the court of the District Judge with a special application to the effect that the case should not be made over to P. Kundan Lal, Sub-Judge, as he had previously expressed his opinion in writing against the views of certain members of the reform party who were conducting the present case. Owing to some transfers in the judicial staff the case, however, came to P. Kundan Lal. The plaintiffs applied for transfer of the case from this court, but the application was rejected. They further applied to the High Court for transfer and put in an application in the court of P. Kundan Lal, informing him that an application had been lodged and praying for the stay of further proceedings in his court pending the High Court decision. The Pandit Sahib, however, proceeded with the case and ordered the plaintiffs on 20th August, 1920, to pay the court-fee on the value of Rs. 50,000 by 30th August, 1920, which date was, on account of the September vacations, extended to 8th October, 1920. The plaintiffs, beside maintaining an active Khalsa Diwan, had to meet the expenses of a well-equipped High School for boys and a Middle School for girls, had built recently a Gurdwara at Tahli Sahib in honour of the 6th Guru and had been fighting out the case of Bawli Sahib. They failed to pay the required court-fee, and their plaint was rejected.

In the meanwhile agitation was in full swing against Mr. Ganda Sinh's appointment, which was clearly an insult to the

Sikh religion. An apostate, who had done away with the sacred keshas and was openly flouting Sikhism, to be in charge of a Sikh temple and give the rule to the worshippers! It was unbearable. The Sikhs of the locality had sufficiently organized themselves to take care of their religious interests. They had heroically fought their case in the courts, but law had utterly failed to help them. They, therefore, decided to help themselves. They had already formed a Khalsa Sewak Jatha and reformed the Gurdwaras in the city. They began to hold weekly and then daily morning services in the Gurdwara of Babe-di-Ber, which is about half a mile from the city. Mr. Ganda Sinh, who feared for his position, began to place many difficulties in their way. A party of *gundas* was daily seen visiting the place just at the time when worshippers from the city would come to hold their musical performance. One of the worshippers, B. Jawahir Singh by name, while crossing a little stream that runs between tbe city and the temple, was set upon and beaten by the *gundas*. Others were threatened with a similar fate. John Hadow, the son of Mr. Ganda Sinh, is also said to have shown his pistol in the Gurdwara. Certain women were also sent to beat and abuse the Sikhs and interfere with the Kirtan.

As agitation increased against the Manager, the Gurdwara began to present a strange spectacle. While Sikhs sat singing hymns, scores of *gundas* hovered about them, ready to pick up a quarrel and create a row. Sardars Amar Singh and Jaswant Singh of Jhabbal came to Sialkot at this stage, and by their lectures counteracted the growing mischief that certain interested parties were spreading among Hindus and Moslems. From this time onwards the whole public was with the reform party. Warrants under Section 107, Cr. P. C., were issued against Bhais Bhag Singh, Jawahir Singh, Nanak Singh, Ram Singh and Mahan Singh, members of the Sewak Jatha. The whole public was horrified at this, and in a big meeting held on the same night people advised the five gentlemen not to give surety and expressed themselves ready to go to jail. Sardar Kharak Singh, who had been all along working in sympathy with the Jatha, also supported the resolution. The Sikhs determined, there and then, not to allow the apostate to desecrate the temple any more.

Next day a body of armed police with one Police Inspector, three Sub-Inspectors, and one E. A. C. came to the Gurdwara, but no Ganda Sinh. Thousands of people thronged the court, when at 10 A. M. the five Sikhs presented themselves before the District

Magistrate. They stated that they would offer no defence and would give no security. October 4 was fixed as the next day of hearing. The District Magistrate ordered under Section 144, Cr. P. C., that for the next two months nobody should interfere with the management of Mr. Ganda Sinh. The people gathered again in the same evening and resolved not to allow Mr. Ganda Sinh to act as Manager. There was great sensation in the community and the Sikhs began to pour in from all sides. After a few days they temporarily took charge of the Gurdwara in the name of the Panth and opened the long-neglected free kitchen.

The case that was pending in the court was withdrawn. On 5th October the Khalsa gathered in large numbers and in a big diwan a committee of thirteen members was elected for the management and control of the Gurdwara. Next day Mr. King, the Divisional Commissioner, came to Sialkot and summoning a deputation of nine leading Sikhs told them that the Government did not want to interfere in the religious affairs of the Sikhs and that the Sikhs were at liberty to manage the affairs of their Gurdwaras as they pleased. As to the income from jagir and land, he said that it would remain with the Government as a trust, until the "two parties" came to a settlement.

In the meanwhile things had begun to hum at the Golden Temple, and the scene of Sikh activities, therefore, shifted to Amritsar.

CHAPTER IX.

THE GOLDEN TEMPLE.

The city of Amritsar with the Holy Tank was founded by Guru Ram Das, the fourth Guru, who settled here about 1574 and obtained a grant of the site with 500 bighas of land from Akbar in 1577. It was Guru Arjan who built the temple in 1589. Its head priest was always appointed by the Gurus. After Guru Gobind Singh's death, when differences arose between the true Sikhs, called the Tat Khalsa, and the Bandei Khalsa, his widow appointed Bhai Mani Singh, the most learned Sikh of the time, to take charge of the Golden Temple in 1721. Soon after, by order of the Lahore Nawab, soldiers were picketted in the neighbourhood of Amritsar and the Sikhs were not allowed to visit their temple. "A proclamation was issued by the Lahore Viceroy ordering a general massacre of long-haired Singhs wherever found. They were hunted like wild beasts, a price being fixed on their heads; thousands were put to death, refusing pardon on condition of renouncing their faith and cutting their hair." "Bands of Sikh horsemen were to be seen at dawn riding at full gallop towards Amritsar, running the gauntlet of the Mohammedan troops." (Gordon).

Bhai Mani Singh, who was held in great esteem by the Mohammedan Qazi of Amritsar, felt emboldened to apply for leave to hold the Diwali fair in Amritsar. The matter being referred to Lahore, permission was granted on the condition that Bhai Mani Singh should pay Rs. 5,000 after the fair. Bhai Mani Singh invited the Sikhs from far and near in 1738. The governor of Lahore sent a force to Amritsar under the pretext of keeping order during the fair, but really it was designed to fall upon the approaching Sikhs and destroy them. After some losses the Sikhs were apprised of the trap and the fair was not held. Bhai Mani Singh was arrested for not paying the sum, which he had hoped to pay out of the offerings of Sikhs, and was condemned to death. He was offered the usual alternative of Islam. But he stoutly refused to barter his religion. His body was cut to pieces, limb by limb and joint by joint.

This reign of terror continued upto 1763. Massa Ranghar, the local governor, used to hold his nautch parties inside the Temple, and the precincts were used as stables. The Sikhs were away from the Punjab wandering in jungles as outlaws. A body of Sikhs in Bikaner learnt of the desecration in 1740, and sent Bhai Mehtab Singh of Mirankot, district

Amritsar, to avenge the insult. He came with a follower, killed the governor and cleared the precincts. He was afterwards martyred. In 1757 and again in 1762 the Abdali invaders demolished the Temple twice and filled up the sacred tank. But the Sikhs soon came back and restored the Temple and the tank in 1763.

When they became supreme and established misals or confederacies, they removed the Udasi custodians of the Temple and appointed Bhai Chanchal Singh, a baptised Sikh, as Granthi. This man used to pare nails before he took charge of the greatest temple of the Sikhs. It was Maharaja Ranjit Singh who adorned the Temple with marble and gold plate and attached to it a jagir for its maintenance. The Bungahs or hospices were built by Sikh Chiefs and Sirdars for the accommodation of the Sikh sangats from their domains. The jagir attached to the Guru ka Langar or kitchen has been appropriated by some former Sarbrah, and a quarry of marble stone, which once belonged to the Darbar Sahib, has been disposed of in some way.

When the British Government annexed the Punjab there was a committee of control composed of baptised Sikhs, but the affairs of the Temple were soon reduced to confusion. In 1859 in order to settle the long-standing disputes of the pujaris or priests about their pay, a meeting of some Sirdars was summoned at the house of Raja Tej Singh in Amritsar. Mr. Cooper, the Deputy Commissioner, was also present. After finishing the main question for which the meeting had been called, somebody put the question : "Khalsaji, can we carry on the management of the Darbar Sahib without the help of the Sirkar?" There could be only one answer to the question in those days of national paralysis, especially when the greatest officer of the district was present. A committee of nine baptised Sikhs was appointed as a committee of trustees with a Government-appointed president called Sarbrah or guardian. From the proceedings published it appears that this committee carried on its work regularly, controlling the administration, authorising the spending of money, and keeping the establishment under discipline. The Sarbrah only carried out their instructions. About 1883, however, the committee was quietly dropped and the whole control came to be vested in the Sarbrah, who received his instructions from the Deputy Commissioner.

In the beginning the whole octroi revenue of the city had been dedicated to the Darbar Sahib. But as the Sikhs are in a hopeless minority in the city, their affairs have never been looked after adequately by the administration of the city, on which upto very recently they had no representation. Gradually the revenue allowed to the Darbar Sahib was cut down, until only 6 pies in the rupee were paid. This, too, was taken away, and now only the lighting expenses of the Temple and the canal charges on the water supplied to the sacred tanks are paid out of the municipal funds. The Sarbarah had to handle lakhs of rupees a year, but he was never called upon to present accounts to the public. In fact he was responsible to nobody except the Deputy Commissioner. The pujaris or priests, who used to have a very respectable position and exercised some check on the administration, were gradually reduced to a very low position. Many of them ceased to perform any duty in the Temple. They adopted other professions such as pleadership or shop-keeping. But they received their share in the income of the Darbar Sahib all the same. Some of them sent their servants to do the service in the Temple. Those who attended their duties were paid only a few pice a day and many of them naturally turned dishonest. They began to harass the visitors for tips, and began to steal loose coins thrown on the carpet before the Holy Book. The ill-paid daroga, whose duty was to keep watch over the money, was bribed by the priests and he, too, began to share in the loot. The Granthis, with the exception of the Head Granthi who had a jagir, had no other source of income except the presents offered to them by generous visitors, and they tried in various ways to increase their income. Instead of making the Holy of Holies the radiating centre of light and devotion, the priests considered it as the practising ground of robbery. The *Karah Parshad* or the sacred food offered by pilgrims for distribution in the congregation was taken away to the houses of magistrates and police officials, or was thrown away before horses or their grooms. The costly scarfs, offered to serve as wrappers for the Sacred Books in the Golden Temple or other temples elsewhere, were auctioned by the Sarbrah or appropriated by the priests for the use of their wives and children.

The precincts began to be used by pandits and astrologers for the propagation of superstitious practices. Idols were openly worshipped in the holy compound. Dirty booklets were sold and shops of all sorts were opened in the premises. On the Basant and the Holi days licentious songs were sung by musicians inside the Temple. Rogues roamed about harassing women. Brothels were opened in the neighbouring houses, where unwary women visiting the Temple were taken for immoral purposes, some sadhus acting as agents.*

In 1905 with the general awakening in the country, the Sikhs felt their grievances keenly and determined to right some of the outstanding wrongs. The idols were removed, and a widespread agitation was set on foot to nationalise the control of the Darbar Sahib. Sardar Bahadur Arjan Singh, an ex-Sarbrah, proposed in a meeting of the Chief Khalsa Diwan that, in consultation with the Panth, the constitution of the Golden Temple called Dastur-ul-Amal should be changed. The resolution was accepted, but nothing came out of it. It became difficult even to get a copy of the Dastur-ul-Amal. Then in the summer of 1906 the *Khalsa Advocate* and the *Punjab* of Amritsar strongly urged that the rules governing the Darbar Sahib and other Gurdwaras should be so altered as to remove certain patent evils. They emphasised that the position of the Mahants and pujaris should not be hereditary, as they never were intended to be, that the appointments should depend solely on efficiency and good behaviour of the incumbents, that the jagirs or other property attached to a Gurdwara should not be considered as the personal property of its

* The *Punjab* of October 1, 1906, also the *Haq Pasand*, a non-Sikh paper, of about the same date.

Mahant, but should be entered in the name of the Gurdwara, so that the Mahant might not be able to sell the property and, when found guilty of misconduct, his ejection might be easy. They considered it most objectionable that the Sarbrah of the Golden Temple should be appointed by Government and that the Sikhs should have nothing to say as to its management. They urged that the Sarbrah should be an able and energetic Sikh, elected by the Panth, and not an old septagenarian appointed by Government, and that in the meanwhile the old Committee of 1859 which had been abolished should be restored. Complaints were also made about the non-publication of accounts by the Sarbrahs in charge of the administration and of the buildings. The latter for many years has kept engaged the artisans in decorating with worthless tinsel a useless room in the upper storey of the Temple, neglecting the buildings which are in perilous need of repair. Even now—as the charge has not been taken from the Sarbrah—you might find a man working there slowly, as if he has to be there for centuries. It is a most irresponsible kind of work.

Many boys were drowned in the Sacred Tank every year. The *Khalsa Samachar* and the *Punjab* set up an agitation to induce the Sarbrah to have an iron railing erected in the water all round the tank, but the Sarbrah to this as to other complaints, however loud, turned a deaf ear. The people in the press and on the platform complained against the callousness of the Sarbrah, whom they asked to resign if he could not do his duty. Under the auspices of the Sikh Young-men's Association a public meeting of the civil and military Sikh residents of Quetta was held on 22nd December, 1906, and it was resolved to ask the Government to hand over the control of the Darbar Sahib to the Chief Khalsa Diwan. In the covering letter complaints were made about the non-publication of accounts, the hereditary system of service and the intolerable evils prevailing in the precincts as well as the Bungahs bordering on the Temple. Following the lead of the Quetta Association similar resolutions were passed everywhere. In May, 1907, the *Punjab* urged the formation of a "Gurdwara Sambhal Committee" or a committee for the control of Gurdwaras. Then followed a period of moral depression consequent upon the general unrest and the measures taken to suppress it. About 1914 the Sikhs again raised a voice in favour of national control, but the War came and the Sikhs set aside all agitation to help the Government whole-heartedly in the hour of its need.

When the War was over the question

of the control of Darbar Sahib was again raised. In the Sikh League of 1919, as we have seen, the Sikhs demanded that the management of the Golden Temple should be handed over to a representative committee of Sikhs, constituted on an elective basis and responsible to the Panth. A Sikh member of the Punjab Council asked questions about the management and requested the Government to shew accounts to the public. Very evasive replies were given, and it was said that the question of management would be determined in the Reformed Council. But the public was very much agitated over it, and demanded some immediate action. Wherever the Sikhs gathered in their daily meetings, in the Singh Sabhas, or at the annual meetings of their diwans, they put forth their demand that the Darbar Sahib, Nankana Sahib and the Khalsa College should be handed over to the Panth. Even the Sikhs of Basra, Baghdad and Maymyo sent resolutions to the Government to withdraw from the control of the Darbar Sahib. The Government, however, in its communique of July 14, 1920, tried to answer all the agitation by quoting the following reply given to a question in the Punjab Council on 13th March, 1920:—

"The question of management of the Golden Temple at Amritsar has been under the consideration of Government for some time. It has been decided to defer the action until the Reforms Scheme has been brought into operation. The elected representatives of Sikh Constituencies will then be consulted as to any changes which may be contemplated.

It should be explained that the action proposed will be under the Religious Endowments Act, 1863, and that it is desired to carry out new arrangements in accordance, so far as can be ascertained, with the general wishes of those who are interested in the temple. The most suitable way of ascertaining these wishes is to consult the gentlemen who will be elected for the Legislative Council as representatives of Sikh Constituencies in the Province, and the Government intend to consult these gentlemen at an early date after the conclusion of elections. With their assistance a Committee will be selected, in whose hands the appointment of the Manager and scrutiny of accounts will thereafter rest. When the Committee has been constituted, it is the intention of Government to stand aside from the management entirely in future."

The Sikhs were not satisfied with this delaying process, nor with the proposed method of selection or the scope of the Committee's functions as suggested in the communique. When the boycott of Councils was preached and the ambiguous definition of a Sikh was published by Government, people despaired of getting any satisfactory committee formed.

The complaints against the conduct of the priests and the Manager grew so loud that the position became intolerable. It was not forgotten that it was under this Manager that the Komagata Maru Sikhs had been condemned at the Akal Takht, and that it was by this Manager that in the days of Martial Law General Dyer was presented with a robe of honour from the Golden Temple, where even Maharaja Ranjit Singh had been condemned and punished for an un-Sikh-like act. People could not put up with the insults offered to their religion in the Temple. One priest openly said that he would mix tobacco with the sacred food. The Sikhs could not turn out the man, as the control was in the hands of Government's Manager. This Manager with the permission of the Deputy Commissioner reinstated an ex-priest who had been expelled some years before and had been convicted in court. One day in August the holy congregation were abused at the Akal Takht and refused the morning service. They came to the Manager's house and complained. He promised to go himself next day at the morning service and make the priest beg pardon. But he never came. Then the people held meetings of protest. The Deputy Commissioner, instead of asking the Manager to retire, sent policemen to forbid a meeting of Sikhs within the precincts of the Temple. The people, however, held a meeting inspite of the police, and passed resolutions against the Deputy Commissioner and the Manager. The Manager was sent on leave for two months. But the public wanted his resignation. It was decided that the Manager's effigy should be taken out like a regular funeral, if he did not resign by 29th August. Thousands of ladies also held meetings and passed resolutions. The Sikhs were holding a meeting in the Jallianwala Bagh, when the Manager came and with folded hands begged the Khalsa to forgive him, announcing at the same time that he had resigned. Thus the old Manager left and another was appointed in his place by Government. The people clamoured for accounts, but who would listen to them ? The retiring Manager was knighted soon after and became Sir Arur Singh *of the Golden Temple.*

The enormities of the priests could be made impossible only if the control of the Temple were handed over to the Sikh community. But it was not done, inspite of hundreds of resolutions being passed by the

Sikh representative bodies all over India. Resolutions came from Canada, Burma, and from Sikh military officers in Mesopotamia.

The Sikhs were tabooed in the Temple. A Sikh, regularly baptised from a low caste, would not be admitted along with other Sikhs into the Temple, but if he became a Christian and came with a hat on, the priests would run to meet him and show him all over the temple. The girl students of Bhasaur were not allowed to sing hymns in the Darbar Sahib and before the Akal Takht. Even big Sirdars, Professors and students of the Khalsa College could not get their prayers offered there, merely because they had reformed themselves. The rule among the Sikhs, as previously shown in this book, is that anybody in the world can become a Sikh,* and after receiving baptism all persons become equal in claiming religious rights. Ever since the modern revival of Sikhism great emphasis had been laid on the conversion of the low-caste people, and different bodies like the Lahore Diwan, the Chief Khalsa Diwan and the Panch Khalsa Diwan took lively interest in the uplifting of the

* Guru Nanak says: There are lowest men among the low classes. Nanak shall go with them. What have I to do with the great? God's eye of mercy falls on those who take care of the lowly.

Sri Rag.

depressed classes. In 1906 the Chief Khalsa Diwan held a very big diwan at Jullundur, the home of Ramdasias and other so-called out-castes, and brought hundreds of these people into the fold of Sikhism. Again in 1919 a large number of them were converted at Amritsar. The Diwan also did much to reclaim the criminal tribes entrusted to it at Moghulpura, and converted thousands of Meghs and Kabirpanthis in Kishtwar. Tikka Jaswant Singh Bedi also converted thousands of Basiths in Mirpur.

There is a religious body in Amritsar, called the Khalsa Brotherhood, which holds annual diwans for the purpose of preaching equality among men and converting men and women of all castes to Sikhism. On 12th October, 1920, a few low-caste men baptised at the annual meeting of this society were brought in a procession to the Golden Temple. The priests refused to offer prayer for them. The Sikhs insisted on the right of every Sikh to get his prayer and the sacred food offered at the Temple. The Holy Book was opened and by a miraculous chance the following words of Guru Amar Das were read out by the Granthi, who himself was among the objectors :—" Brother, He sends grace even to those who have no merit, and takes from them the true Guru's service, which is most noble, as it turns our hearts to the love of God. He Himself forgives and brings us into union with Himself. Brother, how worthless, were we, and yet the perfect and the true Enlightener took us on to His society. My dear, what a lot of sinners He has forgiven by reason of His true Word! How many He has ferried across the world-ocean in the Guru's safety bark! By the touch of the Philosopher's stone, that is the Guru, base metal has become gold. Selfishness has departed and the Name has come to live in the heart. Our light has blended with His light and we have become one with Him."*

The words had a wonderful effect. Hundreds of men in the audience were visibly affected. The priests, too, were convinced and they agreed to offer prayer and accept the sacred food from the hands of the newly-coverted Sikhs. There was no unpleasantness in the whole proceedings and the priests were left to carry on their work.

When the whole party was coming out successful and going towards the Akal Takht, a temple just opposite to the Darbar Sahib, the priests of the Takht fled from their posts, and those who remained refused to offer prayer or accept the offerings consisting of money and sacred food, and then they, too, fled away from the posteran gate.

---

* *Sorath, III.*

The place, founded by Guru Har Gobind in 1609, is one of the greatest importance. The Guru used to receive his Sikhs here and discuss with them important matters connected with the welfare of the community. It was here that he put on the sword, symbolising a new phase in the development of the Sikh character. It was here that the weak and the oppressed came from far and near to seek help against tyranny. Once in the days of the *misals* a Brahmin of Kasur came and laid his complaint before the assembled Khalsa that his bride had been taken away from him by the local Nawab. The Sikhs stood up and vowed under the leadership of one Sardar Hari Singh that they would not rest until they had restored the Brahmin's wife to him. They went and did it. It was also here that later on by a resolution of the Khalsa Maharaja Ranjit Singh, the Lion of the Punjab, was punished for associating with an evil woman. It is the chief Takht or Throne of Authority, from which orders called Hukamnamas are issued to the whole community. The weapons used by Guru Hargobind and Guru Gobind Singh are kept here.

It could not be left vacant. The assembly led by Bhai Kartar Singh of Jhabbar called for 25 volunteers to sit and watch there temporarily without touching the money or property. Sardar Sundar Singh, the Sarbrah, was informed of it and he agreed. The priests were called upon to express regret for having deserted the sacred Throne. They did not come, even when the Sarbrah called them.

The next day on October 13, the Deputy Commissioner sent for the Sarbrah and a few representatives of the Sikhs and the priests to his bungalow to discuss the new turn of events in the Golden Temple. The priests did not attend. The Deputy Commissioner formed a provisional Committee of nine Sikhs, all reformers, including the Sarbrah at its head, to manage the Golden Temple until a permanent one was formed. The priests, chagrined at this, instigated the Nihang Sikhs of the Budha Dal and tried to bring them into collision with the reforming Sikhs. The Budha Dal of the historic fame actually reached Amritsar and created some unpleasantness. The matter reached a crisis on the night of 15th October, when it was feared that the Nihangs might attack the Sikhs in possession of the Takht. Venerable Baba Kehar Singh of Patti, however, amicably settled the difficulty with his usual statesmanlike tact and skill. With his sweet persuasiveness he made the Nihangs agree to a resolution condemning the priests for their desertion of the Takht and desiring that, until the general meeting of the Panth was held, all should wait and let the Sikhs in possession carry on. On the night of Diwali some Nihang Sikhs again wanted to create a row by taking possession of the Akal Takht. Baba Kehar Singh argued the matter with them for a length of time but to no avail. Then two other gentlemen tried to dissuade them, but they persisted. Then the leader of the Akali Jatha in charge of the Takht challenged the Nihangs to try their strength with the Panth if they could. The challenge unnerved the Nihang Sikhs and they quietly withdrew from the Takht.

After this there was no disturbance in the Darbar Sahib except on December 6, 1921, when encouraged by the arrests of Sikh leaders, some mischief-makers instigated an attack on the temple. About a dozen Sadhus dressed in a peculiar fashion attacked the Akal Takht and demanded of the Sikhs in charge to clear out. When the Sikhs, who were only five or six in number, refused to go, the Sadhus began to belabour them with lathis, *chimtas* and iron bars which they had brought with them. One or two went away to inform the Sikhs outside, but the remaining suffered the blows quietly until they fell down unconscious. Another Sikh who had come up was beaten down. His wife, who followed, suffered equally while trying to save her husband. Another lady as well became the target of these men and fell down after receiving heavy blows on her head and other parts of her body. The attack continued for about ten minutes and, when all the Sikhs were down, a large crowd of people came in. Some of the Sadhus, while being disarmed, must have received blows from the crowd; but when the responsible officers of the Shromani Gurdwara Parbandhak Committee arrived on the scene no rough-handling was allowed. As no arrests are permitted in the sacred precincts the Sadhus were removed to a place outside the Akal Takht, whence the police took them away. Some time after one of the Sadhus died. This grievous insult to the premier Temple was preceded by an attempt by Government to disturb the possession of the Shromani Gurdwara Parbandhak Committee by snatching away the Keys of the Golden Temple; but the Sikhs, as we shall see, vindicated their right by taking upon themselves heavy suffering.

The affairs of the Golden Temple were in confusion when the Shromani Committee took its charge. No regular charge of the treasury had been given by Sardar Arur Singh on his retirement, and when Sardar Sundar Singh Ramgarhia, who succeeded him, gave charge of the things he had received from his predecessor, it was found that almost all important papers relating to the period before him were missing and no proper means existed of checking the existence of all the various valuable articles kept in the treasury. The importance of a proper scrutiny can be realised from the fact that, while in one eye of a jewel-peacock a pearl worth Rs. 3,500 is present, in the other there is one worth Rs. 50 only.

At first the direct administration of the Darbar Sahib was vested by the Shromani Gurdwara Parbandhak Committee in a Sub-Committee, including Sardar Sundar Singh Ramgarhia, Sardar Dan Singh, Sardar Jaswant Singh and Sardar Didar Singh. Then in September, 1921, a local committee of nine members, including Sardar Sundar Singh Ramgarhia as Chairman, was appointed. This again was replaced by a larger committee composed of all the members of the Shromani Committee, resident in Amritsar, seven outside-members nominated by the Executive Committee, and five residents of Amritsar, who were non Members. The Chairman, called Member-in-Charge, was appointed by the Executive Committee from among its members. This sub-committee passed a rule that the whole income of the Golden Temple and the attached Gurdwaras should be deposited in the name of the

Shromani Committee, which should be asked to advance money required for the expenses of which a regular account should be presented. The daily income from offerings is registered and watched throughout the day by a darogha, and is counted in the evening by regular officers of the Committee with some member or members in the presence of the sangat, and then it is deposited in the treasury, wherein a register is kept of all the deposits. A regular account is kept in the office. After some days the rupees and the smaller coins are counted in the presence of a few responsible members and office-bearers of the Committee and given to a goldsmith for exchange in currency notes, which are taken to the bank for deposit in the name of the Shromani Committee.

The office and the priestly establishment cost about Rs. 3000 a month. The priests were allowed to work on the old lines for more than a year, but it was found impossible to check theft and irregularity,—corruption had grown so deep-rooted in the system. The Committee was obliged to order that no Granthi or pujari should touch any money of the offerings in the Temple. The Granthis are paid regular salaries. A renowned poet and historian has been appointed Granthi on Rs. 120 per mensem, while the young Granthi belonging to the old system has been offered Rs. 350 per mensem as salary and a big sum and some houses in consideration of the jagir and property now transferred to the Committee.

On 10th August, 1921, the pujaris of Baba Atal were dismissed by the Committee for making and encouraging attacks on the Akalis on duty. The Holy Book was installed in the vacant temple, and other reforms which were overdue were affected. The Udasi Mahant of the Akhara of Brahm Buta, which opens on the Darbar Sahib premises, was persuaded to carry out the necessary reforms. The various shrines located in the precincts were put in good order, and their service was made regular. The old gloomy building of the Jhanda Bungah has been pulled down and, thanks to the venerable saint Bhai Sham Singh and the sangat, a very durable and fine edifice is rising in its place. The wall has been removed eight feet backwards, so that the open space for meetings before the Akal Takht has been extended and the complaint about the narrow passage behind the Banners has been removed.

The sacred tank of Kaulsar has been cleaned, its steps cemented, and its surroundings altogether improved. The holy tank of the Golden Temple is also being cleaned and the buildings repaired. For all this work of building, repairing and cleaning, a Committee is appointed. This body, called the *Kar Sarowar Committee*, with its Secretary, Bhai Jaswant Singh, B. A., is a wonderful organization. It combines in it precision, promptness and economy of the modern days with all the fervour and love for social service that has ever been exhibited by the Sikhs in the past. It has got a vast colony of unpaid workers drawn from all classes and all parts of the country. Those who, like the Ramgarhias, can provide skilled labour have offered their services free, and those who are unskilled are also there in thousands to help in doing any work that may be given to them. The division of work is so well-organized that there is absolutely no over-lapping. In one corner a vast multitude of women is seen breaking bricks into fine concrete. In another hundreds of men and women are seen washing sand. They are told to wash it 25 times before it is ready for use in making tiles. In a third place *kankar*, which has been brought from a long distance, is being washed and burnt and then ground into lime. The most laborious work is the slow grinding of small pieces of marble into the finest powder like antimony. This, mixed with the powder of almonds, pistacia and other precious things, makes the hardest white cement, which is being used in plastering the causeway that leads from the Main Gate to the inner Sanctuary. Not a pice has been spent on all the labour employed. Men and women, whether rich or poor, have thought it an honour to take part in this work which the Guru has given them after 250 years. Relays of ladies and gentlemen are daily seen carrying baskets of mud on their heads, chanting *Sat-Nam-Wahiguru, Sat-Nam-Wahiguru.* Hindus and Mohammedans, men and women, came to share in this noble work. It was a beautiful sight to see a band of 200 Mohammedans working in mud and then after taking their food in the Guru's kitchen reading Nimaz in the Guru ka Bagh, with hundreds of Sikhs looking on and pouring blessings on them. Men came with their families, not only from the Punjab but also from Sindh, from Frontier, from U. P., and from other parts of India, burning with the love of service. They were accommodated in Bungahs and other buildings close to Darbar Sahib. The Guru's kitchen expenses were about Rs. 500 a day, but, thanks to the philanthropy of people, the Committee had no difficulty in finding the money. Thousands of rupees came unasked, and people vied with each other in providing rations for the kitchen. It was proposed to erect a brass railing round the Holy Tank in order to prevent mortalities from drowning. An appeal was made to ladies to donate each 4 chattaks weight of broken brass utensils Bagfulls of brass began to pour in and hundreds of maunds were collected in a short time.

The work done by the Kar Sarowar Committee has called forth the best forces of sacrifice and organization, and is as important as anything else done by the Sikhs during this campaign of reform. It has lifted up the whole community from the low depths of apathy and discord, and has provided a scope for the display of the best spirit of the Khalsa.

With the establishment of the Panthic Committee many of the long-standing evils have been removed. All the shops in the Parkarma, which used to give refuge to men and women of evil repute, have been abolished and the hawkers of all sorts forbidden to carry on their trade within the sacred compound. The pure ceremony of baptism has been restored at the Akal Takht, and thousands have received Amrit since the formation of the Committee.

The whole place has acquired a Sikh look again. It is again the bee-hive of the Sikhs as it once used to be. Holy congregations meeting in the Darbar Sahib where music never ceases and before the Akal Takht where Sikhs receive the idea of their national power, the lofty banners flying, and the Holy Choirs moving nightly round the Golden Temple, again bring visibly before the Sikhs the glories of the Khalsa which are recounted in the daily prayer.

CHAPTER X.

THE SHROMANI GURDWARA PARBANDHAK COMMITTEE.

A Hukamnama was issued from the Akal Takht summoning a general assembly of the Sikhs to meet on 15th November, 1920, in the front of the Akal Takht for the purpose of electing a representative committee of the Panth to control the Golden Temple and all other Gurdwaras. The conditions to be satisfied by each delegate from different bodies were: (1) He must have received Amrit or baptism, (2) must be a regular reader of the Scriptures, (3) must possess the five K.'s, (4) must be an early riser, and (5) must be giving 1/10th of his income regularly for the Panthic cause. The representation was regulated as follows:—

1. Four Takhts — 6 representatives each.
2. Gurdwaras — 1 representative each.
3. Sikh Associations — 5 representatives for 100 members each.

	Managing Committee.	Staff.	Students.
4. Khalsa College, Amritsar	1	2	2
5. G. N. College, Gujranwala	1	2	2

		Managing Committee.	Staff.	Students.
6.	Akal Collage, Mastuana	1	2	2
7.	High Schools	1	1	1 each
8.	Middle Schools	1	1	... „
9.	Primary Schools	1	...	... „
10.	Sikh States	...	5 each.	
11.	Mixed Sikh Cavalries		2 each.	
12.	„ „ Regiments		2 each.	
13.	Purely Sikh Cavalries		5 each.	
14.	Purely Sikh Regiments		5 each.	
15.	Nihang Jathas, whose special duty in the past had been the protection of temples.		5 each for every 100 members.	

But two days before the meeting was held the Government hastened to appoint a Managing Committee, consisting of 36 members—all reformers—for the Golden Temple and other temples, like that of Tarn Taran, affiliated to it. The Sikhs of all shades of opinion from different parts of the country, including the Sikh States, came to the big meeting held on 15th and 16th November and resolved to form a committee of 175 members to control all the temples of the Sikhs, whether in the Punjab or elsewhere. They wisely included the 36 members of the Government-appointed Committee also, and elected them on a sub-committee formed to manage the Golden Temple and the shrines allied to it. As the Governor had said at the time of the formation of the Committee of 36 that they could add any number to themselves and do anything they wanted with their constitution, it was legitimate for the committee of 175 to take their place. The representation was according to districts in the Punjab and according to provinces outside. Members were elected also to represent the Sikh States and Sikh bodies in Burma, Malaya, China, and America. All parties were satisfied with the arrangements. As long as the bigger Committee did not come into existence, Sardar Harbans Singh of Atari, as President of the Government-appointed Committee, with Sardar Sundar Singh Ramgarhia as Manager, carried on the administration.

The inaugural meeting of the Shromani Gurdwara Parbandhak Committee came off at the Akal Takht on December 12, 1920. When all had assembled, the Assistant Secretary read out the names of the members elected, who were taken to the upper part of the Akal Takht and subjected to a strict scrutiny as prescribed before. The five *Piaras**,

* 1 Bhai Teja Singh, M A., LL. B., A. M., (Harvard), Principal, Akal College, Mastuana.

2. Bhai Jodh Singh M.A , Principal, G. N. College, Gujranwala

3. Bawa Harkishen Singh, M. A., Professor, Khalsa College.

4. Bhai Teja Singh of the Central Majha Diwan, and

5. Sardar Balwant Singh, Reis of Kulla.

who had been elected in the last meeting to conduct the scrutiny, asked each member as he came up as to how far he fell short of the standard prescribed. Those who confessed to some shortcomings agreed to undergo suitable religious punishments. The scrutiny over, all the members headed by the 5 Piaras, clad in black and carrying their kirpans on their shoulders, came down singing Shabads and presented themselves before the Sangat, which had been anxiously waiting for them. The scene was most impressive, when Bawa Harkishen Singh, the Assistant Secretary, read out the names of those who were declared duly inaugurated, specifying the respective confessions of those who were found short in any respect. The attention of the audience became most rapt when the name of Sardar Bahadur Sardar Sundar Singh Majithia was announced. The Assistant Secretary explained in detail the position of the Honourable Sardar. He said that, in view of the fact that certain members of the Panth were displeased with the Sardar Bahadur, he had been asked to say in the presence of the Guru, before His very Throne, whether or not he had been prompted in all he had done, as Secretary of the Chief Khalsa Diwan or as representative of the Panth, by motives which in any way aimed not at the unalloyed welfare of his community.

With perfect humility and calm and dignified serenity Sardar Sundar Singh said that in the presence of the Guru he solemnly affirmed that whatever he did he did to the best of his ability and understanding in the best interest of the community, and was not at all actuated by any selfish or unworthy motives that were attributed to him. Still, however, he said, he implored the indulgence of the forgiving Panth in the words of the musician Kirat, whose verses are incorporated in the Holy Granth :—

"I am full of defects and possess no merit.

Forsaking nectar I drink the poison of evil.

Led by false attachment and deluded by superstition and fear,

I have been engrossed in the worldly love of the wife and son.

But I have heard of a noble *Panth* and the Guru's Sangat,

By whose contact the fear of Death vanishes.

I, Bard Kirat, have to offer one prayer only :

'May Guru Ram Das be my refuge.'"

On this the five Piaras had signified their satisfaction. When this was announced in the meeting below, the whole audience was moved to tears. This was the highest consummation of the spirit of democracy among the Sikhs. The very men, who had been loudest in crying him down in the past, proposed and supported his election to the Presidentship of the Shromani Committee. Sardar Harbans Singh of Atari was elected Vice-President and Sardar Sundar Singh Ramgarhia Secretary. A sub-committee including the office-bearers was formed for drafting a new constitution and Dastural-al-Amal of the Darbar Sahib.

The Shromani Gurdwara Parbandhak Committee was registered on 30th April, 1921.

According to the new constitution four-fifths of the members would be elected by different constituencies in the Punjab and outside, and the remaining 1/5 would be nominated by the elected element. The different districts were apportioned a fixed number of seats on the Committee according to the population and religious importance of the Sikhs residing therein. The Sikh States were also given representation. One-fourth of the whole number of seats assigned to a State were to be nominated by its Sikh Maharaja and the remaining to be elected by the Sikh population of the State. As the Committee was the most important religious assembly of the Sikhs and its business was to control temples and determine true form of worship to be observed in them, only those were given the right of voting who could be called representative Sikhs. Every initiated Sikh, who was not less than 21 years old and who observed the elementary rules of Sikh conduct, such as rising early in the morning, reading the Scriptures, giving one-tenth of the personal income, and keeping the baptismal vows, got a vote.

When the rules were prepared and approved, a new election of the Shromani Committee was held in July 1921. In every electorate voting papers were given on application to those who satisfied the prescribed conditions and paid a fee of four annas. The Shromani Committee had sent its own polling officers to different centres to conduct the elections according to rules. The local body would hold a diwan in some central place, where the voters of a particular electorate assembled. After a few nominations were voted the voters were asked to write in their voting papers the names of those whom they wanted to elect. The voting papers were then collected under supervision from each individual elector. In some places the voting papers were collected by the polling officers at a gate from which individual voter was asked to pass. Then the votes were counted in the presence of some respectable gentlemen, and the results declared in the open diwan.

The elected members met at the Akal Takht on 14th August, 1921, to nominate the remaining one-fifth provided in the rules. They had the wisdom to nominate almost all of them, with the exception of a few journalists, out of the moderate party. The nominated members included such eminent workers as Sardar Harbans Singh of Atari, Professor Jodh Singh, M. A., Babas Gurdial Singh and Partap Singh, the Namdhari leaders, Baba Jaswant Singh Bedi, Bhai Sangat Singh of Kamalia, Bhai Hira Singh Ragi, Sardar Man Singh Vakil, Sardar Kahan Singh of Nabha, and S. Ram Singh Kabuli. On 27th August the new members were subjected to the same scrutiny as before by five Piaras. The following office-bearers were elected :—

President :—Sardar Kharak Singh, B. A., L.L.B., Reis, Sialkot.

Vice-President :—Sardar Sundar Singh Ramgarhia, Hony. Magistrate and Reis, Amritsar.

Hony. Secretary :—Sardar Bahadur Sardar Mehtab Singh, Bar.-at-Law, late Public Prosecutor, Government Advocate and Deputy President of the Punjab Legislative Council.

A Professor from the Gujranwala College was made a paid Assistant Secretary.

A strong Executive Committee of 31 members was elected.

A few days later the Executive Committee formed a Working Committee of 7 members and Local Committees for the Golden Temple Amritsar, Tarn Taran and Nankana Sahib. The administration of the different Gurdwaras with their local committees, the Kar or cleaning service of the Sacred Tank, the missionary, the publicity and other departments were put in charge of different members. An Engineer on a salary of Rs. 250 per mensem was appointed to look after the buildings of the affiliated Gurdwaras and advise on the constructions and repairs which were going on everywhere on a large scale. An Inspector has been appointed to report on the condition of different Gurdwaras. In more important cases sub-committees are appointed to do this work. The expenses of the Committee are met from the contributions of the one-tenth part of every affiliated Gurdwara's income, which according to the constitution is due to the Shromani Committee. Owing to financial difficulties this rule has not been strictly enforced. The Shromani Committee helps those Gurdwaras where the income is scanty and the congregations cannot support the maintenance of the priests and the buildings. Financial help has been given to the following Gurdwaras :—

1. Hothian, 2. Teje, 3. Chohla Sahib,

4. Panja Sahib, 5. Samadh Akali Phula Singh, 6. Pir Hayat, 7. Dalhousie, 8. Anandpur Sahib, 9. Nonar, 10. Kâmalia, 11. Gurdwara Bibi Veero at Jhabal.

Some of them are not poor but owing to circumstances help was needed.

The Managing Committees of the following Gurdwaras, among others, are affiliated to the Shromani Gurdwara Parbandhak Committee :—

The Golden Temple Amritsar, Tarn Taran, Nankana Sahib, Babe-di-Ber Sialkot, Anandpur, Chamkaur, Akali Phula Singh's Samadh, Khadur Sahib, Rori Sahib Gujranwala, Nonar Sialkot, Chohla Sahib Amritsar, Teje, Hothian Gurdaspur, Baba Bakala Amritsar, Guru-ka-Bagh Amritsar, Panja Sahib Campbellpur, Khara Sauda, Bhai Joga Singh's Gurdwara Peshawar.

There are hundreds of Gurdwara Committees affiliated to the Central Committee and working in different localities. They are required to report their accounts regularly. The present office-bearers elected on July 16th, 1922, are the following :—

President—Sardar Kharak Singh, (in his absence in jail Sardar Mehtab Singh, Bar.-at-Law, is to act for him).

Vice-President—Sardar Amar Singh of Jhabal.

Secretary—Bhai Jaswant Singh, B. A.

CHAPTER XI.

GURDWARA PANJA SAHIB.

On his return from the western countries Guru Nanak came to Hasan Abdal and stopped as usual at a little distance from the village at the foot of a hill. He sent Mardana, his rebeck-player, to fetch water from a Mohammedan saint called Vali Qandhari, whose seat was on the top of the hill. Mardana came back disappointed, as the saint refused to give water and out of sulkiness threw a big boulder down the hill-side to crush the rival saint. The stone as it came down rolling was stopped by Guru Nanak with his hand, and the spot where he touched it is marked by a figure of the hand cut into the stone. Guru Nanak struck a vein of water-spring even at the foot of the hill, where now a temple stands with a beautiful tiny lake enclosed in marble. The temple has got a jagír worth Rs. 500 a year. There is also some land, and a few water mills. As there are only a few houses of the Sikhs in the village, the affairs of the temple have never been looked after properly.

In 1906 Mahant Mitha Singh got the Gurdwara land transferred to his own name.

The Singh Sabha of Abbottabad and other bodies protested against this misappropriation and called upon the Mahant to publish an account of the income and expenditure, but nothing was done to satisfy the public. In 1915 it appeared from some documents published in the *Panth Sewak* of Lahore that the Mahant, emboldened by his previous success in defying the Panth, had got entered in his own name not only the jagir belonging to the Gurdwara but also the Gurdwara itself. There was a great agitation about it at the Ferozepore Conference, and on June 25, 1916, the Singh Sabha of Rawalpindi called a meeting of the prominent Sikhs of the neighbouring districts to consider the situation and devise some course of action. A committee was formed to sue the Mahant in the court, but after some time the case was dropped for want of funds. The Mahant now began openly to flout Sikhism and its preachers. A missionary association of Lahore, called Khalsa Dharam Parcharak Jatha, wanted to hold a diwan at Panja Sahib, but the Mahant not only refused accommodation for the meeting in the holy place, but also went so far as to press others not to give any facilities to the organizers of the diwan. Inspite of his opposition, however, land was secured on hire from the local Sayyeds, and then to make the meeting impossible the Mahant sent some drummers of the village to beat their drums close to the place of meeting. The police had to be called to remove the drummers. In the autumn of 1920 a committee of enquiry was formed to investigate into the complaints that were constantly made against the Mahant. About 60 people, a majority of whom were Hindus and orthodox Sikhs, brought very serious charges against the Mahant and his management. It was proved beyond doubt, among other things, that the Mahant was of loose character, that he encouraged badmashes to drink and sing lewd songs while sitting over the streams flowing by the temple, and that the sacred food, after being offered at the temple, was sold back to the shopkeepers.

When the active reform of temples began the Mahant began to collect firearms and terrify the congregations with his power. One day the Mahant's brother, named Sant Singh, took out a pistol, when a pilgrim objected to the sacred food being prepared by a smoker and a shop of tobacco being opened on the Gurdwara land. The pilgrim was shot in the thigh, and the incident created a great sensation among the Sikhs.

When Mahant Mitha Singh died in November, the Sikhs assembled at Amritsar decided to make some suitable arrangement with the new incumbent before he was made Mahant. A Jatha of about 25 men started from Amritsar under the leadership of Bhai Kartar Singh of Jhabbar, and Sardar Amar Singh Reis of Jhabbal and reached Panja Sahib on the morning of 18th November, 1920. The police arrived a few hours later. Sant Singh gave rations to the Jatha and also some utensils for cooking food. Next day the Jatha performed kirtan (sacred music) in the temple, after which a partisan of the Mahant stood up and, without any mention having been made so far as to the reform of management, declared in an excited speech that the Sikhs had got no concern whatever with the temple. The situation grew critical, and Sardar Amar Singh came away to inform the outside public. Certain leaders from Rawalpindi, Abbottabad and other places came in the meanwhile with men and money, and then negotiations began with the widow and the brother of the late Mahant. They were told that if they agreed to work under a committee affiliated to the Shromani Committee, the Mahant's widow and Sant Singh would be given sufficient pay to maintain themselves and their family, and the late Mahant's son would be educated up to B. A. at the expense of the Committee. Sant Singh consented and an agreement embodying these terms was drawn up in the presence of five respectable Hindu residents of the place one of whom was President of the local Arya Samaj. Sant Singh was going to sign the document, when a Brahmin who used to get something out of the Gurdwara income under the old system, called him out. When he came back after a few minutes, he was quite a changed man. He refused to sign the paper. The assembled sangat charged him with breaking his solemn word given in the sacred presence and refused to let him enter the Gurdwara as a *tankhahia*, unless he begged pardon for his fault and got the *tankhah* removed. At night the villagers met and resolved to eject the Sikhs, as according to them the Gurdwara did not belong to the Sikhs. Next day they came in large numbers with *lathis* to attack the Gurdwara, where the Mohammedan D. S. P., who had arrived on that day, was standing to watch the proceedings. The D. S. P. whistled to the police, who came and prevented the people from attacking the Sikhs. He also asked the police to clear the Gurdwara of those assembled in it. Bhai Kartar Singh Jathadar ordered the Sikhs not to leave the Gurdwara. Then the police officer said, "Drive out the others, who are not Sikhs." This was done. A police guard was posted and the crowding of village people was forbidden in the temple. Then the mischievous people sent some bold women, who surrounded the temple, harassed the Sikhs, and would not go even up to very late in the night. Their husbands, however, came and took them away. The Khilafatists of Pindi came personally to call off the hostility of the Mohammedan villagers, who behaved admirably ever afterwards.

Next day the Deputy Commissioner came to the place and enquired from the Jatha as to who had sent them. Bhai Kartar Singh was able to show two telegrams, which he had received just then from Sardar Harbans Singh of Atari and Sardar Sundar Singh Ramgarhia, promising support in the undertaking. The Deputy Commissioner proposed a committee of three, of which the Mahant and Chaudhri Ram Singh of Rawalpindi were to be members and over which the Deputy Commissioner himself was to preside. The Sikhs rejected this on the ground that no official could be accepted as President and the Mahant could not be taken as a member as long as he was a *tankhahia* or under a religious ban. The Sikhs insisted on a committee of five, which was not accepted by Sant Singh. On this the Deputy Commissioner ordered Sant Singh not to go to the temple and asked him to go to court if he had got any complaint.

On Guru Nanak's birthday a big meeting was held at Panja Sahib, to which came representatives from the neighbouring districts of Peshawar, Campbellpur, Hazara, Rawalpindi and Jhelum. A committee of management, including such leading men as Chaudhri Ram Singh, President, S. Sohan Singh Reis, S. Teja Singh Vakil, Malik Dewa Singh, etc., was appointed. Sant Singh, who had never been made Mahant, filed a suit under Section 145 Cr. P. C. against Chaudhri Ram Singh, Secretary, Singh Sabha, Rawalpindi, B. Kartar Singh Jhabbar, Malik Dewa Singh of Abbottabad, S. Sohan Singh Reis of Rawalpindi, and others who had taken part in the reform. The new Deputy Commissioner, Mr. Miles Irving, dismissed the suit on 29th December, 1920.

Under the Panthic Committee the Gurdwara has improved a great deal. The jagir belonging to the temple is not paid to the Committee, which has to meet, in addition to the normal requirements, great expenses in maintaining the free kitchen, which was never kept before, and in erecting new buildings and carrying out other improvements, which have vastly increased the comfort of visitors.

CHAPTER XII.

SOME MORE CASES.

CHOMALA SAHIB.

In August, 1920, there was some agitation about the 6th Guru's Gurdwara called Chomala Sahib in the Bhati gate, Lahore. The income of the Gurdwara was very poor. The Granthi Hari Singh did not allow accommodation to pilgrims in the building, which had been built at the public expense and which he was letting out on hire to meat-sellers and cowherds. He did not know how to perform the duties of a priest. In fact he did not know how to recite even Japji and Rahras, the morning and evening services. The Gurdwara was full of dung and dirt. The Sikhs decided to put an end to this state of affairs. The Khalsa Parcharak Jatha held diwans in the Gurdwara, but the Granthi sent his women to attack the singing parties and lodged a complaint in court. The Sikhs suspended the Granthi on September 27 and assured him that, if he improved himself he would be reinstated. They appointed a Managing Committee of 12 leading Sikhs including S. Sohan Singh

Secretary, Sri Guru Singh Sabha, Lahore; Sardar Amar Singh, editor of the *Loyal Gazette*; Sardar Mehtab Singh, Bar-at-Law; S. Sohan Singh, editor of the *Sikh*; Sardar Sardul Singh Caveessieur; Sardar Sundar Singh Reis; Master Sundar Singh Lyallpuri; Sardar Sant Singh, President, and Sardar Sadhu Singh, Secretary of the Khalsa Parcharak Jatha; Mahant Teja Singh of Gurdwara Dera Sahib of Guru Arjan; Sardar Gurdit Singh and S. Gurbakhsh Singh. This Committee appointed 14 men, including S. Sant Singh, President, and Sardar Sadhu Singh, Secretary, of the Parcharak Jatha, to take charge of the Gurdwara. The Granthi brought another complaint under Section 107, Cr. P. C., and then on November 4 he filed a civil suit for permanent injunction against the Sikhs, in which he obtained an *exparte* degree in his favour on January 6, 1921. He had also filed a complaint under Section 145, Cr. P. C., in the court of the Deputy Commissioner, but it was dismissed. The Sikhs in the meanwhile carried on the administration of the Gurdwara and were not ousted from their position.

THAM SAHIB.

The affairs of Gurdwara Tham Sahib in the village Jhambar Kalan of the Lahore District were falling into disrepute. The

Gurdwara was sacred to the 5th and 6th Gurus, and had always been under the control of the village sangat. It had got 136 Killas of land endowed by Maharaja Ranjit Singh. The Mahant, named Prem Singh, was wasting the income and encumbering the Gurdwara with debt. In order to check the evil, the Sikhs of the village held a meeting and formed a committee to control the income and expenditure of the Gurdwara and the lands attached to it. After the Mahant had reported to the Police and seen nothing good coming out of it, he agreed to work under the committee. But when the rules and regulations were made for the conduct of management, the Mahant changed his front. Originally there was no intention of ejecting the Mahant, but when it was found that the reform of the Mahant was impossible, the sangat dismissed him and appointed Baba Bela Singh Nihang in his place. A regular panchayat-nama signed by the leading men and the lambardars was given to the new Mahant. Prem Singh filed a criminal suit under Section 448, I. P. C., against Baba Bela Singh on December 3, 1920, which was dismissed on February 15, 1921, by the Sub-Divisional Officer of Kasur. The five arbitrators, to whom the complaint of Prem Singh had been referred, also decided in favour of the sangat.

KHARA SAUDA.

This is the place where Guru Nanak had made his *Khara Sauda* or Good Bargain. When he was still young his father had sent him with a few rupees to make a good bargain. He went and spent the money in providing food and clothing to a few needy men he met in the jungle. In the Sikh days one Baba Raya erected a platform round the *Van* tree under which the Guru had sat, and watched over the sanctity of the pond lying close to it. A Sikh of Chuharkana is said to have come to harm for desecrating the pond by bathing his horse in it. From that time the fame of the place increased, and the Sikhs raised a Gurdwara over the platform. The Sikh Government endowed a jagir to the place, and in the course of time some land was also attached to it. The Mahant was always appointed by the Sikh villagers, and the turban of Mahantship was tied by a representative of Baba Raya's family.

In 1917 complaints were made through public notices and in the press against the conduct of the Udasi Mahant named Narain Das. It was also observed that he kept in one of the side-rooms of the temple paper images of Guru Nanak and his two companions, and worshipped them. A Namdhari

Sikh, Narain Singh, who objected to image-worship, was beaten by the Mahant. One day a few students of the local Khalsa School went to the temple and one of them, named Thakar Singh, refused to take the sacred food which had been first offered to the idols. Other students did likewise. The Mahant flew into rage and after abusing the students drove them away. The students complained to Bhai Kartar Singh of Jhabbar, Manager of their school, who resolved not to go to the Gurdwara until it was reformed.

On December 24, 1920, Lal Das, chela of Narain Dass, informed Bhai Kartar Singh that the Mahant was dismantling the Gurdwara and had already taken away two cartloads of Gurdwara property to his village Kaloke. Akali Jathas were beginning to be formed in those days. One of them led by Bhai Kartar Singh reached Khara Sauda on the morning of December 27. The Mahant, when openly charged with living with another's woman, admitted his fault. Another Sadhu, who was a *gurbhai** of the Mahant, also confessed to have attacked the chastity of a stranger woman, who had come about three months before to visit the temple. The Sikhs announced to the Mahant and his gurbhai that they were *tankhahias* and, as

---

* A fellow-disciple of the same Guru.

long as they did not exonerate themselves before the general assembly of the neighbouring sangat which was summoned on 30th December, they were debarred from the performance of service in the Gurdwara. The offerings, cattle and other property of the Gurdwara were, of course, not disturbed. The Mahant in anger went to the thana and informed the police. But he himself never came back. On 30th December a big sangat collected from the neighbouring villages and heard the whole story of the Mahant's misconduct. The woman, whom the Mahant had left behind, was sent away safely. The sangat elected a committee of 15 members to carry on the management of the Gurdwara. The report of the proceedings was sent every day to the Shromani Gurdwara Parbandhak Committee, Amritsar.

In January there was an unpleasant scene created by the orthodox Hindus of Gojra. A Sikh baptised from Ramdasias was sitting in the local Gurdwara at the morning diwan. Some Hindus rushed with lathies to force the Sikhs not to distribute the sacred food when the Ramdasia was present. In the same month the Gurdwara of Rori Sahib in Eminabad, where Guru Nanak had stayed to meditate on God, was reformed.

Gurdwara Chohla Sahib.

Guru Arjan once came to this village, which in those days was called Bhaini. A Sikh woman found the Guru hungry, and seeing that he could not wait for a full dinner, she prepared for him a dish called *chohla* or broken bread mixed with butter and sugar. He was very much pleased with the sweet crumbs and wanted to remember the hospitality. He enquired the name of the village, and was told that it was Bhaini. The Guru said: "The name of this place should be Chohla." He also sang a hymn of thankfulness in the Dhanasri measure. There is jagir attached to the Gurdwara. Beside this there is also an income of about 600 rupees a month.

The Sikhs on January 13, 1921, came to an understanding with the Mahant named Karan Dass, who agreed to serve under a committee in consideration of a regular salary for himself and his son and some property being granted to him. Inspite of the fact that for a long time, on account of extreme business elsewhere, the Shromani Gurdwara Parbandhak Committee could not turn its attention to the registration of a formal deed and the election of a regular committee of management, the Mahant continued loyal to the first agreement. He wrote to the Collector of Amritsar that the jagir money, which since January last had been kept in deposit in Government Treasury should be paid to the Shromani Committee, to which he had handed over the Gurdwara. He also tried several times to get the deed registered, but the District authorities have not complied with his request.

The Shromani Committee paid off the debt of the Mahant, which amounted to about Rs. 14,000, and also spent about Rs. 2,440 in providing a new house for him as Manager. The following are the terms of settlement finally agreed upon between the Shromani Committee and the Mahant :—

(1) Mahant Karan Das is appointed Manager of Gurdwara Chohla Sahib on Rs. 175 per mensem.

(2) For the management of the Gurdwara there shall be a committee consisting of nine members, four from the village, three from the neighbourhood, one representing the Gurdwara Committee, and one Mahant himself.

(3) As Mahant Karan Das has borne good conduct and has behaved well with the public; as inspite of instigations to mislead him, he has maintained a proper attitude towards the Panth; and as his financial condition is weak on account of his honesty in the past, the Committee grants him a sum of Rs. 10,000 to improve his position, Rs. 5,000 being given at once and the remaining Rs. 5,000 to be given

within next three years. He is also given a house in Amritsar, so that if at any time he ceases to be Manager of the Gurdwara, he may find a house for himself.

(4). All immoveable property belonging to the Gurdwara should be entered in the name of the Gurdwara under the management of the Shromani Gurdwara Parbandhak Committee.

(5) The Mahant shall be responsible for the income and expenditure of the Gurdwara and its property.

(6) The ritual and ceremony observed in the Gurdwara shall be according to the rules of Sikh religion.

(7) In case of misconduct or corruption, the Mahant can be removed by the Shromani Gurdwara Parbandhak Committee, but his dismissal shall have no effect on the payment of Rs. 10,000 granted to him.

After this occurred the Tarn Taran Tragedy, which will be described in a separate chapter. Mahant Raghbir Singh of Gurdwara Ram Dass, in District Amritsar, where Baba Budha was born, agreed in writing to hand over control of the Gurdwara and its lands to the Shromani Committee in return for a subsistence allowance of Rs. 300 a month. But he changed his mind afterwards. The Udasi Mahant of the Gurdwara of Guru ka Bagh, in Amritsar District, also came to terms with the Shromani Committee. The place is sacred to the memory of Guru Arjan and Guru Teg Bahadur. The Sikhs of the neighbourhood had been complaining for a long time about the character of the Mahant. On 31st January a Jatha of Akalis under the leadership of Sardar Dan Singh proceeded to the spot and after some talk was able to bring round the Mahant. An agreement was signed by the Mahant to the effect that he would put away his mistresses and marry one of them, and also that he would serve under a committee of eleven. A great trouble rose later on which will be described towards the end of this book.

In the same month the Mahant of the Gurdwara of Batala in Gurdaspur District, famous as the place where Guru Nanak's marriage had been celebrated, came to terms with the reforming party and agreed to work under the control of the Shromani Gurdwara Parbandhak Committee.

KER SAHIB.

Nanak Saran, the Udhasi Mahant of this place which is near Khara Sauda, was living with a widow and there were general complaints against his character. He kept no free kitchen, although a dozen squares of land were attached to the Gurdwara for the very purpose. On about 8th February, 1921, a big annual meeting was held at Khara Sauda to commemorate the day of Guru Nanak's Good Bargain. The sangat went from Khara Sauda to pay their respects to Ker Sahib, but they found that the Mahant had fled away. A committee of management was formed, and in the place of Nanak Saran, his Gurbhai Dev Datt was appointed Mahant. After the Nankana Sahib Tragedy, when the policy of the Government changed and Sikh leaders began to be arrested, this new Mahant began to scheme against the reform party. Finding him incurable the Sikhs ousted him too.

MACHHIKE.

This Gurdwara was erected in honour of Bhai Guria, one of the needy men whom Guru Nanak had fed at Khara Sauda. Maharaja Ranjit Singh gave the whole village as jagir to the temple. The evils of the Udasi Mahant, named Gulab Dass, were crying for reform. The whole sangat of the place, supported by his two nephews, one of whom was his chela, petitioned the Jatha of Khara Sauda against the enormities of the Mahant. On 9th February, 1921, Bhai Kartar Singh of Jhabbar went with the sangat of the neighbourhood to Machhike, where in an open diwan a nephew of the Mahant complained about the latter's character. It was clear from the evidence of the villagers that the Mahant was keeping a Mahommedan weaver woman, was in the habit of drinking wine with the villagers, and was wasting the income of the Gurdwara on useless litigation. Next day when the Mahant came, he was told by the sangat that if he removed his defects and promised to live in future a better life under a committee, he would be allowed to remain. On his refusal his chela and nephew, Dhian Dass, who agreed to these conditions, was appointed Mahant.

GURDWARA SHEKHUPURA.

When Maharani Nakain, mother of Maharaja Kharak Singh, came to reside in Shekhupura fort, she made arrangements for the people within the fort to live outside. She built a mosque for Mahommedans, a temple for Hindus and a Dharamsala for Sikhs. To the Dharamsala she assigned a jagir consisting of four villages, three of which, on account of the keepers' negligence, have been confiscated and only one remained. Many complaints were made against the character of the late Mahant. When at last he married, he began to live on mere official recognition and did not allow free access to people in the Dharmsala, which was the only place of worship for the Sikhs in the whole village.

The Jatha of Khara Sauda came from Machhike on 11th February and reminded the Mahant of the promise he had made to accept the rules laid down by the Shromani Gurdwara Parbandhak Committee. He willingly signed an agreement to work under a committee, affiliated to the Shromani Committee, and helped in making a list of property which he signed. After the committee was appointed the Jatha went away.

At the Nankana Sahib Massacre, however, the Mahant expressed great jubilation and, when the Sikh Leaders were arrested and the Sikh cause seemed to be humiliated, he went back to his old ways and refused free access to the Sikh worshippers. Bhai Kartar Singh Jhabar on his release approached the Deputy Commissioner and showed him the papers connected with the Gurdwara. The Deputy Commissioner called the Mahant and asked him to abide by his written promise. The Mahant himself nominated Sardar Kharak Singh and Sardar Mehtab Singh of the Shromani Committee, as arbitrators, to decide upon his maintenance. But when he was summoned by these two Sardars he refused to accept any agreement. The Sikhs kept the possession of the Gurdwara, which they had got with the aid of the Deputy Commissioner, and have continued to manage the Gurdwara up to this day. Free food and comfortable accommodation is provided to all visiters.

KHADUR SAHIB.

This is the place in Amritsar District, where Guru Angad lived. Maharaja Ranjit Singh granted the revenue of the village for the maintenance of the Gurdwara. Seeing the Reforms coming, the custodians of the temple put up a managing committee for themselves in December, 1920. When the Sikhs were reforming Chohla Sahib the priests of Khadur Sahib came to them and offered to abide by the rules of the Shromani Committee. A sub-committee was appointed to make a settlement with the priests, who came to Sardar Harbans Singh of Atari and Baba Khem Singh, Secretary of the Shromani Committee, on 12th February, but refused to sign an agreement to affiliate their Committee to the Shromani Committee. On the same day a Jatha went to Khadur Sahib and tried to effect an understanding. But the priests were truculent and did not care even to talk to the Jatha. Temporary possession was taken next day. After this the tahsildar began to harass the Sikhs and threatened to impose a police chouki on the village. But the Pujaries were brought round, especially by Baba Parduman Singh, Vakil of Multan, to get their Committee affiliated to the Shromani Committee, and so on 17th March, 1921, the charge of the Gurdwara was given back to the old party. The relations of the Local Committee with the Shromani Committee are not what they should be, but an early reconciliation is expected.

On 15th February, 1921, Mahant Hari Singh of Babek Sar in Amritsar willingly placed the Gurdwara under the control of the Shromani Committee and, when later on complaints were made against him, he again agreed in writing on 13th August, 1922, to abstain from allenating any property of the Gurdwara.

NAURANGABAD.

It is a famous Gurdwara connected with the name of Baba Bir Singh, a great Saint of Sikh days. When Prince Dalip Singh became Maharaja the two parties at the Court, trying to put up their own candidates, became openly factious in 1844, and Bhai Bir Singh would not let the Princes Kashmira Singh and Peshaura Singh, who had taken refuge with him, be attacked. He tried to stem the tide by calling upon both the parties not to fight, as they were Sikhs. "Brothers ! Do not attack brothers", he said. But nobody would listen to his words of peace. S. Attar Singh and Prince Kashmira Singh were slain and Bhai Bir Singh was also killed by a cannon shot striking his thigh.

There were many complaints against the Mahant of this place. One of them was that he kept a mistress. In February 1921 he was persuaded to put away the woman and work according to the wishes of the Shromani Committe. After the Nankana Tragedy, when the new policy of the Government led to the wholesale arrests of Sikhs, this Mahant, like others, fell back to his old ways and called back his mistress. A few Akalis from Tarn Taran went to remonstrate with the Mahant on April 30th, 1921, but the Mahant had collected a large body of men from the neighbourhood, and there was a danger of serious developments. A body of Police had also arrived on the scene. A few members of the Shromani Committee, including Baba Kehr Singh, who were at Tarn Taran, hurried to the spot and called off the Akalis, as they had gone there without any authority.

CHAPTER XIII.

TARN TARAN TRAGEDY.

The city and the temple of Tarn Taran were founded by Guru Arjan in 1590. Beside being a place of worship and devotion, it was a great refuge for lepers, who came in thousands to get cured at the hands of the Guru. A big jagir was attached to the Gurdwara, and there was some land reserved for the maintenance and support of the lepers. A large sum had been granted by the Sikh Government for raising four tall towers at the corners of the sacred tank, but after one tower was built the money was embezzled and was never spent for the intended purpose. The land assigned for the upkeep of lepers also went out of the Sikh control and is at present under the custody of a Christian mission!

The Gurdwara was under the same management as the Darbar Sahib of Amritsar, but the control of the Sarbrah, exercised from Amritsar, was lax and the priests were more independent. They divided the whole income among themselves, while most of them were following other professions fn the city. Nothing was spared for the daily musical service and the lighting of the Parkarma.

The condition of the Gurdwara was as bad as that of the Golden Temple at Amritsar, and the morals of some of the priests were most shocking. Sometimes the priests came drunk to the temple. Some of them were seen sitting before the Holy Book with quails in their hands. They openly called the temple their shop. Theft was most common among them. No woman's honour was safe in the temple.

The educated and reformed Sikhs were interdicted here as at Amritsar. When towards the end of 1920 Sardar Lachhman Singh, who was afterwards martyred at Nankana Sahib, came with the girls of his school to pay his respects at Tarn Taran, the priests prevented the girls from singing hymns in the temple, and drove them out as belonging to Singh Sabha. Other bodies in favour of Reform were similarly treated. On January 11th, 1921, the Sewak Jatha of Tarn Taran was forbidden to perform kirtan in the temple. Since the issue of Commissioner King's letter* calling the priests' interests in the religious endowments as their *established rights*, the priests of Tarn Taran

---

* Even Sir Valentine Chirol declared about this letter "that in the circumstances it would have been wise to add an admonition to the effect that legal rights also involved duties and responsibilities which must be properly discharged."

had assumed a very truculent attitude towards the Panth and had felt encouraged to resist all attempts at reform. Rumours were afloat that, seeing the fate of other Gurdwaras, the priests of Tarn Taran had approached Mr. King, the Commissioner of Lahore, who "inspite of his long experience of this district and probable knowledge of the doings of these pujaris, instead of telling them to realise the true significance of this movement of reform, is said to have told them that if need be they might apply to the Almighty Sarkar for support. Sardar Mohan Singh, a highly respectable leader of the town, wrote to Mr. King on 3rd January and asked him to publicly contradict these rumours, which were detrimental to public tranquility. No reply was ever vouchsafed to Sardar Mohan Singh, not even an acknowledgment."*

On 24th January before a general meeting of the Sikhs at Akal Takht a woman stood up to relate the sufferings her family had undergone at the hands of the priests of Tarn Taran. Her son had been thrown, she said, into the sacred tank with stones tied round his neck. Her daughter had been harassed in the temple. She also described how a Hindu girl had been kissed within the

* Report of the Tarn Taran tragedy by Dr. Kichlew, Lala Bhola Nath and Lala Girdhari Lal of Amritsar.

Holy of Holies. Her speech created a great sensation in the audience, and Akalis, then and there addressed a prayer to God, asking for guidance as how to reform the temple.

About 40 of them under the leadership of Bhai Teja Singh of Bhuchar proceeded to Tarn Taran by the morning train and reached the temple there at about 8 A.M., when the morning service was going on. For two hours they listened to the sacred music, and then the leader of the Jatha, seeing some excitement among the priests, tried to allay their fears by telling them that the Jatha had come not to disturb their possession but to induce them amicably to remove the public grievances. The youthful among the priests, whose number was about 70 at the time, tried to provoke a fight by abusing and attacking the Akalis. But the latter kept quiet. The older priests spoke calmly, welcoming the object of the Akalis' visit, and promised to do their best to bring about a peaceful settlement. It was mutually agreed to meet in a small conference at 4 P.M. The pujaris named as their representatives: Bhais Nihal Singh, Gurbakhsh Singh, Gurdit Singh, Sewa Singh, Sundar Singh and Teja Singh. The Akali Jatha nominated Bhai Teja Singh Jathadar, Sardar Balwant Singh of Kulla, Sardar Dan Singh, Bhai Kartar Singh Jhabar and Hakim Bahadur Singh

The following leading citizens of Tarn Taran and its neighbourhood were also asked to participate in the conference :—Bhais Mohan Singh Vaid, Sant Singh, Mehtab Singh Headmaster, Sundar Singh, Bishan Singh Lambardar, Gian Singh and. Dharm Singh, Reis of Usma.

The Sikh residents brought articles of food for the Jatha people, who dispersed to different bungahs and other places in the vicinity to cook their food and take rest. The pujaris in the meanwhile sent their men to the neighbouring villages to bring up their supporters, and began themselves to make secret arrangements for attacking the Akalis. It appears from the evidence of Pujari Surjan Singh and a manufacturer of fireworks that even at 9 A. M. certain pujaris had ordered some explosive balls to be bought for them. But when their leaders appeared before the Jatha people, they were all sweetness and humility, as if butter would not melt in their mouths.

The representatives of both parties met in Bungah Dhotian at 4 P.M., and the following five conditions were laid before the priests for acceptance :—

(1) That the management of the Gurdwara Tarn Taran be carried on according to the rules laid down by the Shromani Gurdwara Parbandhak Committee ;

(2) that a small local committee affiliated to the Shromani Committee be formed to supervise the management;

(3) that all the existing defects be removed and in future no chance of any complaint be given to the Panth;

(5) that all those among the priests who have broken the religious law to accept any punishment imposed by the sangat; and

(4) that only those be appointed Granthis who conform strictly to the rules of baptism.

By 5-30 P. M. the representatives of the priests agreed to these demands, but they wanted time to consult their friends. They went into the temple where the rest of them were gathering in large numbers, and the Jatha people came to join the diwan which was being held in front of the temple. While Bhai Kartar Singh was exhorting the people to give time to the priests, Sardar Dan Singh pointed out to the audience that certain rough men were collecting in Gurdit Singh Pujari's building adjoining the Jhanda Bungah on the left of the main entrance, and two women were going up and down repeatedly with a lamp and seemed to be storing something in the upper storey. The gas lamp in front of the temple also began to grow dim for want of oil. The Jathadar gave instructions to all the Sikhs present to remain firm and not to retaliate under any circumstances.

At about 8-30 P. M. two pujaris cam from inside to the meeting and announced that all had agreed to accept the terms of reform, and asked the Sikh leaders to bring a fair copy of the document to be signed by the pujaris who were sitting in the temple. Sardar Dan Singh said that the appearances were suspicious and that they should come out. But the representatives laughed at the suspicion as groundless, and said that as all the priests were collected inside their signatures could be taken at once. Bhai Mohan Singh Vaid was sent out to copy out the terms of agreement; and he informed of it the Tehsildar, the Circle Inspector and other Government officials who were present outside the main gate of the temple.

In the meanwhile the representatives of the pujaris had agreed that the priest who performed the work of Granthi was by character unfit for the post, and that, until a better man was appointed in his place, Bhai Saran Singh of the Jatha should be allowed to officiate. Some members of the Jatha, including Sardar Balwant Singh of Kulla, accompanied Bhai Saran Singh into the temple, which was full of pujaris and their hired men. A moment later, as Bhai Bahadur Singh Hakim was addressing the diwan outside, an explosive ball burst near him. Then four or five more balls fell and burst in different places among the audience, wounding several with the small pieces of iron and nails. These balls and bricks fell from the roofs of Gurdit Singh Pujari's house and other bungahs close to it. They were a signal for the beginning of an attack on the Akalis who had gone inside.

Sardar Balwant Singh was bowing his head before the Holy Book, when a blow fell upon him and his arm was almost severed from his shoulder. Bhai Hazara Singh of Aldinpur, who bowed next, received a mortal wound in the belly and fell prostrate on the ground. As he was receiving blow after blow he was heard to say : "Brothers, you may kill me ; I will not attack a brother"* Hukam Singh got four *chhavi* blows on his head. Others who got badly hurt were Bhais Gurbakhsh Singh, Labh Singh, Bela Singh and Ishar Singh. The whole attack lasted only for a few minutes, and in all about 17 Jatha men were wounded. The pujaris had thrown down the door screens and had blown out the lamp. In the confusion caused by the explosions outside nothing

* The words used by Bhai Bir Singh, a great Sikh martyr of Naurangabad, who was killed in 1844, while giving shelter to the Princes Kashmira Singh and Pashaura Singh.

was known to the people in the diwan about the tragedy, until the wounded Sikhs staggered out and hastily told the tale of woe. The Jathadar ordered all the outlets to be guarded at once. When the horrified Sikhs entered the temple, they found the sacred place full of blood and two of their men lying on the ground. The priests were drunk* and looked wild. Many of them had already fled, some swimming away across the tank. The remaining were secured and bound down with their own scarfs or turbans. After a few minutes it was considered wiser to let them off and they went away on their own legs without showing any signs of injury. The wounded were carried by school boys and others to the hospital, where they were attended by Dr. Sundar Singh and Dr. Harnam Singh. The Tehsildar and the Police Inspector came at about 10 P. M., and went in to see what had happened. The Naib-Tehsildar and a Sub-Inspector went to the houses of the pujaris to see if any belonging to their party had been wounded. But nobody complained of any injuries received. At about 12 in the night a priest in a drunken state was brought on a charpai to the officers. He said that he had on him many serious wounds made by an axe; but the officers laughed at

* An empty bottle of wine was found lying on the floor.

him and told him, like the famous prophet, to take up his stick and walk off. And he did so. It was next day that on the advice of the police the priests brought 13 men on charpais as wounded to the hospital. Most of them had blue marks, which could have been got by tying wet cloth round the spots.

Next day the Sikhs washed and cleaned the blood-stained temple, and held the usual morning service. How many tears must have mixed with the water used to remove the blood! It was the first blood shed in the cause of Gurdwara Reform, and fitly in the temple of Guru Arjan who was the first martyr in the Sikh history.

The District Magistrate and the Superintendent of Police came from Amritsar and interviewed the leaders of both parties. They expressed sympathy with the Akalis for their suffering and asked them to sue the pujaris in court for attacking and wounding them. But the Akali leaders replied, "We have yet to reform many Gurdwaras and might suffer the same fate everywhere. Instead of taking cases from us, give us our temples." The District Magistrate next asked if there was any danger of further attack to them in the temple. The Akalis, who had been attacked again at night with brickbats, said that there was danger. The pujaris were told that if they came to harm it would be for their own foolish high-handedness. They were put on security not to enter the precincts of the temple, "until the matter was finally decided by the Parbandhak Gurdwara Committee."* Those of them living in houses bordering on the Parkarma were also bound down to prevent the throwing of stones, etc.

On the same day the pujaris came of their own accord to Dr. Kitchlew and Lala Girdhari Lal (who had come to make enquiries), and publicly confessed their serious crime. Later on they handed over a written apology and placed themselves at the mercy of the Panth. The Sikhs forgave them and, at their request, promised not to sue them in court. The pujaris, too, admitted that they were so much in the wrong that their going to court was unthinkable.

Bhai Hazara Singh, who had been wounded overnight, died in the afternoon, and his funeral, which took place on the 28th, was attended by thousands from far and near. Almost all the villagers of Aldinpur came with the martyr's mother, who felt proud of her son and blessed him. The people, too, who formed a long procession, showed a remarkably calm and orderly spirit. They walked in regular rows, which the Govern-

---

* Government communique, dated 9th February 1921.

ment calls 'military formation,' and chanted hymns of praise and thanksgiving. There was not a curse, not even a bitter word uttered at the insensate cruelty of the priests. In a truly prayerful mood the loss was taken as a pure sacrifice. Bhai Hazara Singh in freeing the Tarn Taran temple proved worthy of his ancestor Baghel Singh, who had used all his power in freeing the sacred places of Delhi. Another Akali, named Bhai Hukam Singh, succumbed to his injuries on 4th February.

A provisional managing committee, consisting of the following prominent Sikhs, was formed to control and manage the Gurdwara, until the Shromani Committee made another arrangement :—

1. S. Balwant Singh Subedar of Kulla, President.
2. S. Dharm Singh, Reis of Usma, Vice-President.
3. S. Mohan Singh, Vaid, Municipal Commissioner, of Tarn Taran.
4. S. Mehtab Singh, Headmaster, Khalsa High School, Tarn Taran.
5. S. Bishan Singh, Lambardar.
6. S. Sundar Singh, Manager of a factory.
7. S. Sant Singh, Secretary, Singh Sabha, Tarn Taran.
8. S. Amar Singh, Reis of Jhabal.
9. S. Teja Singh, Jathadar, Akali Dal

10. S. Kishen Singh of Bhuchar.
11. S. Hazara Singh of Jamarai.
12. S. Harnam Singh of Nowshera.
13. S. Teja Singh of Pandori.
14. Baba Kehar Singh of Patti.
15. S. Teja Singh Burjanwala.

A free kitchen was opened to provide food to all visitors belonging to any caste or creed.

The District Magistrate ordered a case to be started and the police took up the investigation. Ultimately there came up three cases in the Court of Mr. F. A. Connor, Additional District Magistrate of Amritsar: The first was under Sections 148, 149 and 304, Indian Penal Code,* in which the pujaris were held accused, and the second under Section 148, I. P. C., against the Akalis, in which the pujaris were said to have been attacked and wounded. There was a third case due to an application by the pujaris under Section 145, Cr. P. C., for having been deprived of possession of their

* It was evidently a murder case, but the usual official theory prevailed. The District Magistrate is alleged to have admitted to a Sikh editor 'that no doubt it was a clear case of 302, I. P. C., but as the Akalis refused to co-operate with the authorities and give their statements furnishing proper evidence or a case under Section 302, I. P. C., the case was challaned under Sections 148, 149 and 304, I. P. C.'
Khalsa Advocate, 14th October, 1921.

temple and apprehending a likelihood of a breach of the peace. The pujaris in this case stated that their ancestors had founded the Gurdwara of Tarn Taran to commemorate Guru Arjan and that the offerings belonged to them as of hereditary right. The Akalis on the other hand emphasised that the Gurdwara was the property of the Sikh community, and that the pujaris had themselves handed over a written apology to the Shromani Gurdwara Parbandhak Committee, in which they had agreed to submit to the authority of the Committee. The judge fearing no breach of the peace rejected the petition of the pujaris on July 9, 1921.

The other cases in the meanwhile had dragged on for many months, until on 4th July, 1921, about a dozen leading Sikh citizens of Tarn Taran and other places were also added to the list of Akalis who were being prosecuted. That was the time when indiscriminate arrests of Sikhs in connection with Gurdwaras and Kirpans were going on in several other places and the Akali movement was supposed to be on the wane. The only part that these leaders of Tarn Taran newly prosecuted had taken in the temple affair was that on the day of the occurrence they had been trying their utmost to maintain peace. It was mere harassment, calculated to terrify respectable men away from the popular movement. Among the Akalis, too, only those men were included who had been wounded in the temple and had the misfortune to go to the hospital. Others who had been hurt by the stones and brickbats, thrown from the bungahs, were not touched.

After a lull of several months, in October, 1921, charges were framed against 16 pujaris and 17 Akalis, and on 9th January, 1922, 15 pujaris were sentenced each to 3 years' rigorous imprisonment and one of them was fined Rs. 50. Out of the Akalis ten, including Bhai Mohan Singh Vaid and Bhai Mehtab Singh Head Master, were acquitted, while the rest were sentenced each to one year's rigorous imprisonment with a fine of Rs. 50. The Sessions Judge on 20th February reduced the sentences of the pujaris to nine months each, and of the Akalis to six months each with a fine of Rs. 50. The High Court rejected the appeals of both parties. Sardar Balwant Singh Kulla's sentence was remitted by the Governor.

CHAPTER XIV.

NANKANA SAHIB TRAGEDY.

Nankana Sahib, originally called Talwandi, is the birth place of Guru Nanak, the Apostle of Peace and Goodwill. Beside Janam Asthan, the house of Baba Kalu where Guru Nanak was born, there are several other places in the town associated with the different events of Guru Nanak's boyhood. There is one place, called Bal Lila, where Guru Nanak used to play with children. There is another place, called Kiara Sahib, where the Guru had made up the loss of a farmer who complained that the Guru's buffaloes had broken into his field and spoilt the green crop. The third place is called Mal Sahib, where a snake is said to have innocently spread its hood to shade the lamb-like Guru. The fourth place is connected with the Good Bargain made by Guru Nanak and is called Tamboo Sahib. When the Guru returned after feeding poor men with the money he had been given for making some profitable business, he was afraid of his father and took shelter within a tree, which even now covers the ground like a tent. There is also a place sacred to Guru Har

Gobind, who had come and tied his horse to a tree which is still preserved. There is a place called Patti Sahib or Attari, where Guru Nanak is said to have conned his lessons over a *patti* or a wooden tablet.

The most important place, however, is Janam Asthan. Even towards the end of Guru Nanak's life the house had been given up by his family. The Guru had two sons. One of them, named Sri Chand, against the injunctions of his father, turned an ascetic. He went away from home and lived in Barath, district Gurdaspur, and in Chamba. The second son, Lakhmi Das, was a householder, but he lived at Kartarpur in the Gurdaspur district, and after him his son, Dharam Chand, founded Dera Baba Nanak, where he and his descendants lived.

Sri Chand lived for a long time quite estranged from the successors of Guru Nanak, but he founded no sect and made no disciple. After some time he forgot his imaginary grievances and was gradually drawn more and more closely towards the Gurus, until he came round to their views completely, and before dying in 1629 he bestowed his mitre and necklace on Baba Gurditta, the eldest son of Guru Hargobind. The words of Sri Chand addressed to Guru Hargobind at the time of this adoption were: "The Guruship was already with you. I had only the fakir's mitre, and now that, too, is given over to your family." Baba Gurditta was a married man, but he was a hermit too. He wore the same kind of dress as was worn by Guru Nanak during his *udasis* or preaching tours. In 1636 he was asked by his father to appoint four masands or preachers, whom he invested with the same peculiar dress. Their names were : Almast, Phul, Gonda and Bal Hasna, the last being named Hasna as he had laughed out when he was given the queer dress to wear. They founded what are called *Dhuans* or hearths, and were very zealous preachers of Sikhism. As the masands or missionaries appointed by the earlier Gurus grew more and more corrupt, this new order of preachers grew more prominent and was especially useful in spreading Sikhism in far and difficult places. Beside the four *Dhuans*, there grew up in the course of time many other similar centres of missionary work, called *Bakhshishes.* Dharam Chand, the grandson of Guru Nanak, converted Bhagat Gir, a Bairagi monk, into a Sikh and, renaming him Bhagat Bhagwan, appointed him to preach Sikhism in the east, where he established 360 gaddis, most of which are still intact. Another Bakhshish, called Sangat Sahib, is after the name of Bhai Pheru, who was a devoted Sikh of Guru Har Rai. The Guru, after training him as a preacher, made him masand. When Guru Gobind Singh was punishing the masands who had grown corrupt, Bhai Pheru was also summoned. He came in extreme humility, holding his beard in his hands, and the Guru, being charmed with his devotion, was pleased to bestow upon him one-half of his own turban and the title of Sangat Sahib or the Guru's companion. He was also called the Truebeard. He was given the charge of preaching in the Nakka district between the rivers Ravi and Beas. There was a third Bakhshish, called Ramdaske, granted by Guru Tegh Bahadur to Baba Gurditta, a great-grandson of Baba Budha. The successors of this preacher are found at Ramdas, Muradabad, Nainakot, Teje, etc. The fourth Bakhshish was named after Bakht Mal, a masand in the time of Guru Gobind Singh. Seeing that other masands were being punished for their sins, he put on female clothes with bangles and a nose-ring, and took refuge with the ladies of the Guru's house. He was spared on their recommendation. His successors still wear female bangles in memory of the event, and are found at Chak in the district of Jullundur. The fifth Bakhshish was of Mihan Sahib, who was so named for supplying water in *rainlike* abundance to the congregations of the ninth Guru. Guru Tegh Bahadur appointed him to the Bakhshish at Dhamtan in Patiala. After some time Mihan Sahib appeared before Guru Gobind Singh with a kettledrum and was rewarded for his devotion with a flag and one-half of the Guru's turban. There were two other Bakhshishes, one named after Ajit Mal who was a masand of Guru Gobind Singh at Fatehpur in the South, and the other after Dakhni Rai, a Sodhi of Gharacho in Patiala.

These preachers were called *Udasis*, a name which had already been used for Guru Nanak's preaching tours. They were no sect, but a class of missionaries, like the masands, sent out by the Gurus for the spread of Sikhism. They believed in the same Holy Granth as other Sikhs and offered the same prayer in which the same Gurus from Guru Nanak onwards were invoked. They remained in constant communion with the Gurus and even fought for Guru Gobind Singh loyally like other Sikhs. When in 1699 the last Guru instituted the initiation by baptism, most of these people took the new ceremony and joined the Khalsa. But some of them remained without it, being engaged in distant places, where it was hard to get five *Piaras* for initiation. In the hard struggle that followed the death of Guru Gobind Singh and Baba Banda, when to be a Khalsa was considered a crime, their separatism was a protection against danger, and so they were confirmed in their distinction.* They, however, worked very zealously for Sikhism and like other Sahjdharis did not call themselves a sect, but only Sikhs who could not afford to put on the baptismal forms. In all other respects they believed and practised the same things as other Sikhs. Else how could they have found support and encouragement from the Khalsa? One sect does not support the preaching of another sect.

Janam Asthan remained deserted for several generations, during which time it was occasionally visited by some one from the town, who would come to light a lamp to ward off distress or beg for some gift. It was Guru Har Gobind, who marked out the sites of Janam Asthan, Bal Lila, Malji Sahib and Kiara Sahib for preservation, and enjoined upon the Sikhs in the city to take care

* Some of them, like Pritam Das and Santokh Das, who went in 1753 to the east, found that their simple dress did not bring so much respect and influence as the complicated garb and symbols of the Bairagis. So about 1765 they were led to adopt the matted hair and waist chain, etc. of the Vankhandias. After some time they also began to carry an ash-ball before their processions. They are now represented by some Udasis in Nepal and those living in the Sangalwala Akhara at Amritsar. In 1783 they dug the Hansli to supply water from the Ravi to the sacred tanks of Amritsar.

of the places. Long after this a visit was paid to the city by Diwan Kaura Mal, a staunch friend of the Sikhs in their days of persecution. He came from Multan and stopped at Bal Lila. Finding the place neglected he raised a temple over it and built two sides of the tank. He also left thirteen of his Sikh horsemen to take care of the sacred places. The present Pattidars of Bal Lila and Kiara Sahib are descended from those thirteen Sikh sowars.

After Diwan Kaura Mal Maharaja Ranjit Singh paid a visit to Nankana Sahib. He had with him Baba Sahib Singh Bedi, a great descendant of Guru Nanak, who drew the attention of the Maharaja to the neglected state of the Gurdwara. The Maharaja told the Baba Sahib to go next morning on horseback into the adjoining lands, and promised to give over to the Gurdwaras the whole land that he was able to go round with his horse before the time of dinner. Baba Sahib Singh eagerly ran his horse to the north and to the east, and a great deal of land was taken in, but when he turned towards the south, he thought that the time of meals had arrived, and that he should return, lest the Maharaja should think that he was too greedy. He came back and found that he had come an hour earlier. The Maharaja gave the whole land as jagir to the Gurdwaras and ordered that a beautiful temple be raised over the Janam Asthan. A big kitchen was also built for free distribution of food to the visitors of all castes and creeds. The well which is situated in the compound was also planned at that time. The Maharaja appointed certain Udasi Sikhs to look after the place and conduct religious service in the temple.

As long as the income of the Gurdwara was small the Mahants consulted the wishes of the Sikhs, who paid a yearly visit to Nankana Sahib. But when with the opening of the canal the value of the land increased enormously, the Mahants grew corrupt and began to look more to the friendship of revenue and other officers than to the restraining influence of the public. What can we expect from a professed ascetic, who has to administer and enjoy an income of two or three lakhs a year without feeling any check or control from public ?

In the time of Mahant Sadhu Ram the affairs of the temple fell into disrepute. The Sikhs, as we have seen, tried to exercise some check, but the influence of the local officials was too much for them. The Mahant was a notorious drunkard and adulterer. He had contracted a dirty venereal disease, which did not allow him even to walk steadily. Kishan Das, who succeeded him, was no better.

He produced a great scandal by living with the rich widow of a well-known Sardar and having a son by her. He invited dancing girls on his nephew's marriage, and a nautch party was held even in the Janam Asthan. The marriage party, including the Mahant, for drinking were given a shoe-beating by the people of the bride's village. This Mahant was carried away by the same venereal disease which had killed his predecessor. When Kishan Das was dying at Lahore, Narain Das, who was one of his disciples, took the temple keys out of his pocket and, coming hurriedly to Nankana Sahib, took possession of the treasure. The money paved his way to Mahantship.

At the time of his appointment, however, he declared to the convened sangat, in the presence of a Magistrate, that the conduct of his predecessor had gone with him in his pyre and that he, the new Mahant, would never tread in his footsteps. He also declared in writing that, if any fault were proved against him, he would abdicate at the bidding of the sangat.

He, however, falsified all his promises and began to live as loosely as any of his predecessars had done before. He kept a low-class Mohammedan drummer's woman, who had already lived with some priests and other men. He had by her two boys and two girls, for whom he built two houses, one at Nankana Sahib and another in Ram Gali at Lahore. In August, 1917, the whole Sikh community was scandalized to learn that dancing girls were invited to Nankana Sahib, and their dancing and singing was permitted even in the Janam Asthan. There was great agitation in the press, and resolutions were passed in Singh Sabhas, expressing indignation at the sacrilege and asking Government to take some steps to prevent such actions on the part of the keepers of Janam Asthan. The people felt so helpless that in some quarters it was suggested that, while asking for reforms from Government, the Sikhs should also demand the control and management of their much-corrupted Church. In 1918 a retired E. A. C. of Sindh came to visit the Gurdwaras in the Punjab. First he came to Nankana Sahib, and was accommodated at the Janam Asthan. In the evening, when the Rahras service was going on, his daughter of 13 years was raped by a priest, but the Mahant refused to take any action. In 1918 six women of the Jaranwala ilaqa came to make an offering on the Full-moon day at the Janam Asthan and put up at the temple. All of these women were raped at night. These are only a few out of many instances of sin and sacrilege which were going on in the place, where Guru

Nanak was born to eradicate sin from the world.

About the beginning of October, 1920, a great diwan was held at Dharowal and the deplorable condition of the Nankana Sahib temple was discussed. A resolution was passed, calling upon the Mahant to reform his ways and the administration of the temple. But the Mahant, instead of doing anything to remove the grievances of the public, began to make preparations for violence. He collected about 400 desperate men daily from the Kots to guard the Gurdwara, and engaged several notorious cut-throats like Ranjha, Rehana, etc. In consultation with Baba Kartar Singh and other friends he decided to hold a meeting of Sadhus and Mahants at Nankana Sahib. In the meeting which was attended by about 60 men, including Baba Kartar Singh, it was decided that the Mahants should not recognise the Sikh Committee, but should have one of their own. A committee was actually constituted with Mahant Narain Das as President, and Mahant Basant Das of Manak as Secretary. About Rs. 60,000 were collected for expenses, and a paper called *Sant Sewak* was started at Lahore for propaganda work.

Four or five days before Guru Nanak's birthday fair in November the Mahant collected about 400 'good fighters' and armed them with *chhavis* and *takwas* to give a suitable reception to any Sikhs who might dare to come on the day of their Guru. He had also ordered that no Sikh with a Kirpan should be allowed to enter. Bhai Lachman Singh, a tall and handsome Sardar of Dharowal, came with a few people of his village to pay his respects at the temple. As soon as he entered the precincts a body of desperadoes sprang out of a side-room and were ready to attack the Bhai Sahib, but the day of martyrdom was not yet, and the intervention of the Deputy Commissioner and the C. I. D. Superintendent 'averted what might have been even a worse tragedy than what actually happened on the 20th February'.* Most of the hired men were sent away after the fair, but some of them, like Ranjha, Shamu, Kahna, etc., who were servants, remained with the Mahant.

After that the Mahant approached H. H. the Maharaja of Patiala who was at Lahore, but he was told that the best thing for him was to form a representative committee of genuine Sikhs to control the Gurdwara. He also sought help from Government, but the Commissioner told

---

* Mr. King's statement in the Legislative Council on 15th March, 1921.

him that the matter being religious, the Government did not want to interfere. He was, however, shown the letter which Mr. King had issued some time before and in which he had told the Mahants that, if they apprehended attacks on their shrines, they could apply for police protection for which they would have to pay. He wanted a force of police which should be armed with rifles and authorised to fire, but the Government refused. Seeing that no help was forthcoming to support him in his defiance of the Panth, he fell back upon the main force, which could be easily bought for money. The C. I. D. report cited in the Nankana Sahib case admits that the Mahant collected number of 'supporters,' and the Commissioner in his explanatory speech in the Punjab Council on 15th March, 1921, referred to certain rumours to the effect that ever since October, 1920, the Mahant had been secretly collecting weapons. He was so impressed with the gravity of the situation on his visit to Nankana Sahib towards the end of January that he 'at once wrote to the police authorities asking that a police station should be established at Nankana as soon as possible.' But the police being too busy with the preparations for the Duke of Connaught, the establishment of a choukie at Nankana Sahib could not be carried out.*

The Sikhs knew of the Mahant's preparations and referred to them in their meetings and the press,† but they did not want to fight. They adopted the only possible non-violent method of effecting their purpose. On 24th January, 1921, they passed a resolution in the Shromani Gurdwara Parbandhak Committee that the whole Panth should gather in a diwan at Nankana Sahib on March 4, 5 and 6, and call upon the Mahant to reform himself. A printed notice was also circulated asking the Punjab Government, the Sikh Princes, the Sikh public and all others interested in the matter to exert their influence to secure the Panthic control of the Gurdwara. On February 6, a committee of Bhais Lachhman Singh of Dharowal, Dalip Singh of Sangla, Teja Singh of Samundri, Kartar Singh of Jhabar and Bakhshish Singh, was appointed to make feeding arrangements for the lakhs of people who were going to gather at Nankana Sahib.

Now the Mahant saw that he would have to do something. He began to make military preparations, but at the same time he tried to negotiate with the Sikhs. He

---

* See the statement of Mr. King in his libel case against the *Akali*.

† See the *Akali* of Lahore, October 8, 1920.

met Bhai Kartar Singh of Jhabar at Lahore and proposed that he would agree to a committee, if (*i*) he were not ousted, (*ii*) if he were made a member of the committee and (*iii*) if instead of pay he were given a share in the income of the Gurdwara. He was assured that if he promised to reform himself, his first and third conditions would be accepted, and about the second he was told that the matter lay with the Shromani Committee, which would be consulted. Bhai Kartar Singh related the result of his negotiations to the Shromani Committee. A sub-committee was appointed to talk to the Mahant, and he was called to an interview at the Khara Sauda diwan.

The Mahant, instead of meeting the Sikhs, engaged 28 Pathans on Rs. 20 a month each, with rations, and armed them with lathis. His nephews also brought a large number of stout men from Manjha. Several desperadoes from Bhai Pheru also came to help the Mahant. The old wooden gate of the temple was replaced by a strong one made of iron with holes to fire through. The walls of the rooms surrounding the shrine were also pierced to admit of shooting through them. When the whole thing was ready, the Mahant's paper, *Sant Sewak*, openly threatened that if the Sikhs came to Nankana Sahib they would be well-peppered.

About February 7, the Mahant summoned a meeting, in the Janam Asthan, of his supporters, including the Bhatti Mussalmans who live in the neighbourhood of Nankana Sahib, and took solemn oaths from them to aid him in fighting the Akalis. Hari Nath, one of the murderers who made a very important confession, said that a Bawa Bedi and Mangal Singh Kuka also spoke on this occasion.

Sundar Das, Hari Das and others came to Khara Sauda on behalf of the Mahant and informed the Sikhs gathered there that the Mahant would not come to Khara Sauda that day, but that he would present himself at Sheikhupura on February 15. When Bhai Kartar Singh Jhabar reached Sheikhupura on the night of February 14, he found that Mahant Narain Das had not come, but Mahant Jiwan Das was there to inform him thet the Mahant would like to meet him and Sardar Buta Singh at Lahore. These two gentlemen went to Lahore by the morning train, and 10 A. M. was fixed as the time of meeting at the house of Sardar Amar Singh, editor of the *Loyal Gazette.* The Mahant did not come. A reliable Sikh, who had been appointed to watch the movements of the Mahant, came to inform that on the evening of the 14th a meeting had been held, where it was resolved that, when on March 5 the whole Panth would collect at Nankana Sahib, the Sikh leaders would be invited for settlement into the Janam Asthan, where all of them would be murdered by the hired ruffians.

These news staggered Bhai Kartar Singh. He came to Khara Sauda and informed his Jatha, who hastily resolved to prevent the Mahant from executing his horrible purpose on the leaders by going to Nankana Sahib before the date fixed. Bhai Lachhman Singh of Dharowal and Bhai Buta Singh of Lyallpur were sent for. They came on the 17th. It was arranged that Bhai Buta Singh should go to Nankana Sahib on the morning of the 19th, and on the same night Bhai Lachhman Singh with his jatha should reach Chandarkot, a few miles from Nankana Sahib, where he would be joined by Bhai Kartar Singh with his jatha.

Bhai Buta Singh went to Lyallpur and consulting a few friends went to Nankana Sahib as bidden. When Sardar Harchand Singh, Sardar Teja Singh of Samundri and Master Tara Singh, B.A., came to know of it, they disapproved of the idea and at once proceeded to Lahore, where they reached on the morning of the 19th. In a meeting convened at the *Akali* Office, where they were joined by Sardar Sardul Singh Caveessieur, Master Sundar Singh, Sardar Jaswant Singh of Jhabbal and Bhai Dalip Singh of Sangla, it was decided that no Jatha should go to Nankana Sahib before the fixed date. Bhai Dalip Singh and Sardar Jaswant Singh were sent to dissuade Bhai Kartar Singh from going to Nankana Sahib. They reached Khara Sauda on the same day at 1 P. M. and by 8 P. M. were able to persuade Bhai Kartar Singh to abide by the decision of the sangat. Then Bhai Dalip Singh undertook to go and prevent Bhai Lachhman Singh from entering Nankana Sahib. With three horsemen from the Jatha of Bhai Kartar Singh he went to Chandarkot, but not finding Bhai Lachhman Singh there, he returned to the factory of Sardar Uttam Singh, which is about half a mile from the Janam Asthan. After meeting at the *Akali's* Office Master Tara Singh and S. Teja Singh of Samundri came to attend a meeting of the Shromani Committee on the same day. It was informally decided that Master Tara Singh and others should go as soon as possible and prevent people from going to Nankana Sahib.

Bhai Lachhman Singh in the meanwhile had started late in the evening of the 19th with six men from his village. He had also got two women with him. One was his own wife and the other a school mistress. Another woman is said to have joined them on the way. About 19 men came from Devasinghwala, 11 from Dhannuwal, 7 or 8 from Chelawala, 6 from Thothian, 5 from Mulasinghwala, and others from different villages in the canal region, until a jatha of about 150 was made up. A little before 6 A. M. they came to the kilns situated to the north of Janam Asthan and were met by a messenger of Bhai Dalip Singh. He gave a letter written by Dalip Singh to Bhai Lachhman Singh, asking the latter to go away and not to set his foot in Nankana Sahib. Bhai Lachhman Singh, who greatly revered Bhai Dalip Singh, obeyed the orders and turned back. But he was persuaded by Bhai Tahl Singh, one of the jatha, to go at least for *darshan*. He was told that it was the day of Guru Har Rai, who had kept armies and wore arms, but inspite of provocations had never used them. The Mahant at the worst would kill them. But it did not matter at all, when they were resolved not to provoke or retaliate. They decided to pay their respects at the temple and then come away peacefully. The women went to the Gurdwara of Tamboo Sahib, whence they returned home later, and the men went to bathe at the tank outside the Janam Asthan. At 6 A. M. they entered the temple.

Five or six days before the occurrence the Mahant had removed his family and property to Lahore. According to Hari Nath he had also sent his men to a police officer at Kasur to make his own position secure by reporting that Rihana, Amli, Kandi, Vaisakha, and other notorious men were with him and asking that their presence should be connived at.

Narain Das had to attend the Mahants' Conference at Lahore which was fixed for the 19th and 20th, but he came every day to Nankana Sahib. He had sent Amli, Gomi, and others to bring more men from Majha and elsewhere. When they were brought he took them to Nankana Sahib on the morning of the 19th. At 3-44 P. M. he got into the train for Lahore, but he got out at once when a Mohammedan woman told him that a jatha had arrived at Buchiana. He came back and distributed a large number of battle-axes and iron-shod sticks to his men. He stored a great quantity of wood and kerosine oil in the outer rooms. He had got three breech-loading guns and one muzzle-loader.* A lot of cartridges were especially bought from Lahore and sufficient lead was provided to Rihana to manufacture

* A six-chambered revolver, presumably belonging to the Mahant, was recovered from the Janam Asthan tank on July 24, 1922.

bullets. Several heaps of brick-bats were piled on the roofs in different places. He supplied wine to his men. Sardar Uttam Singh, factory owner, who had seen the Mahant distributing axes and heard him threatening to kill the Sikhs with them, sent a letter about it to the Deputy Commissioner on the morning of the 20th, but it was too late.

The temple is a small four-doored room built on a platform, with a verandah on the front. There is a low path running round the platform, and the whole open space is bordered with rooms, with only two outlets beside the main gate facing east, which is called the Darshani door. The southern gate faces the bazar and is called the Bazar door.

The Mahant had placed his Majha men in his *baithak* or the sitting room, which lies close to the west. The men from the Kots were posted, some in the verandah in front of the Bazar gate and some inside the Gurdwara in a verandah near the Darshani gate. The Pathans guarded the two main gates from outside.

When the Sikhs entered the Darshani gate, they raised the usual religious shout of Sat Sri Akal, which means God the deathless is true. They repeated the shout on reaching the front of the temple. The men who were posted at the gate went out and the doors were shut. The few priests, who were sitting inside, also went away one by one. Bhai Lachhman Singh sat before Guru Granth Sahib and the jatha began to sing the morning hymns. In a few minutes about 25 men were seen on the roofs of the verandah towards the southern gate. Four of them, including Ranjah and Rihana, began to fire at the Sikhs with guns, while a Mohammedan supplied ammunition. The rest of the men, sadhus and all, began to throw bricks at the Sikhs, some of whom ran to take shelter in the side room or the Darshani porch. Some who went to the north of the sanctuary were shot at from the western wall. Those who stayed calmly suffered themselves to be shot, and thus about 25 were killed in the compound. Even the Holy Book was riddled through in several places. The rest of the Sikhs, about 60, went into the sanctuary, called Chaukhandi, and shut the doors from inside. Then the Mahant's men came to the roof of the Darshani porch and began to fire at the Sikhs below. After killing and wounding several with shots and bricks the Mahant's men came down the two stair-cases. The Darshani and the Bazar gates were opened and many Pathans and other men of the Mahant came in from outside.

About 5 or 6 Sikhs were found taking refuge in the enclosed verandah of the Darshani porch. A few shots were fired at them, and then the wounded were finished off with chhavis and takwas. Afterwards a great quantity of minced flesh was found at this place. The side-rooms were also searched, and about 25 Sikhs who were found there were despatched.

Some more Sikhs had arrived outside by this time, and hearing their shouts of Sat Sri Akal the Mahant's men rushed out of the Darshani and the Bazar gates. Some also got themselves upon the roofs. It was here that some wounded Sikhs got out and escaped. Two Akalis, who had gone up the stair by the southern gate, were attacked with chhavis, and after being wounded were thrown down outside the wall. The Mahant had a *chaddar* wrapped round his face and was riding a horse. He was urging his men to spare no long-haired Sikh in the whole vicinity. The newly arrived Sikhs came from the north to the road leading from the Bazar gate to the potters' kilns. The Mahant called out, "Kill them." He himself fired his pistol and killed one man. Rihana aimed his gun at another, but a Sikh hit him on the arm and the gun fell down. About 6 Sikhs were killed here. The remaining were pursued by Ranjha and some Sadhus to the railway line, where an old man and two others were killed and burnt. One or two were killed in the fields.

Then somebody shouted that the Chaukhandi doors were shut and that there were many Sikhs inside. A host came in for a fresh attack. Two of them had guns and others had chhavis. A Sikh who was hiding in a tomb was shot and killed. One man started to fire through the silver-plated door on the west of the Chaukhandi. Others, cutting away the fence in front of the northern door, pulled it down with chhavis. Ranjha and one other man began to fire through this door.* A Pathan made a hole in the western door with his axe for two men to fire through. A Sikh from inside called out, 'let me out.' A Mahant's man replied, 'we shall do so.' The Sikh came out, but was shot dead. When all were wounded or killed inside, the Pathans and others entered and dragged out the bodies. All, about 60, were despatched. Only a boy of 12 who had taken refuge under Guru Granth Sahib was spared.

The Mahant came in and said that all the bodies lying in the compound, except four, should be collected and burnt. He carefully ordered his men not to burn the

---

* After the event several hundred marks of bullets were counted on the walls, and pieces of marble had come off from a niche.

bodies of three Sikhs* and one sadhu who had been admittedly shot by mistake by some one of the Mahant's party. From this he wanted to make out that men had been killed on both sides. Wood and oil was brought from a side room and fire was lighted in the open space to the north-west of the Chaukhandi. Before the bodies were put on fire, they were searched by Pathans, who took away whatever valuable was found on them, *e.g.*, money, kirpans, blankets, etc. Wood and oil proving insufficient a great quantity was brought on carts from the bazar. It appears from the confessions of the culprits that some Sikhs got up alive from the burning heaps, but were beaten down with sticks and chhavis. There is also some evidence to prove that some Sikhs were burnt alive. At least one seems to have been tied to a tree and burnt. Those who were killed outside the Gurdwara were thrown into a potter's kiln and burnt there.

The story of Bhai Dalip Singh's martyrdom is very pathetic. Hearing that, inspite of all his attempts to prevent him, Bhai

---

*These were of Hazara Singh, Mangal Singh and Atma Singh. Mangal Singh, an ex soldier, had suffered imprisonment for wearing kirpan and was therefore given the title of Kirpan Bahadur. He had been a Mazhabi before receiving baptism and was adopted by Bhai Lachhman Singh as his dearest son.

Lachhman Singh had gone with his jatha to the Janam Asthan, Bhai Dalip Singh decided to go himself to save the Sikhs or die in the attempt. He was told that the firing had begun and that the Sikhs were being murdered. But he would not desist. He thought that the Mahant, who knew and respected him, would give up the massacre when he would make a personal appeal to him. He took with him Bhai Waryam Singh, a man of romantic antecedents, who had joined the movement out of pure love for sacrifice. They came to the Darshani gate, when an attack was going on against the newly-arrived Sikhs and the Mahant on horseback was urging his men not to spare a *keshadhari* Sikh. With folded hands Bhai Dalip Singh implored the Mahant to desist: "Cease ! O cease ! Let this carnage cease ! Even now I shall get you pardon from the Panth." The Mahant, who was drunk with the murder of innocents, replied: "Are you not a Sikh?" Bang went his pistol and the saintly Sikh fell dead on the ground. The same fate was met by Bhai Waryam Singh at somebody else's hands.

After finishing the work of the day, the Mahant and his men went to their places and tried to drown their fears in drink. The whole city was deserted.

When the sound of firing was heard and it was ascertained that murder was going on in the Janam Asthan, other Sikhs living in the vicinity began to fear for their lives. At 8-15 A. M. Mr. N. S. Sandhu, District Engineer, sent a mounted messenger to the Deputy Commissioner, who was in camp at Mangtanwala, 12 miles off. At 9-12 A. M. Sardar Uttam Singh wired the terrible news to the Governor, the Commissioner, the Deputy Commissioner, the Superintendent of Police, and the different Sikh centres. The Patwari and the Sikh Station-master also sent wires in all directions. Although Lahore is only about 40 miles from Nankana Sahib, no prompt action was taken by Government. The Deputy Commissioner arrived at 12-30 P.M. and went into the temple with the Mahant, but without police he could not do anything. He wired for troops. A Sub-Inspector of Police came at 2 P. M. and was ordered to extinguish the fire and record the injuries of the dead and the wounded. The booking of tickets for all stations within 20 miles of Nankana Sahib was stopped. Even roads, bridges and ferries near the locality were guarded, and no man was allowed to proceed to Nankana Sahib. The Commissioner and the Deputy Inspector-General of Police with 100 British and 100 Indian soldiers arrived from Lahore by a special train, at 9-15 in the night, and Mahant Narain Das, with two of his henchmen and 26 Pathans, was arrested and sent to Lahore. He had a gun with him when he was arrested. Two more guns and a pistol were recovered from his house. The Gurdwara was attached and placed under a military guard.

The sensational news spread a thrill of horror and indignation all over the country, and resolutions of sympathy were passed by all communities. Wherever the Sikhs heard of it they were struck with grief and reverence for the martyrs. Thousands proceeded at once to Nankana Sahib. They came as far as they could by rail and then on foot, but none were allowed to go near the Gurdwara. People, who were thirsting for information, got conflicting news from different sources. Some telegrams sent by Sikhs described the occurrence as a cold-blooded massacre and put the number of the killed at above 150, while certain Anglo-Indian papers started the campaign of misrepresentation by calling the heinous crime as a 'fight', a 'riot', an 'affray' and 'a disturbance of a sectarian character', and tried to belittle the number of the killed. The Deputy Commissioner of Amritsar telephoned to the Khalsa College on the 21st that only 20 men had been killed at Nankana Sahib. Later it was given out in a Government communique that the number was not less than 67, and then a week later it was admitted to be 130. The Government claimed to have secured order at the shrine by a show of military force !

Six Sikh leaders from Lahore, including Sardar Bahadur Mehtab Singh, Public Prosecutor, had already reached Nankana Sahib in the troop train on the 20th, and about 9 more leaders from Amritsar, including Sardar Harbans Singh and Sardar Sundar Singh Ramgarhia with three doctors and others, arrived on the morning of the 21st by motor. Then the temple was entered at 8 A.M. and the investigation began. The Gurdwara presented a terrible scene of carnage. The whole place looked like a vast cremation ground. The greater portion of the flooring was covered with blood and the traces of bodies having been dragged on the ground. Long hair and combs were found scattered here and there. There were four dead men lying near the sanctuary and five big heaps of charred bodies to the north-west. Without disturbing them 56 distinct skulls were counted. Outside in the kiln six iron bracelets were found in the ashes, to which the martyred Sikhs had been reduced. On the roofs of the side-rooms 24 heaps of brickbats were found. The police also recovered from the roof eight empty boxes of cartridges, each of which was marked to contain 25 cartridges, together with 63 empty cases of cartridges picked up from various places. From the *baithak* of the Mahant, beside other incriminating articles, a sieve, some lead and iron, and an iron pot, apparently for melting lead, were found. In another room were found five empty bottles of country wine, one cartridge and some buckshot. Several cartridges and other things were also recovered later on from the tower where the Pathans used to live.

On the evening of the 21st the Commissioner yielded to a strong pressure put by the Sikh leaders, and handed over the keys of the Gurdwara to a Committee of seven members with powers to co-opt. Sardar Harbans Singh, as president of the Committee, took charge of the Gurdwara in the name of the Shromani Gurdwara Parbandhak Committee of Amritsar. The military guard was removed. The Sikhs, who had been kept away so far, entered the Gurdwara and wept bitterly to see their brethren mercilessly slaughtered and disgracefully burnt. By the order of Sardar Harbans Singh, however, large crowds were not allowed to gather inside the temple to facilitate the medical enquiry. Next day thousands of Sikhs came from far and near to pay their respects to the martyrs. They found—and the police evidence agrees—that almost all of the inhabitants had fled from the place even before the Sikhs had come. So they collected the cattle, which would have died otherwise, and placed them in a pound. They also protected the deserted houses from burglars and thieves by keeping watch over them. They announced by the beat of drum that the people of the place were welcome to their homes and that all fear had vanished with the arrest of the culprits and the removal of the military.

His Excellency Sir Edward Maclagan, accompanied by his Executive Councillors and Ministers, came to Nankana Sahib on the afternoon of February 22nd to show his sympathy with the victims of the outrage. He seemed to be much affected by the sight and promised that no efforts would be spared to discover and punish the perpetrators of the crime. He also sent a message of sympathy through the members of the Legislative Council to the relatives and friends of the victims.

By the evening of February 23rd, which was fixed for the funeral, thousands of Sikhs had mustered on the spot to pay their last homage to the holy martyrs. Many of them, owing to the stoppage of trains on the 21st and 22nd, had to walk for miles in dust and sun. The scene inside was most pathetic. Relations and friends were moving about to recognise their dead. A woman was sitting by a heap of ashes and bones, pressing the hand of a half-burnt body. She said it was her son's. She had lost five sons and one grandson. Another woman had lost two sons; another one brother. And they did not weep.

When all the remains were collected from different places, 130 heads were easily counted. The rest were reduced to ashes or small pieces of bones, and were not distinguishable. A big funeral pyre was erected in the same place in the compound where a majority of the martyrs had been thrown by the culprits for burning. In a touching oration Professor Jodh Singh, M.A., exhorted the Sikhs to bear the suffering like their forefathers as a sacrifice, without a reproach or curse. The crimes committed in the holy temple required a flood of innocent blood to be washed away. And they have been washed away. "As for the criminal, his own sins are sufficient to ruin him." The daily prayer of the Sikhs contains these words: "Those who died for their religion, were cut away limb by limb, or were burnt on heated plates think of them and call on God." These familiar words, uttered in the funeral prayer that day, went to the hearts of the assembled Sikhs with a new meaning. It was as if a page of the old Sikh history had been turned again. From that day the following words have been added to the standard Sikh prayer and are repeated daily in all congregations:

"Those who, to purge the temples of the long-standing evils, suffered themselves to be shot, cut up, or burnt alive with kerosine oil, but did not make any resistance or utter even a sigh of complaint: think of their patient faith and call on God!" When the Holy Book was opened it gave out the most appropriate verse: "Those whom God wanted to honour as His servants have been picked out." By a resolution passed in the light of the big funeral fire it was resolved to hold prayer meetings everywhere on a fixed day. It was also decided to found a suitable memorial to the heroic sacrifice of the martyrs. A Martyrs' Fund was opened to which all Sikh families were requested to contribute at least one rupee per head.

The police carried on its investigation and, inspite of the advice of Mahatma Gandhi, who visited the place on March 3, to seek no justice from Government, the Sikh Committee continued to give assistance, and it was appreciated in the beginning. But soon it became clear that the presence of the Sikhs at Nankana Sahib was not relished by the police, who wanted a free hand to make anything they wanted of the case and did not take down the statements of witnesses as they were made. The Sikhs, therefore, dissociated themselves from the enquiry and took no interest in the case, which was started on April 5. Many of the prosecution witnesses turned away from their previous statements made before a Magistrate, and the official witnesses gave evidence in a spirit distinctly hostile to the reform party among the Sikhs. The three assessors (one Hindu, one Sikh and one Muhammedan) found the Mahant guilty of murder, and the Sessions Judge, who delivered his judgment on October 12, 1921, sentenced the Mahant and seven others to death, eight to transportation for life, sixteen Pathans to seven years' rigorous imprisonment, and acquitted the remaining sixteen. In the High Court, however, Mr. Hassan Imam of Patna fought heroically for the Mahant and his sweeping cock-sure arguments prevailed. In defending the Mahant's order to kill all the Sikhs, he went so far as to say that 'even if the number of deaths were 130 thousand and not 130, the Mahant would have been justified in giving that order.'* The Judges of the High Court, who delivered their judgment on March 3, 1922, held that in view of his failure to secure protection from Government, the Mahant was fully justified in taking steps for his own protection both by engaging Pathans

---

* Reported in the *Tribune* of January 26, 1922.

as guards and by importing men, who were reported to be good fighters, such as Ranjha and Rihana. 'He was,' in their Lordships' opinion, 'suffering doubtless under a deep sense of wrong and helplessness, and it was not surprising that he lost his head and acted as he did.' His sentence of death was reduced to one of transportation for life. Only three sentences of death, *i. e.*, against Hari Nath, who had made full confession, and against Ranjha and Rihana, were maintained. Out of those who had been sentenced to transportation for life, only two got their sentences confirmed. All others, together with the Pathans, were acquitted. This decision created a great sensation in the country.

In May, 1921, in view of an apprehension of a breach of peace between the Mahant's party and the Gurdwara Committee about the lands attached to the Gurdwara, the District Magistrate called upon the parties to state their claims as to the actual possession of the said lands. He decided that the claim of the Gurdwara Committee was true and that it was entitled to the possession of the lands until ousted by the courts of law.

A civil suit was filed against the Gurdwara Committee, and on the day following the decision of the High Court, the Deputy Commissioner of Sheikhupura informed the Manager of the Janam Asthan that the jagir money was to be kept in deposit by the Government as long as the Civil suit was not decided, and ordered him, under threat of legal proceedings, to pay up the arrears within fifteen days.

In April, 1922, the Mahant's people tried to get a Receiver appointed for the Janam Asthan. But the court did not allow it.

The Gurdwara Committee was successful in making an arrangement with Mahant Kirpa Ram of Malji Sahib at Nankana Sahib, by which the Mahant consented to give charge of the Gurdwara and its property to the Committee. A very generous consideration was shown to him. He was granted a monthly salary of Rs. 1,000, with houses worth Rs. 80,000 for perpetual possession. About Rs. 45,000 were sanctioned to pay up his debts. He also got for himself and his male descendants 3 squares of land, which will revert to the Gurdwara when his descendants cease to exist. After his death his children, male and female, will get Rs. 500 a month, and his grand-children Rs. 250 a month. Inspite of temptations and threats by mischievous parties, the Mahant has continued to be loyal, except once in June, 1921, when he made an abortive attempt with a band of ruffians dressed in Akali clothes to take possession of Malji Sahib; but he soon recovered his balance and, when a few months later, the Udasin Mahamandal of Hardwar in a letter threatened him with excommunication for his sympathies with the Akali movement and told him clearly that if he alienated any part of the Gurdwara property he would be sued in the court, he refused to be led away from the path of duty and reaffirmed his belief in the Panth.

The management of the Gurdwaras and their land was placed in the hands of Sardar Narain Singh, Bar-at-Law, who ably conducted the affairs, inspite of many difficulties that are natural in the beginning. The income of the Gurdwaras of Janam Asthan and Malji Sahib for the last year was Rs. 3,26,325. Out of this Rs. 1,33,330 were deposited in banks and with Sahukars, and the remaining sum was utilized in erecting a fund for the relief of the martyrs' families, and in maintaining a free kitchen, missionary propaganda, a hospital, and two schools, one for boys and the other for girls. Beside other things tailoring and weaving are taught in the boys' school. The whole sum collected in the Martyrs' Memorial Fund upto 31st July 1922, amount to Rs. 2,48,461-12-3. In September, 1921, upto Rs. 700 a month was sanctioned for giving pensions to the families of the martyrs and Rs. 25,000 towards the payment of their debts, out of which Rs. 13,000 have already been paid. The relief, which is paid regularfy every month, varies from Rs. 10 to 30 per family. At present Rs. 546 are spent in this way. More demand is being made. Most of the proposals received about the Martyrs' Memorial suggested a missonary seminary for the purpose of training preachers, and the sub-committee appointed by the Shromani Committee to recommend what form the Memorial should take has also made the same suggestion.

Great improvements have been carried out in the land surrounding the temple by laying out lawns and gardens. New buildings for public use have been erected and more are being planned. Good arrangements have been made for the reception and acccommodation of visitors. Those who saw the celebration of Guru Nanak's Birthday in November, 1921, will bear witness to the unprecedented enthusiasm with which the service of each other and the mission work was carried on by the people. There were regular mission camps held, of which those belonging to the Shromani Gurdwara Parbandhak Committee, Chief Khalsa Diwan, Sheikhupura Khalsa Diwan, Ramgarhia Khalsa Diwan, Lahore and Gujranwala Khalsa Diwan and Dhuri Khalsa Diwan were most prominent. Feeding arrangements for thousands of people were made most successfully.

CHAPTER XV.

AFTER NANKANA.

After the Nankana Sahib tragedy, owing to the personal pique of some officers, the attitude of the Government changed altogether towards the Sikhs, Mr. King, who had been Commissioner of Lahore Division, became Assistant Chief Secretary, and from that point of vantage began to take very active interest in the Sikh movement. Instead of showing any practical sympathy with the Sikhs several Government officers actually showed their anxiety to belittle the gravity of the happening. The Deputy Commissioner of Shahpur dismissed one clerk and treated others as absent without leave for having gone to Nankana Sahib, and he is alleged to have used insulting language towards the martyrs. The police became suddenly active in taking up cases, however slight, against the Sikhs, and the Associated Press lent its services for spreading misrepresentations about them. The Government became too nervous about the public criticism of its officers. Without making any enquiry into the grave allegations, about some of which even Pandit Malviya expressed himself satisfied, it hastened to declare the conduct of its officers immaculate in connection with the Nankana affair and threatened to take legal action against any body who made unjust accusations against them. S. Sardul Singh Caveessieur, who at the time of the Nankana massacre had been illegally forbidden by the District Magistrate to leave Lahore, was hauled up for writing seditious articles about Nankana Sahib in the *Akali*, and was sentenced to five years' transportation. Several others were gagged at Lahore. The *Akali* also was prosecuted for publishing certain allegations against Mr. King and Mr. Bowring, the Superintendent of C. I. D.

An attempt was made through the official evidence in the Nankana Sahib trial to prejudice the case against the reform party by irrelevantly referring to the excited condition of the Sikhs who visited Nankana Sahib after the tragedy. The officers complained, as the Government did in its communiques, that the Sikhs terrorized the people with their large numbers and their kirpans, and that when the Governor arrived on 22nd February "they were calling out that they desired justice." To all reasonable men it must appear but natural that the Sikhs should at least feel excited over the cruel murder of so many of their brethren. And what harm did they actually do in this excitement? They could be angry with the Government for having taken no adequate measures to prevent the massacre, and with the men of the Mahant's party for having played a part in the savage crime. But it is admitted by the Government that when the Governor arrived with his retinue, including Mr. King, "there were a large crowd of Sikhs gathered in this enclosure, who, although greatly excited, were obedient to their leaders and under their control, so that although there were no police present His Excellency and his party were able to move all over the shrine without difficulty." The Mahant's people were also safe from any injury. Mr. P. L. Orde, Superintendent of Police, who was on special duty at Nankana, when asked if it was unsafe for the Mahant's adherents to go about, admitted in court that they suffered no bodily injury. As to the flying away of Nankana people from fear of Sikhs, it is sufficient to say that they had fled even before the Sikhs were allowed to enter the place, so that when Mr. Mercer, D. I. G. of Police, came to Nankana Sahib on the night of 20th February, he found it practically deserted and saw only two or three men in the town. It is significant to note that at the time, when the Sikh terrorism was alleged to be at its highest and when a few cases of dacoity were also registered against the Sikhs, the largest number of the so-called arms captured from the Sikh visitors was 74 takwas (with which the Sikhs cut *datans* or tooth brushes) and 114 sticks (which included many gentlemen's walking canes and old men's only supports in life).

There was a general campaign of misrepresentation in the Associated Press and the Government communiques, and the specific charges mentioned were that the Sikhs were tyranising over the population in and about Nankana, molesting women, violating sacred shrines of the Hindus and Muslims, defacing images, robbing people of their property and desecrating graves. This created a great tension between the sister communities. On the basis of these allegations Government sent to Nankana about one thousand soldiers to keep peace and order.

In the opinion of the Sikh leaders these charges were mainly without any foundation. They requested Hindu and Muslim leaders to go to the place and make enquiries on the spot. The Sikh members of the Legislative Council also visited the place and made a statement about these allegations to His Excellency. The Khilafat Committee deputed Agha Safdar, Malik Lal Khan, Sardar Habib Ullah and Maulvi Ghulam Qadir Sahib for the investigation; Swarajya Ashram sent

Mehta Anand Kishore and Lala Sham Dass; Syed Habib, editor, 'Siyasat' and Raizada Hans Raj, Bar-at-Law, President, Congress Committee, Jullundur, also visited Nankana Sahib for the same purpose. The result of their enquiries is given below. The allegations have been divided into four parts, first Government communiques are given, then follow the results of the enquiries of these gentlemen. We leave it to the public to judge of the facts from these extracts and form their own opinion about the Government Communiques.

1. TYRANNY OF THE SIKH CROWDS.

Government Communique.

The investigation is being greatly hampered by the presence at Nankana of crowds of persons who have come to see the site of the tragedy. Among these crowds are bad characters whose presence has alarmed the inhabitants of neighbouring villages to the extent of causing many of them to desert their homes. To meet this situation a detachment of cavalry has been detailed to patrol the affected area and it is hoped that this will restore confidence.

The Associated Press Special Correspondent.

The indignation aroused by the atrocity has caused great excitement and Sikhs patrolling the countryside in military formation with battle-axes. Their formidable numbers and high state of excitement are seriously hindering the investigation of the tragedy. At the same time their violent demeanour is causing much alarm among the peaceful Hindu and Muslim population of the locality which is beginning to fly in terror. Numerous stories are told of beating and arresting of individuals without any justification and the commandeering of supplies and fodder.

SIKH MEMBERS OF THE PUNJAB COUNCIL.

There are large areas of land attached to the Gurdwaras. Gurdwara Committee, being put in charge of the Gurdwaras by the Government, made arrangements for collection of crops and possession of lands. There were serious differences with Government officers who objected to these acts of the Committee. The Government has now agreed neither to oust the Committee from these lands nor to interfere with the management. The rumours that crops have been forcibly appropriated or lands seized do not appear to have any better foundation than this.

We found that there was absolutely no need of the military being sent on the spot a second time and we actually saw people of the old village leaving it with their belongings, who, on being questioned, told us that they were doing so owing to the fear of bombardment.

THE KHILAFAT DEPUTATION.

The fact is that on the second day of the tragedy a large number of the Sikhs had come to Nankana from out-stations. This, coupled with the arrests made by the Police and the military, had frightened the people there. In this panic they left their houses and ran away. Even now many of the houses are locked up, and it appears that the whole population has not yet come back to the village. No body can claim for all the Khalsas' immunity from every sort of immoderation. In our opinion it would be against nature that all should be perfectly calm and peaceful. More than one hundred and fifty of their brethren had been butchered most mercilessly, necessarily their hearts must have been filled with anger and the spirit of revenge. But after seeing that, barring a few complaints of petty nature, no complaint had any foundation at all, we are obliged to offer praise for the calmness and restraint displayed by the Khalsa.

SWARAJYA ASHRAM DEPUTATION.

We are told in the Mandi that when there was a great crowd of the Sikhs, and the enemies began to spread various rumours, people were informed by the beat of drum that if there were any trouble to them they should inform the Gurdwara Committee of it. The Committee received about fifty letters thanking them for their good management. We too add our appreciation of such a good behaviour displayed by so many people.

Syed Habib, Editor, "Siyasat."

All those who live in Mandi and others explained to me that the Sikhs robbed no one; rather when the people had fled on account of panic, they kept strict guard over their property.

Lala Hans Raj, Bar-at-Law, President, Congress Committee, Jullundur.

The members of the Akali Jatha are holy persons. Whatever their past life, now they are filled with an enthusiasm born of religious fervour.

Hindu-Muslim Meeting.

The Nankana Hindus and Mohammedans passed the following resolution on the 11th of March in a public meeting :—

"That from the time the Sikhs have come to Nankana their treatment of Hindus and Mohammedans is sympathetic and praiseworthy; they do not interfere in the religion of others, and we strongly repudiate the false rumours spread by enemies."

II.—VIOLATION OF SHRINES, MOSQUES, IMAGES, Etc.

Associated Press Special Correspondent.

It is even stated freely by panic-stricken villagers that Sikhs have violated the shrines of Shiv near Daria station.

Government Communique.

In Nankana houses have been seized and Hindu images desecrated.

Sikh Membrrs of the Council.

There were a few small receptacles like Samadhs of some of the Mahant's predecessors within the four walls of the Gurdwara. The victims had taken refuge in these receptacles. Ruffians smashed the thin doors with axes, cut the victims into pieces, leaving pools of blood inside, and roasted the dead bodies outside these Samadhs. During the rush at the cremation ceremony crowds pulled down these Samadhs. These were not temples, nor were there any gods or idols in them. No one, at least from amongst the Sikh pilgrims present or visiting Nankana Sahib, desecrated any temples. The Sikhs respect the Hindu temples and consider them sacred.

Swarajya Ashram Deputation.

After making investigations we are convinced that there was no Shivling in the Gurdwara Janam Asthan, nor were there any marks of an idol having been displaced.

There were some broken idols in the compound of the Gurdwara. These were found about a hundred yards back from the Dhaular mound. These idols are like those found in the Museums. The Pandits informed us that these idols were never the objects of worship of the Hindus.

Some of the images in the house of Baba Harnam Dass have been scratched. These images were in good condition when the Sikhs gave charge of this house to the Mahant. The images are those of Baba Nanak, Mehta Kalu, Bibi Nanaki, Raja Janak, Harnakash and thirteen saints, and of others. There are some images on the top of those mentioned above. These were intact and contained images of Mahant Kishen Das and Baba Sujan Singh Bedi. As these images were desecrated after the Mahant got the posssession of the house from the Committee, we cannot regard this as the work of the Sikhs. Had the Sikhs any hand in the affair, they would not have touched the images of Guru Nanak and would not have left untouched that of Mahant Kishan Das.

Khilafat Deputation.

We went to the mosque which was said to have been pulled down. We found it in perfect condition and without any harm having been done to it.

Syed Habib, Editor, "Siyasat."

The mosque is quite in a good condition and no damage has been done to it..... I have seen pictures and images of Hindu deities in the office of the Gurdwara Parbandhak Committee. No one has done any harm to these. Some of the images have been desecrated in the private house of the Mahant and the temple of Harnam Das. Amongst these images are those of Guru Nanak, his father and mother, Bhagat Kabir and his wife..... No Sikh could have done this...... Harnam Das was arrested. His house remained in charge of the Sikhs for ten days. No images were desecrated during that time. When the Sikhs handed over the charge to the Mahant and the Police came in, it was then that these images were injured.

III.—DESECRATION OF GRAVES.

Associated Press Special Correspondent.

It is even stated freely by panic-stricken villagers that Sikhs have dug up a Mussalman grave.

Sikh Members of the Punjab Council.

The Sikhs respect every grave and consider the graveyards sacred grounds. They have the greatest respect for the feelings of the sister communities, and any rumours that any of them dug up any grave is absolutely false and baseless. Such false rumours and even such sacrilege of mischief-makers are not unknown in times of commotion and excitement in order to set one community against another.

Khilafat Deputation.

We went to the graveyard; many of the villagers were with us. In the whole of the graveyard there was only one high grave built with white lime and bricks. Only a small portion of its plaster was found displaced. It appeared to have been struck during the last four or five days by some one with a stick. Nobody could tell who had done this; nor could it be thought that it was done with a view to dig up.................... It is these which are said to have been dug up. We have come to know from the men there that after the tragedy hundreds of the Khalsa had gone to the graveyard in search of the assassins hidden there. It is possible that the earth was pressed low because of this visit. Anyhow it did not appear to us that anyone had tried to dig up the graves and desecrate the dead bodies.

SYED HABIB, EDITOR, "SIYASAT."

I myself went to the graveyard. All the tombs were in proper condition...... I regard allegations against the Sikhs as utterly untrue.

IV.—MOLESTATION OF LADIES.

GOVERNMENT COMMUNIQUE.

It is stated that men have been seized and maltreated and women molested, in so far that in some villages the residents have deserted their homes.

SIKH MEMBERS OF THE PUNJAB COUNCIL.

It is common knowledge that women of the Sikh community always attend the big and crowded communal gatherings like the Sikh Educational Conference. No one ever heard any complaints of women being molested in such gatherings. Several Sikh Members of the Council have been going to Nankana Sahib from time to time ever since the tragedy and they have always found the Sikhs on the spot in a condition of deep and sacred grief. People who go for such purpose as they did hardly molest or ill-treat womenfolk. There is no true basis for rumours that women have been or are being molested.

Khilafat Deputation.

Some people informed us of the rumours about the molestation of ladies, but nobody could tell us with certainty of any instances. Many persons explained to us that these rumours were without any foundation. In our opinion there is no room for distrust of the Sikh community on the basis of these false rumours.

Swarajya Ashram Deputation.

We made special enquiries into this allegation. We could not find a single man in the whole of the Mandi and Nankana Sahib who could support this charge. It appears that some friends are at the back of these rumours in order to bring the Sikhs into disrepute.

Syed Habib, Editor, "Siyasat."

All the persons whom I saw on the spot said on oath that they have not even heard that any Sikh molested any woman, Muslim or Non-Muslim.

Lala Hans Raj, President, Congress Committee, Jullundur.

Those who charge them (the Sikhs at Nankana) with theft and disrespect towards women cannot be others than enemies of truth and country.

It is noteworthy that out of the 55 cases of excesses alleged to have been committed by Sikhs in and around Nankana Sahib only four were brought for trial to the courts. It will be interesting to look into the reality of these cases.

On February 20, at 11 A. M., Bhai Kartar Singh of Jhabar, while sitting in the Gurdwara of Khara Sauda, received a wire from Bhai Uttam Singh of Nankana Sahib that Sikhs were being butchered and burnt in the Janam Asthan, that Bhai Dalip Singh had been killed already, and that he himself was in danger of his life. Bhai Kartar Singh at once despatched about 40 men to different villages to carry the news of the happening, and himself started with about 50 men for Nankana. When at about 10 P. M. he reached the Bridge of Chandarkot he found himself at the head of a jatha of thousand Sikhs. Half an hour later they saw a bright thing drawing towards them. When it came near, it was found to be a motor car. They shouted to the driver to stop, but he would not. Their suspicions having been roused, they stood before the motor and stopped it. It was found to contain three men with Deva Das, who was a chela of Mahant Narain Das and who was alleged to have taken a prominent part in the day's work. The self-restraint of the Sikhs at that time of rage and grief may be measured from this that they did not move even a finger to hurt him. They simply detained these four men in order to hand them over as suspects to the police. When the Sikhs began to light fire to warm themselves, Deva Das felt terrified and implored them on his knees not to burn him. He offered to give eight lakhs of rupees and a house if they spared him. They reassured him by saying that they were not so cruel as he was alleged to have been to their brethren.

The Mahant had been arrested and a force of British and Indian soldiers was guarding the Janam Asthan. The inhabitants out of fear of the army—for the jathas had not yet entered the town—were flying from Nankana Sahib. One of them, named Sant Singh with his wife on horseback, was coming along the canal on the morning of the 21st, when he was overtaken by a body of Sikhs who were coming like Bhai Kartar Singh to Nankana Sahib. This new jatha held up Sant Singh as a suspect, for he was known to some men in the jatha to be connected with the temple. He was brought before Bhai Kartar Singh, who sent away the wife on horseback to her parents' village, Kotwar, in the company of five respectable men of that village, who had come to offer food to Bhai Kartar Singh's jatha. She reached her destination safely with all her precious ornaments on her. Sant Singh with Deva Das and his party was brought to village Khipwala, where a Mohammedan with a gun and 72 cartridges was found. He, too, was taken along as a doubtful man. Here Bhai Kartar Singh came to know that a box of ornaments had beon taken by a man of Lyallpur, who belonged to the jatha which had taken Sant Singh into custody. Bhai Kartar Singh asked this man to be careful about the box and hand it over to the police at Nankana Sahib without fail. At this place they received a written order from the Deputy Commissioner not to advance any further. But the jatha in their eagerness to see the Martyrs did not mind the order and went on. When they came near Nankana Sahib they met Sardar Bahadur Sardar Mehtab Singh on horseback, who asked them not to go towards the Gurdwara, as it was guarded by the military with machine-guns and nobody was allowed to go near it. But Bhai Kartar Singh insisted that it was their duty to see the desecrated Gurdwara and take care of the holy Martyrs. The jatha, however, agreed to stop for some time, during which Sardar Mehtab Singh went to consult the Commissioner who was at the Railway Station. Sardar Mehtab Singh urged on the Commissioner to give the control of the Gurdwara to the Sikhs and allow them to go where they pleased. Mr. King, the Commissioner, yielded to the pressure and agreed to give the keys of the Gurdwara to a Committee of seven members of the Shromani Committee who were present there. The army was removed and the Sikhs went to see the Gurdwara.

The five men, who had been brought in custody, were handed over to the police. But Bhai Kartar Singh became so busy with the arrangements about guarding the dead-bodies and keeping peace among the Sikhs that he forgot everything about the box of ornaments. He remembered it, however, a few days later when Tirath Das, an ex-Granthi of the Janam Asthan and a brother of Sant Singh, mentioned it to Sardar Harbans Singh, who asked about it from Bhai Kartar Singh. Bhai Kartar Singh now tried to find out the man with whom he had seen the box, but he was told that the man had gone to Lyallpur. On March 7, he went to Lyallpur and sought the help of Dr. Kishan Singh and others, who found out the man and brought him to Bhai Kartar Singh. But the man totally denied having received any box. Bhai Kartar Singh had to go to Lahore next day to meet the Government about the situation at Nankana Sahib, and he came away from Lyallpur, entrusting the matter of the box to the above-mentioned gentlemen. When he returned to Nankana Sahib he was arrested soon after on 11th March. This is what is called the Chandarkot case, in which Bhai Kartar Singh was charged with dacoity and sentenced, five months later, to seven years' rigorous imprisonment with three years' police surveillance after release.

On February 28, Mahant Tirath Singh, the head custodian of Bal Lila, had voluntarily presented a written application to the Gurdwara Committee, requesting it to take over the management of Bal Lila Gurdwara and stating that he was willing to work in accordance with the wishes and instructions of the Committee. On March 4, another application was presented to the Committee by Tirath Singh, Buta Singh and Santa Singh to the effect that certain lands belonging to the Gurdwara had been entered in their personal names in the revenue records, but that they desired that those lands be transferred to the name of the Gurdwara, and that they and their families be granted maintenance. These two applications were duly laid before the Committee on March 6, and the Committee decided that the management of the Bal Lila Gurdwara be taken over by them, and that the Committee should appoint certain persons to work at the Gurdwara. Tirath Singh handed the keys of the Gurdwara to the Secretary of the Gurdwara Committee.

The charge of the Gurdwara of Kiara Sahib had also been given similarly to the Gurdwara Committee. On March 10, Bhai Kartar Singh was appointed by the Committee to detail some men to take charge of the Gurdwaras of Bal Lila and Kiara Sahib. He sent a few men to Bal Lila and about ten men to Kiara Sahib. A sentry standing at the Kiara Sahib shrine reported the matter to Mr. Orde, S. P., who wired to the District Magistrate and the D. I. G. of Police, and proceeding to Kiara Sahib with a detachment of troops took down the names of the Sikhs who had been sent by the Committee to serve at the shrine. Next day a report was obtained from one Sant Singh, who complained that he had been ousted from his mahantship and that a dacoity had been committed at his Gurdwara, from which a canopy, a gold *chhaba* (an ornament) and several sacred scarfs, belonging to the Holy Book, had been taken away. The Commissioner and the Deputy Commissioner hurried to Nankana Sahib in a special train and with a fine show of military force eleven Sikhs were arrested and handcuffed: Bhai Kartar Singh from Janam Asthan, Bhai Uttam Singh, factory-owner, from his house, and eight men from Kiara Sahib. Bhai Lakha Singh, who was also wanted, went and surrendered himself. When S. Jogendra Singh, who had gone there, questioned Mr. Dunnett, the Deputy Commissioner, as to the charge agianst these respectable Sikhs, he was horrified to learn that it was 'dacoity and being members of an unlawful assembly.' After the arrests of Sikhs found in the Gurdwara the holy place was attached, which created great indignation in the Panth.

Next day Mr. Orde, with a military and police force, went to Bal Lila and arrested 16 men from there. Even women sitting in the temple were driven out and the Gurdwara was attached. Bhais Kartar Singh and Lakha Singh were charged in this case also.

As to the charges of unlawful possession and dacoity, it will be interesting to read the following statement by Mahantni Indar Kaur, widow of Mahant Ishar Singh of Kiara Sahib, before three M.L.C.'s, who were also Honorary Magistrates, and before the Commissioner of Lahore Division :—

"I manage the Gurdwara Kiara Sahib, and after my husband's death the Gurdwara has remained under my charge. My husband's brother Sant Singh and his son Ujagar Singh lodged a civil suit against me regarding the

Gurdwara. It was decided in my favour three years ago. With my voluntary consent I made over in writing the management of my Gurdwara about 20 days ago to the Gurdwara Committee, Nankana Sahib. Since then the management has been in their hands. Day before yesterday when the police arrived to take my statement ....asked me that my statement should agree with theirs regarding the forced possession by the Sikhs, pulling down of Samadhs and the theft of the *chhaba*, canopy and other articles. Because it was all false, I refused to make such a statement; and, on the other hand, I stated that I had voluntarily made over possession to the Sikhs, who knew nothing about the pulling down of Samadhs, and that the gold *chhaba* and the canopy were lying in my house, and nothing had been stolen. I did not give any of the above-mentioned articles to the police. I kept them in the Mandi and the police went away. Because I fear that I shall be molested, I have brought these articles to Sardar Seva Ram Singh to send my statement to the officers. I have voluntarily made this statement before you. I herewith make over the *chhaba*, canopy and the *rumals* to Sardar Seva Ram Singh. Nothing of the Gurdwara has been stolen.

Read out to me and certified to be correct."

The dacoity charge was dropped after some time. But Bhai Kartar Singh was convicted in both cases under Section 452, I. P. C., and got two years' rigorous imprisonment in each case. Three others in Bal Lila case and nine in the Kiara Sahib case got one year each. Bhai Uttam Singh had been released after some weeks for want of evidence.

After Bhai Kartar Singh's arrest in connection with the Bal Lila and Kiara Sahib cases, the Chandarkot and Attari cases of dacoity were also brought against him, though these had occurred about three weeks before his arrest. In each of them he got seven years. Bhai Kartar Singh had nothing whatever to do with the Attari case. Attari or Patti Sahib was in charge of Nirmala Sikhs. When the great tragedy occurred, the Nirmalas fled away for fear of their lives, leaving cattle and other property unprotected. Somebody reported to the Committee that the cattle were dying without food and water. The Committee deputed Bhai Mool Singh to take care of the animals and make a list of the property left. It was done. A free kitchen was also opened in the place. On March 12, Bhai Mool Singh was arrested for having committed a dacoity and Bhai Kartar Singh, who has upto now never stepped into the place, was added as a co-accused. Bhai

Kartar Singh was sentenced to five years' rigorous imprisonment under Section 395, I. P. C., and two years under Section 452, I. P. C., both sentences to run concurrently. Bhai Mool Singh was sentenced to three years' rigorous imprisonment under Section 395, I. P. C., and one year under Section 452, I. P. C., both sentences to run concurrently. These sentences were passed about five months after the arrests, although the accused, by way of protest against the treatment of Mr. Keough, the Additional District Magistrate, had non-co-operated.

These cases belong to Nankana Sahib. There were similar cases going on at the same time in other places. The Government had issued instructions to District Magistrates to attach a Gurdwara whenever there seemed to be an apprehension of interference on the part of Akalis. There began a regular campaign of arrests, and even old cases were dug up against the reforming Sikhs. There is a specimen of Government's own efforts to relieve tension by appointing managing committees in disputed Gurdwaras. On March 13, 1921, a meeting of some Sikhs of the Ferozepore District was convened at Muktsar in the presence of the Commissioner and the Deputy Commissioner, who announced their intention of withdrawing from the management of the Muktsar temple and relieving the official president, the Naib-Tahsildar, and the official Secretary, the local Sub-Registrar. A committee of 18 members, twelve of whom were priests, was appointed for the management of the Darbar Sahib.

The new policy of Government had the effect of encouraging opposition to the Sikh cause from all sides. Even the Bhatti Mohammedans living round Nankana Sahib sent a memorial to the Government to hand over the Janam Asthan to them. The Mahants and priests were emboldened to seek independence of the Sikh Panth. Certain Udasi Mahants,* in their memorial to the Government, went so far as to say that the Udasis were not Sikhs at all, but a sect of Hindus, like the Sanyasis and Bairagis. Others, especially in Sindh, made a hero of Mahant Narain Das, and began to exclude the Sikh congregations from their temples. One such case occurred at Lahore.

Within the Sheranwala Gate in Lahore there is a Gurdwara sacred to the memory of Bhai Sadhu Ram, a great Sikh of Guru Arjan. It was in the custody of Mahantni Nand Kaur

* A great many Udasi and other Mahants, however, especially those in Shahpur District, protested against the dishonest attempt of certain Sadhus to deny Sikhism and declared themselves as the followers of the ten Sikh Gurus They also expressed themselves in favour of the present movement of Gurdwara reform.

and her chela Hari Das, against whom there were some complaints as regards his character. After the Nankana tragedy the attitude of Hari Das towards the Sikh congregations became truculent. He declared that the temple was his private house and no Gurdwara. He actually began to make preparations to convert it into a Thakurdwara. He went so far in his hostility towards the Sikhs that he expelled those Sikh tenants who were living in the Gurdwara houses on rent. The Sikhs who went to remonstrate with him were ill-treated. At last the Sikhs, with the permission of the local Gurdwara Parbandhak Committee, decided to hold a diwan in the temple on 6th March. When the sangat went to the place on the fixed day they found it locked. The man had gone to bring the police. The meeting was, however, held in an adjoining temple, where Hari Das came and begged pardon for having insulted the sangat by shutting them out of the temple. The people after imposing a *tankhah*, which he readily accepted, went with him to the Dharamsala and re-assured the Mahantni by telling her that there was no intention of ousting her. Hari Das also agreed to work according to the wishes of the Gurdwara Committee, and the sangat went away. On March 9, when the sangat went again, they found the temple closed against them and a posse of about 100 policemen standing on guard. The sangat insisted on their right of entering the Gurdwara, but the police refused to let them enter. The District Magistrate arrived in the morning and declared that the Gurdwara was attached, but that the Sikhs could enter for worship. The sangat went in and held their diwan. The Nishan Sahib or the flag, which is usually found in Gurdwaras, and which was lying down in a dilapidated condition, was raised up. When on March 10 Mr. Browne, Deputy Superintendent of Police, came to the Gurdwara, he was much enraged to find the flag upraised, and ordered it to be taken down. Some weak-kneed Sikhs carried out the order, which was an unnecessary interference with a religious custom of the Sikhs. In the evening the three Sikhs, who had helped in the desecration of the flag, expressed their regret and the flag was hoisted again.

On March 11, when the morning service was going on, the Superintendent of Police and Mr. Browne came with a force of police and ordered the congregation to disperse. The Sikhs resented this interference with their worship, but did not move from the place. Twenty one persons were arrested, of whom seven were released by the District Magistrate. They were charged under

Sections 143 and 148, I. P. C. Mr. J. E. Keough, the trying Magistrate, showed the same objectionable attitude in this case as in other cases. He held that the shrine in dispute was not a Gurdwara but a place of Udasis, with which the Sikhs, who called themselves Akalis, had got nothing to do. The District Magistrate, Major Ferrar, also exhibited great nervousness by ordering the arrest of Sikh visitors to the court who wore kirpans. He would not admit any Sikh with a kirpan into his presence. Of the 14 accused, who had refused to defend themselves, Bhai Bhagat Singh was sentenced to 9 months and the remaining to 6 months' imprisonment, except one who was acquitted.

When the case of Sadhu Ram's Dharamsala began an old case, which had happened in Lahore six months before, was also raked up. Bhai Sant Singh, President, Khalsa Parcharak Jatha, Bhai Sadhu Singh, Secretary, Bhai Gurbakhsh Singh and eight others, who had been deputed by the local Gurdwara Committee to take charge of the Gurdwara of Chomala Sahib in September, 1920, were sent to jail on 21st March, 1921. They were put on trial under Sections 145 (rioting), 448 (taking forcible and illegal possession of property) and 342 (wrongful confinement) of the Indian Penal Code. A charge of dacoity under Section 395, I. P. C., was added afterwards, but it was quashed. The City Magistrate tried them in the Borstal Jail. They refused to defend themselves, and two of them were convicted, getting 6 months' imprisonment each.

Another old case came up about the same time, and was tried by Mr. Keough. We saw how in December, 1920, the sangat of Jhambar Kalan in Lahore District, exercising their ancient right of appointing incumbents of their Gurdwaras, had ousted Mahant Prem Singh from the Gurdwara of Tham Sahib and the lands belonging to it. After the Nankana tragedy on March 13, three Lambardars, three Pattidars, and nine other Sikhs, including Bhai Teja Singh of Bhuchar, were arrested for having taken forcible possession of Tham Sahib, Manak Chauk and Chah Nihanganwala. They were also charged with dacoity for having taken away six kirpans from Manak Chauk to Akal Takht and a pony of the Mahant. Three of them were released, and after about five months the remaining 12 were convicted of both the charges. Bhai Teja Singh of Bhuchar was sentenced to five years' rigorous imprisonment, including three months' solitary confinement, under Section 395, I. P. C., and to two years' rigorous imprisonment under Section 452, I. P. C., the two sentences to run consecutively. Three others were each sentenced to three years' rigorous imprisonment, including three months' solitary confinement, under Section 395, I. P. C., and to one year's rigorous imprisonment under Section 452, I. P. C., the sentences to run consecutively. The remaining accused were each sentenced to two years' R. I. under Section 395, I.P.C., and one year's R. I. under Section 452, I.P.C., the sentences to run concurrently,

Mr. Keough tried another case in which a Mahant was encouraged by the new Government policy to break with the Panth. Manak near Raewind in the Lahore District is a Gurdwara sacred to Bhai Prithi, a missionary Sikh of the eighteenth century. It was entered as a Gurdwara in the Settlement papers of 1892-93 and 1912-13. The Mahant, named Basant Das, took a very prominent part in Mahant Narain Das's conferences held before the Nankana tragedy. He was the secretary of the Sadhus' Association which had been formed in November, 1920, to oppose the Sikhs, and of which Mahant Narain Das was the president. After the tragedy he became nervous about his position, and on 1st March applied in writing to the Lahore sangat, through Sardar Ujagar Singh Vakil and Sardar Mehar Singh Chawla, to get the Gurdwara affiliated to the Shromani Committee. The astute Mahant also volunteered to get himself baptised and began to sign himself as Basant Singh. Some Lahore Sikhs, accompanied by a few local Sikhs, went to Manak and the Mahant voluntarily gave charge of the Gurdwara to them. There arose, however, some differences about the details of management and the Mahant went away to Lahore on March 9 to report the matter to the authorities.

The District Magistrate issued an order of attachment under Section 145, I.P.C., and sent a Sub-Inspector of Police to eject the Sikhs. The Sikhs, who did not understand the trick of the Mahant, refused to vacate the place, saying that they were there on the explicit invitation of the Mahant and that the matter being purely religious the police had no ground to interfere. On the night of March 12 the District Magistrate, accompanied by the Senior Superintendent of Police, a Magistrate and a force of 100 police, proceeded to the spot by a special train and arrested 21 persons early in the morning. S. Ujagar Singh Vakil had already been arrested at Lahore on the 11th. Nine more were arrested later on. The Gurdwara was attached under Section 145, I. P. C. Three accused were discharged on August 6. Of the remaining 28 accused, five including Bhai Lahora Singh were charged under Section 452, I. P. C., with having committed the offence of house trespass and having made preparations for causing hurt, and under Section 395, I. P. C., for dacoity, and the remaining under the former Section only.

The Mahant during the trial declared definitely, in opposition to his statement in a Sialkot court and the official records, that he was not a Sikh and that the place was a Sadhus' dera and not a Gurdwara. The Magistrate also went out of his way to condemn the Akali movement, as he had done in the other similar cases before him. Although he would not permit the defence counsel to touch on the question whether the Mahant was a Sikh and the disputed place a Gurdwara, he himself in his judgment made a dogmatic pronouncement that the Udasis were not Sikhs and that the institution was an Udasi dera and not a Gurdwara. While citing the old Revenue Records of 1868 and a report by a Deputy Commissioner in favour of the place being called a dera, he carefully ignored the Settlement papers of 1892-93 and 1912-13, which had been quoted by the defence counsel and in which it was called a Gurdwara. The defendants declared in vain that the Mahant had himself handed over the institution to them and that they had gone there to take charge at his own invitation. They in vain presented a document in which the Mahant had clearly stated that, before leaving Manak on March 9, he had not been harshly treated by the Akalis. Twenty out of 28 accused were convicted on September 17. Bhai Lahora Singh, being the leader, was sentenced to 7 years' R. I. under Section 395, I.P.C., and to two years' R. I. under Section 452, I.P.C., the two sentences to run consecutively. Bhais Sawan Singh and Hazara Singh got 4 years each under Section 395 and 2 years each under Section 452, I.P.C., the sentences to run consecutively. The remaining 17 were sentenced to two years' R. I. each under Section 452, I. P. C. Eight accused, including S. Ujagar Singh, Pleader, were acquitted.

In the beginning of September, 1921, after the Chief Khalsa Diwan deputation had failed and after the newly-elected Shromani Committee had confirmed on 28th August the resolution of non-co-operation passed by the old committee in May last, the Government saw reason to release 32 prisoners out of those who had been sentenced in the abovementioned Gurdwara cases. The sentences were suspended on the understanding that the released persons would remain of good behaviour during the term of their sentences. The Shromani Committee and the Panth did not approve of this action of the Sikhs who had accepted release on such a condition. The

Sikhs arrested in the Manak case were not released, as their case was still pending when the order of release in other cases was given. But the promised release did not come even when their case was decided and the false alarm as the Gurdwara Teje, which was given at the reason for withholding the concession, had been judicially proved a mere hoax. The omission was the more glaring in the cases of S. Mangal Singh, B. A., and S. Partap Singh, B. A., B. T., editors of the *Akali*, S. Amar Singh of Jhabal and Sardar Sardul Singh Caveessieur, who had been sentenced for writing or speaking in connection with those Gurdwaras.

CHAPTER XVI.

GURDWARA BHAI JOGA SINGH.

In Peshawar there is a temple called Bhai Joga Singh's Gurdwara. The Bhai Sahib, in whose honour the temple was built, was a Sikh who had received baptism from Guru Gobind Singh himself. He was so devoted to the cause of Sikhism that once, when his marriage ceremony was being performed, summons came from the Guru and he left his bride in the midst of the ceremony and joined his Guru at Anandpur.* He is also called Jogan Shah by Hindus and Mohammedans in the Frontier. In those districts it is customary to call a saint a Shah. Another origin of the epithet Shah is given in the *Tales from Sikh History* (p. 60). Once a Durrani Governor's daughter was cured by a visit to this temple. She began to frequent the temple, which was not liked by her father. But when she persisted against all attempts of her father to dissuade her, the Governor ordered that every one should pronounce Jogan Shah instead of Joga Singh, and gave it out that he was a Sayyed Faqir.

---

* See Macauliffe : *The Sikh Religion*, Vol. V, p. 138; also *Suraj Parkash*, Chapter 36, Rut 4.

A mosque was raised by the side of the Gurdwara and a well was also dug to carry conviction to the ignorant masses.

The Sikhs in Peshawar are in a very small minority and in that Province of the summary law they are not able to look after their interests properly.

Some time back, while the reform movement among the Sikhs had not yet touched Peshawar, a Granthi named Bhai Tara Singh was removed on account of his ill fame and another baptised Sikh was appointed in his place. A committee had also been proposed to govern the temple. It was to be composed of four baptised Sikhs and four Sahjdharis, and Rai Bahadur Karam Chand, who called himself a Sahjdhari, was nominated to act as receiver in connection with the accounts of the temple, pending the formation of the above committee. Unfortunately the committee never came into existence, and the said gentleman continued to look after the accounts as receiver, while the management of the temple remained in the hands of the Granthi and the sangat.

When the reform of Gurdwaras began in 1920 the Hindu leaders held a meeting in the Gurdwara of Mai Raji. They impressed on the people that all Gurdwaras were really meeting places for Hindus and Sikhs, where all could perform their rites.

This alarmed the Sikhs. They held that even if the Sikhs were Hindus, nobody but themselves should be in charge of the Sikh temples. The Jains, the Brahmos, the Arya Samajists were Hindus, but they would not allow the Sikhs or men not belonging to their sects to interfere with the management or the ritual of their temples. The Hindus said that, as they had been supporting the Sikh temples along with the Sikhs, they had the right of sharing the management. The Sikh view was that 70 per cent. of the people who visit and worship the Shrine of Sakhi Sarwar are Hindus, but this fact would not persuade the Mohammedan managers of that place to give control to the Hindus. Besides the Sikhs also have been supporting the Hindu shrines. Their demand was that at least in their temples they alone should have control. Besides the rule has been that the Sahjdharis may call themselves Sikhs and enjoy the right of praying, receiving the communion food or listening to discourses in the Sikh temples, but they have always accepted the leadership of baptised Sikhs in matters of ritual. They have never followed any other ritual except that prescribed in Sikhism. Therefore those at Peshawar, who were insisting on the introduction of Hindu worship in the Gurdwara, were not Sahjdharis but Hindu aggressors who wanted to impose their customs on Sikhs and to convert the latter's Gurdwaras into Thakurdwaras.

Any reasonable man will admit that it is impossible to perform both Hindu and Sikh rituals in the same temple. As long as both were backward committees they might make all sorts of combinations of religious practices, but when they have reformed themselves it is most desirable for them to confine their rituals to their separate temples. They have become self-conscious and, whether rightly or wrongly, their religious sympathies and interests are no longer identical. They cannot be forced to amalgamate themselves. Separation of religious interests is bound to happen. Then in the interest of the wider unity awaiting us, why should we not do it decently ?

The Sikhs came in a deputation to the house of Rai Bahadur Karam Chand to persuade him to make peace. On 21st December, 1920, the Hindu and Sikh leaders met together at the house of S. Ram Singh, a Sikh banker, for settling the question. But the Hindus were inexorable. It was openly said that Bhai Joga Singh was a Hindu ascetic and no Sikh, that his temple belonged to the Hindus alone. Every day in the temple meetings anti-Sikh literature began to be distributed and the Sikh worship was disturbed. At the same time, other Sikh temples in the city met the same fate. Their doors were closed against the Sikhs and prayers suspended. The Sikh Scriptures were removed from some and other books or images substituted. Here and there a lonely passing Sikh was jeered at, abused or beaten.

The Akali Jatha which was in those days at Panja Sahib, midway between Rawalpindi and Peshawar, heard of the troubles of the Peshawar Sikhs and came to their rescue. They with their leader Bhai Teja Singh of Bhuchar put up at Bhai Joga Singh's temple. It was reported to the authorities that the Jatha people were Bolsheviks and that they had come with the purpose of looting and terrorising the people. The Deputy Commissioner issued orders that Bhai Teja Singh with his party should leave Peshawar within 24 hours. These orders were at once withdrawn, when the Deputy Commissioner discovered that he had been misled. An application was filed under Section 145, Cr. P. C., and the leading Sikhs of Peshawar and the Akali Jatha were summoned as respondents to the Court of the City Magistrate on 28th December at a few hours' notice. On both parties giving assurance that there would be no breach of the peace the application was dismissed.

The Sikhs kept the promise. But the attacks on them continued as before. Once a Kabuli Sikh, named Jagat Singh, was set upon in a street and almost done to death. Attempts were made to set fire to the temple of Bhai Joga Singh.

In the beginning of February an attempt was made by Lala Lajpat Rai and Giani Sher Singh to make peace between the parties, but they were not allowed by Government to proceed to Peshawar, and were stopped at Attock. Then on February 20 Hindu and Sikh leaders of Peshawar and Pindi met Mahatma Gandhi and Lala Lajpat Rai at Rawalpindi, and it was proposed to refer the question to a court of arbitrators composed of five Sikhs and five Hindus, but the terrible news of the Nankana tragedy put a stop to all deliberations.

Just before the Holi festival, on March 17, a compromise was arrived at in the presence of the Deputy Commissioner. Both parties agreed that, pending the settlement of the whole Gurdwara question by legislation or otherwise in the Punjab, the Gurdwaras of Mai Raji and Kakran should remain in the hands of Hindus and the Gurdwara of Bhai Joga Singh should remain in the hands of Sikhs, who were also required to send away all the jatha people, except five to remain in charge of the temple.

On March 22 the jatha was sent away to the Punjab and only five men were left in the Gurdwara. The next day the Hindus, forgetting the compromise made in the court, made a serious attempt to capture the Gurdwara. They came about noon to the temple and, according to the published testimony of an eye-witness who is a Hindu gentleman, began to shout the *Jai* of Mahant Narain Das and Bawa Kartar Singh Bedi. They wanted to celebrate Holi in the Gurdwara. The few Sikhs who were there refused to allow them. The Hindus went away, but after 15 minutes a large crowd with a big banner and armed with lathis and knives made a rush at the Gurdwara. A Sikh standing in the doorway was overpowered. He called for help. Only three Sikhs attacked the menacing crowd in return and threw them into confusion. The mob wanted to run away, but their retreat was made difficult by the whole street being full of the Holi crowds. The Sikhs plied their lathis freely and cleared not only the Gurdwara but the whole lane of all males; their females were all the while throwing stones and showering abuses on the Sikhs. Three Sikhs and 13 Hindus were said to have received injuries.

The police and the Deputy Commissioner appeared on the scene, and a large number of Sikhs, too, hastened to the Gurdwara. No

Hindu was touched, but about 40 Sikhs, including the members of the jatha and those Sikhs who had come to the spot after the affray, were arrested. The Gurdwara was attached and put under a military and police guard. No Sikh was allowed access to it. The Sikhs, especially military men, protested against the attachment of their Gurdwara. They wired to the Gurdwara Committee and the Sikh Press, but their telegrams were stopped. They had to send a special messenger to Lahore and Amritsar in order to inform the Sikh public outside Peshawar. The arrested Sikhs were released next day.

It was notified by the Deputy Commissioner of Peshawar that nobody should go about in the city with a kirpan or any other weapon. Those Sikhs, who could not part with the kirpan as a religious obligation, went away to the Sadar where the order was not promulgated. A free kitchen was opened in the Sadar Singh Sabha to feed the refugees. A big diwan was held on the evening of 24th March to protest against the high-handed action of the Deputy Commissioner. Giani Sher Singh, who had arrived by that time, went to see the Deputy Commissioner at his bungalow on the 26th to protest against his order about the kirpan, but the Giani was told to put off his kirpan before he entered the Deputy Commissioner's room. The Sikh leader refused to see him under that humiliating condition, and was then allowed to come in with the kirpan. On the matter being put to him, the Deputy Commissioner said that the Sikhs had been deprived of the kirpan in many places in the Punjab too. He was told that at Nankana Sahib, where even little sticks and canes had been taken away from Sikhs, nobody was deprived of his kirpan. The Deputy Commissioner wanted time to consult the Deputy Commissioner of Lahore, and about 1 P. M. the order against the wearing of kirpans was withdrawn. After much agitation against the attachment of the Gurdwara, it was freed on April 12.

After being dragged about in courts for some time, the Sikhs obtained a firm possession of the Gurdwara, and now it is being controlled by the Sri Guru Singh Sabha of Peshawar City, which has appointed a sub-committee of five members to carry on the management. There is perfect amity between Hindus and Sikhs now.

CHAPTER XVII.

KAMALIA, SATLANI, TEJE, HOTHIAN, KAPURTHALA AND FARIDKOTE.

At Kamalia in the Montgomery District there is a well-known Gurdwara named after Bhai Prem Sati, a Sikh saint. It has got the revenue of the village attached to it. Bhai Taru Ji, Mahant of the place, feeling very old, in 1909 appointed Tikka Ram Kishan Singh of Una as his general Attorney. This gentleman, who already possessed a great estate, wanted to add to it the revenues of this place also. As he was a married man, he could not himself acquire the gaddi; therefore he got his minor son, Devindar Singh, appointed as chela of the Mahant. But this young man, who got married, never attended to his duties, and the purpose for which the Mahant had made these arrangements was never fulfilled. The daily service, the free kitchen, the repairs of the buildings, were all neglected, and the old Mahant himself was not cared for. On February 10, 1921, Bhai Taru Ji applied to the Shromani Gurdwara Parbandhak Committee to take charge of the Gurdwara and make some provision for his living. The Shromani Committee sent three men to get the thing done and a deed was properly registered on March 8, 1921, by which the Gurdwara and the property were transferred to the name of the Shromani Committee, which made a comfortable provision for the Mahant. This was, of course, not very palatable to Tikka Ram Kishan Singh or his supporters in the town. He came on April 5 and put up in the upper storey of the Gurdwara. Next day a large number of persons attacked the unresisting Sikhs who were holding a memorial diwan in the temple, and a repetition of the Nankana tragedy was averted only by the timely interference of two local gentlemen and the police. The Sikhs felt deeply wronged, but were persuaded, in the interest of Hindu-Sikh unity, to forgive their attackers and take no action. The matter seemed to have been settled once for all, when many months later to the surprise of all honest men, all the leading Sikhs of the place, including the old Mahant, seven in all, were required by the Magistrate to furnish securities for keeping the peace and being of good behaviour. They refused and were sent to jail. The irony of fate is that the Sikhs were the party attacked and they form an infinitesimal minority in a vast population of Hindus at Kamalia. These seven Sikhs were practically the whole of the local Managing Committee of the Gurdwara.

The Shromani Committee sent a number of workers under responsible men to carry on the management of the Gurdwara and its landed property. But all of them, about 24, were arrested on February 27, 1922. The Shromani Committee was in session when the news was brought, and the Executive Committee at once proceeded to Kamalia to take the matter in hand. After this for a long time batches of Sikhs from different places had to be deputed to keep the work of the Gurdwara going. On April 6, 21 of the accused along with their Jathadar Bhai Buta Singh, Assistant Manager of Nankana Sahib, were sentenced each to 6 months' R. I., and other two who were quite young were sentenced each to one day's R. I.

The temple of Gurusar Satlani in the Amritsar district is an historical Gurdwara, sacred to the 6th Guru. Bhai Bulaqa Singh of Guru Gobind Singh's time was its first Mahant. His son Bhai Basti Ram, although a renowned personage, was not an Amritdhari Sikh; and so were his descendants for some time; therefore the Gaddi came to be administered by Amritdhari Sikhs, one of whom, Bhai Kooma Singh, was a great Sikh who refused to accept a jagir from the State. Bhai Bir Singh, the predecessor of the present Mahant, was also called Nihang Singh and Dilli-tor Singh, nd Sir Charles Aitchison wrote about him that to know him was to love him. Its present Mahant Bhai Kirpa Singh boasted in a court that he had acquired control over more than three hundred Gurdwaras and that he was the Shri Mahant of all the Gurdwaras in Northern India. According to him one sign of his over-lordship of so many temples was that all the *bhang* consumed in them was supplied by him out of the two boat-loads which he got exempted from Government.*

Without any attempt on the part of the Sikhs the Mahant vacated the temple about the beginning of February, 1921. The sangat of the surrounding villages gathered at the place on March 6, 1921, and gave charge of

---

* See the Punjab Government notification No. 8 (Revenue), dated 20th January, 1903. By this notification the Lieutenant-Governor exempted *bhang* obtained for the supply of the Gurdwara of Satlani from the duty imposed upon the transport of *bhang*, provided (1) that it was obtained from Gurdaspur district, (2) that the quantity obtained in any one year did not exceed 350 maunds, and (3) that it was consumed only by the Mahants and the Sadhus resident at Satlani and other Gurdwaras subordinate to the gaddi, of which 93 are mentioned in a schedule attached to the notification.

The morality of the exemption apart, could 350 maunds of *bhang* be consumed by all the Nirmalas, whose total number in the Punjab at the census of 1911 did not exceed 378 all of whom could not be Mahants and Sadhus, and most of whom did not drink *bhang* at all.

the temple to an Akali jatha. A committee was appointed, and a list of the articles found in the Gurdwara was prepared and reported to the Shromani Committee. A few days later the Deputy Commissioner summoned the members of the local committee and told them that the Government did not want to give back the possession to Kirpa Singh, but that the man should be allowed to visit the temple. He came on the night of April 16, and refused to leave the temple. The Sikhs did not want to use force and the officers refused to oust him, so he remained in possession in the teeth of all popular opposition.

Then in July, 1921, a few leading Sikhs of the ilaqa, including Risaldar Ajapal Singh Zaildar, S. Bhagat Singh Lambardar, Sardar Mota Singh Reis, S. Surain Singh Jagirdar and Bhai Sadhu Singh, a chela of the Mahant, applied to the Deputy Commissioner for permission to institute a civil suit against Mahant Kirpa Singh. They made grave allegations against his character and exhibited a photograph in which the Mahant had got himself portrayed along with a woman of questionable character. They also filed the alleged love letters of the Mahant in the civil suit which was decided on 5th October, 1922. There was plenty of evidence to show that the character of the Mahant was bad, and about this complaints had been made even in courts in 1898 and 1912. He was now found to be given to wine drinking and womanizing. He kept mistresses at the temple and attended nautch parties of public women. Although professing asceticism, he married at the advanced age of 52 a mere child girl of 12. He spent much time in making calls on Government officials and was suspected of acting as a tout between clients and some corrupt officers. The poor house attached to the temple was neglected. The Mahant openly declared in court that he was not a Sikh, but a monk belonging to the sect of Nirmalas who, according to him, were non-Sikhs. He declared the Gurdwara property to be his private property. The judge found almost all the charges of misconduct and unfitness proved against him. He quoted the Privy Council judgment, reported as 45 Madras 565 (July 1922), wherein it was held that when the custodian of a temple with trust property claims as his own lands found to belong to the temple, he is liable to removal from his post; also the Punjab High Court decision in civil appeal No. 117 of 1917, given on 1st August, 1922, to the effect that a Mahant's denial of the waqf nature of the property attaching to the temple and his setting up an adverse claim to it was sufficient in itself to render him an unfit person to continue in the office of Mahant.

The Judge ordered that Kirpa Singh be removed from the gaddi, that a new Mahant be appointed by the Nirmala Sikhs in consultation with the leading Sikhs of the ilaqa, and that a committee of management consisting of the following gentlemen be formed to assist the Mahant in the management of the Gurdwara :—

(*a*) The head of the Sandhanwalia family of Raja Sansi or his representative.

(*b*) The head of the Attariwala family or a representative of that family.

(*c*) The Sikh Lambardar of Hoshiarnagar.

(*d*) One elected representative of the Shromani Gurdwara Committee of Amritsar, with 3 years' tenure of office.

(*e*) One resident Nirmala Sadhu of Satlani to be elected by the Nirmalas, with 3 years' tenure of office.

(*f*) The Sikh representative of the Bhai family of Lahore or lineal descendant of Bhai Basti Ram.

(*g*) The Mahant of Satlani Sahib *ex-officio.*

The Mahant will be the religious and executive head of the institution. He will not be regarded as a servant of the committee, but he will abide by the decisions of the committee in regard to the management of the property and income.

The court also decreed that the ex-Mahant, Kirpa Singh, be paid Rs. 75 p. m. out of the Gurdwara income as maintenance for his life and a house in Amritsar for his residence until his demise.

A similar case occurred at Wazirabad. The Mahant of the historical temple of Bhai Abinasha Singh had been openly charged with misappropriation and mismanagement of the trust, and his alleged love letters to his own aunt were published in the Press. But the Mahant took no notice. The permission being secured from the Collector of Gujranwala a civil suit under Section 92, C. P. C., was filed on March 31, 1921, for the removal of the Mahant. The case is still pending.

Mahant Dhian Das of Gurdwara Teje, sacred to Baba Budha, in the district of Gurdaspur, was mismanaging the gaddi and wasting the income, which was about Rs. 14,000 a year, on drink and mistresses. Public opinion forced him to make over the management by a deed dated 17th February, 1921, to the Shromani Gurdwara Parbandhak Committee. He was reappointed Mahant on certain conditions, one of which was that if he misconducted himself in future or broke any other condition laid down on his appointment, he would be dismissed. He defied the local committee, which had been appointed for his guidance, and broke almost all the conditions. The matter was reported to the Shromani Committee, which appointed a sub-committee to look into the matter and take action. The Mahant issued a handbill defying the whole Panth, which, he said, had no concern with the Gurdwara. On September 23, the sub-committee visited the temple and found two of his mistresses actually in his bed-room. Tobacco and wine were also found in the Gurdwara. The Mahant was dismissed at once.

The police came, and also hundreds of the Mahant's supporters, who surrounded the Sikhs in the Gurdwara and began to throw stones at them. The besieged Sikhs received injuries, but did not retaliate. One of the Sikhs, who was found outside, was beaten mercilessly before the very eyes of his comrades. The Working Committee of the Shromani Committee reached the spot in a motor car and showed the agreement signed by the Mahant to the District officers, who declared that in face of the agreement they were not prepared to interfere. The suit filed by the Mahant under Section 145, Cr. P. C., was dismissed by the District Magistrate of

Gurdaspur. A Committee consisting of the following gentlemen was appointed to manage the shrine:—Sardar Kharak Singh, B. A., LL. B., Reis of Sialkot, Sardar Mehtab Singh, Bar-at-Law, Sardar Bhag Singh, B.A., LL. B., Sardar Amar Singh of Jhabal, Sardar Dan Singh Reis of Vachhoa, and Sardar Teja Singh of Alavalpur.

After this another Gurdwara in the district of Gurdaspur came into the possession of the Panth. Mahant Nanak Saran, in charge of Guru Arjan's Gurdwara of Hothian, was squandering the income on his low pleasures. On the night of 30th September, 1921, he fled away, secretly removing from the Gurdwara four she-buffaloes, 2 horses, furniture, and every other article of value. The greatest sacrilege he committed was that he stole away two copies of Guru Granth Sahib, one of which was a beautiful old manuscript. Next day the sangat were thunderstruck to find the Gurdwara deserted and the Sacred Book removed. A few Namdhari Sikhs took charge of the place and carried on the worship upto 4th October, when they went away of their own accord. The prominent Sikhs of Hothian and the neighbourhood assembled in large numbers in the Gurdwara on that day, and after condemning the conduct of the Mahant signed a stamped punchayatnama authorising the

Shromani Gurdwara Parbandhak Committee to control and manage the institution. They handed over the control temporarily to a committee of eleven Sikhs under Jathadar Gajjan Singh.

The Mahant reported to the police that he had been forcibly evicted from the *Akhara* on 30th September. The Sikhs in charge of the Gurdwara were arrested and handcuffed, which was absolutely in contravention of the law, as the Section 145, Cr.P.C., is not an offence for which attendance can be enforced. The District Magistrate, the same who had decided the Teje case, ordered on October 26th that the possession should rest with the Mahant and that nobody should come and interfere in his possession.

The Executive Committee of the Shromani Committee, which was in session on 29th October when it heard the news, at once proceedad to the spot and told the District Magistrate that his orders were indefensible and that the Mahant would not be allowed to take possession. The District Magistrate fumed and fretted, but the Sikhs held their ground.

On March 17, 1922, the District Magistrate informed the Shromani Committee that he intended to enforce the order passed on October 26, and wanted to discuss the matter with the Committee. Two members went and interviewed the Magistrate on March 31 and April 25. But the possession has remained with the Sikhs.

The Sikh community was glad to hear in October, 1921, that the Sikh State of Kapurthala had taken up the question of Gurdwara reform in real earnest. A diwan was convened at Kapurthala on 28th August, 1921, in which certain proposals about the reform of Sikh temples in the State were made for the consideration of the Darbar. Another meeting of the Sikhs, invited from all parts of the State, was held on 1st October, 1921, in which Major General Puran Singh, C.I.E., announced the following decisions of the State about the Gurdwara reform :—

(1) That all historic Gurdwaras and Dharmsalas would thenceforth be under the direct management and control of an elected General Committee of Sikhs inhabiting the Kapurthala State.

(2) That all village Gurdwaras and Dharmsalas would be managed and controlled by local Sikh Committees.

(3) That all property (moveable and immoveable) attached to historic and other village Gurdwaras and Dharmsalas, which had hitherto been shown in Revenue Registers against Sadhus and Mahants, would at

once be mutated in favour of Sri Guru Granth Sahib.

(4) That all Sadhus and Mahants leading vicious and wicked lives or not following the main principles of Sikhism as laid down by the Panth would be, after having been given an opportunity to reform themselves, at once turned out of the Gurdwaras or Dharmsalas.

(5) That the General Committee would manage its work in accordance with the wishes of the Tehsil sub-committees, the members of which will be elected according to the rules prescribed by the Shromani Gurdwara Parbandhak Committee.

The Gurdwara of Babe-di-Ber in Sultanpur, which used to be managed by Mahants, was placed in the hands of the Committee. It is a Gurdwara situated on the Bein river which flows by the town of Sultanpur, where Guru Nanak had spent some time as storekeeper of the Lodhi Nawab, and the spot is sacred as the place where Guru Nanak had meditated for three days on the future career of his mission.

In January, 1922, it was learnt that the management of two other Gurdwaras, Chaunta Sahib and Domeli, connected with Guru Har Gobind, were given over to the Representative Committee.

This example was followed up by Faridkot State. A Central Gurdwara Parbandhak Committee, consisting of officials and non-officials, was formed in April, 1922, to manage and control the historical Gurdwaras in the State. The Gurdwaras which badly stood in need of monetary and other assistance, such as those at Kot Kapura, Bahbal Kalan, Mahma Sewai and Lakhi Jangal, received the immediate attention of the Committee. Local Sub-Committees were formed to manage them and funds were collected to complete the unfinished buildings or to put up new ones.

CHAPTER XVIII.

THE GURDWARA BILL.

In the beginning of the Gurdwara reform movement the Government remained neutral. But after the Tarn Taran tragedy, as the events began to thicken and the movement became more rapid, it resolved to take some action. A communique was issued on February 16, 1921, in which the Government announced that a Committee of Enquiry was contemplated 'to consider the existing management of Sikh Gurdwaras, shrines, etc., and the efforts being made to alter such management and to report on the best method of settling disputes and of regulating future control of the institutions.' To arrange for certain preliminary enquiries a conference between the Reformers, as represented by the Shromani Committee, and the Mahants, as represented by Bawa Kartar Singh Bedi, was proposed to be held at Lahore as early as convenient. It was to be presided over by Sheikh Asghar Ali, C. B. A., I. C. S., who was a Secretary to the Government of the Punjab. But close upon the proposal came the horrible tragedy of Nankana and the conference was never held.

Then the Government 'in order to ensure the overhauling of the position of Sikh shrines' proposed the adoption of l islatio in the form of appointment of comm ioner on the lines of Charity Commissioners in England. But as a full-fledged act would take some time and the need for action was immediate, an Ordinance was suggested to serve in the meanwhile. On March 14, Mian Fazl-i-Hussain, Minister of Education, move the following resolution in the Punjab Council :—

"That this Council moves the Local Government to take early steps to introduce a Bill overhauling the law relating to charitable and religious endowments in the Province, and pending the presentation and passing of the legislation, it moves the Governor-General to make and promulgate an ordinance on the subject, so that the movement to alter and reform the existing management of such endowments may cease to threaten the peace and good government of the Province ; *provided that on the expiry of the ordinance the jurisdiction of civil courts, or of such courts as the Bill which it is proposed to introduce may establish, shall not be ousted.*" (The italicised words were added as the result of Raja Narendra Nath's amendment).

In moving his resolution Mian Fazl-i-Hussain admitted that the existing law was not adequate. They had the Regulation 19 of 1810, the Regulation 7 of 1817, Act XX of 1863, Act VI of 1890, Act XIV of 1920, and certain provisions in the Civil Procedure Code. Of these the first two did not apply to the Punjab, the third should be left out of account, because the religious endowments referred to in that Act did not exist in the Punjab, and the Act of 1920 was only an enabling Act. The provisions of the Civil Procedure Code were the only provisions that could be utilised. But the procedure laid down, he said, was expensive and dilatory. Further on the Hon'ble Minister said that wherever there was a man unworthy of holding the position of a trustee, or who did not fulfil the objects of the trust, there should be an effective machinery of law to replace him. But the existing legal provisions of law—which were embodied in the Civil Procedure Code—were too costly and took too long to work.

The Gurdwara Commission which was to be appointed under the proposed Ordinance was to consist of three Members, two of whom were to be non-officials and Sikhs. Its function was to be to take charge of the contested Gurdwaras temporarily and make provision for the men who lived in them and who had a right to do so. Raja Narendra Nath, who proposed an amendment which was incorporated, said that Section 145 of the Cr. P. Code was sufficient to meet the requirements of the situation. Some Hindu members raised the question of the so-called sects in Sikhism, and wanted an adequate representation for them on the proposed commission. Mr. Ganpat Rai who was the legal adviser of Mahant Narain Das and who declared himself to be a Sikh (!), went further and desired representation for Hindus and Mohammedans too, who, he said, had endowed some of the Gurdwaras in the past. The Sikh members protested againt the wording of the resolution and repudiated the suggestion that there were any sects among the Sikhs. They were sceptical about the purpose of the Ordinance, which made no distinction between ordinary charitable trusts and the Sikh Gurdwaras, which must be managed according to Sikh principles; and they chose to stand aloof. The resolution was, however, passed without their votes.

The Government, under these circumstances, could not proceed with the Ordinance, and decided to introduce a Bill instead, for which the Legislative Council was adjourned till 5th April. In the meanwhile the Government proposed a demand of

Rs. 1,15,217 for an additional force of police necessitated, as alleged, by the disturbed state of the Central Punjab and particularly by the disputes regarding the management of Gurdwaras. In vain did Sardar Mehtab Singh protest against the use of police in Gurdwaras, which gave rise to nothing but misrepresentation and repression of Sikhs. In vain did he appeal to Government that the Sikhs were the same who had shed their life's blood in Britain's cause all over the world. The demand was sanctioned.

Before the Council met the Sikhs were asked to present their views as to the form of legislation which would satisfy them. A big representative meeting was held at the Akal Takht on 20th March under the auspices of the Shromnai Gurdwara Parbandhak Committee. Beside the members of the Commitee other important Sikhs, including the Sikh members of the Punjab Council and the press representatives, were invited to take part in the momentous debate. In view of the wholesale arrests of Sikhs going on at the time there was a strong feeling in favour of Non-co-operation with the Government in the matter of Gurdwaras, but a compromise was effected when moderate gentlemen, like Professor Jodh Singh, Sardar Harbans Singh of Attari and Sardar Mehtab Singh, wanted to give another chance to

Government to show its sympathy with its old friends, the Sikhs, in their travail for reform. The following resolutions, among others, were passed :—

(1) That all Sikhs arrested by the authorities in connection with the Gurdwaras should be released.

(2) That the Panth strongly resents and condemns the action of the authorities concerned in arresting the Sikhs from Gurdwaras in various places and handing over the same to their previous Mahants and Pujaris.

(3) That pending the enactment of legislation on the lines suggested by the Shromani Gurdwara Parbandhak Committee for the management of the Gurdwaras and other religious charitable institutions of the Sikhs, the control and management of Gurdwaras be left in the hands of those who were exercising such control at the time when the arrests of the Sikhs began in various places.

(4) All efforts of the Panth to make the Government alive to the pressing need of reform in the Sikh Gurdwaras and charitable institutions having failed, the Panth standing before the Akal Takht in the presence of the Guru resolves solemnly that if the innocent Sikhs arrested are not released and a satisfactory legislation of the Gur-

dwaras is not passed upto the 10th of April, 1921, the Sikhs will consider it an interference with their religious rights and will be compelled to resort to all necessary means of reforming the Gurdwaras themselves.

(5) The Guru Panth calls upon every Sikh to join the Akali jathas to effect the reformation of their Gurdwaras.

(6) As by the grace of the Guru, the Sikhs during this hour of trial have shown he greatest fortitude and self-control, so the Guru Panth ordains that in future, too, they should similarly maintain their calmness and self-restraint in the face of even greater hardships and should never be prompted by an idea of revenge or retaliation. Thus should they remain faithful to Sikhism up to the last breath.

(7) The Shromani Committee requests all Sikhs not to interfere in the existing management of any new Gurdwara upto 10th April next.

By another resolution a standing Committee of 12 Sikhs was appointed to discuss matters with the Government and the members of the Punjab Legislative Council, if asked to do so. But the only reply the Government gave to the demand about the release of prisoners was the arrest of more leaders. One of them Sardar Amar Singh of Jhabal was arrested under the Seditious Meetings Act for repeating and explaining a resolution of the Gurdwara Committee about kirpan to the congregation at the Akal Takht on March 20. He was sentenced to six months' R. I. Others were prosecuted for wearing kirpans and harassed for possessing little axes and sticks. The Gurdwara Bill, too, when published, was a sorely disappointing document. The following is the full text of the Bill as it emerged from the Select Committee, which reported on 8th April.

THE SIKH GURDWARAS AND SHRINES BILL.

PREAMBLE.

Whereas it is expedient to make emergent provision for the administration and management of certain Sikh Gurdwaras, and shrines in the Punjab, and, with a view to future legislation relating thereto, to provide for inquiry into these and other matters;

And whereas the previous sanction of the Governor-General has been obtained under Section 80 A (3) of the Government of India Act to the passing of this Act;

It is hereby enacted as follows :—

SHORT TITLE AND EXTENT.

1. (1) This Act may be called the Sikh Gurdwaras and Shrines Act, 1921.

(2). It extends to the whole of the Punjab.

Definitions.

2. In this Act—

"Disputed Gurdwara or shrine" means a Gurdwara or shrine in respect of which a declaration has been made under section 3.

"Prescribed" means prescribed by rules made by the Local Government under this Act.

"Gurdwara" means a Sikh place of public worship erected by or in memory of or in commemoration of any incident in the life of any of the 10 Sikh Gurus.

"Shrine" means a Sikh place of public worship erected in memory of a Sikh martyr or saint.

Declaration that a Shrine is a Disputed Shrine.

3. Where on enquiry the Local Government is satisfied that any dispute has arisen or is likely to arise with respect to the administration or management of, or succession to any office in, or the title to any property belonging to, any Sikh Gurdwara or shrine, it may by notification declare such Gurdwara or shrine to be disputed Gurdwara or shrine.

Effect of Declaration.

4. Upon the making of a declaration under section 3 in respect of any Gurdwara or shrine, such Gurdwara or shrine shall be

deemed to have been attached by the Local Government; and the Local Government shall appoint a Board of Commissioners in the manner hereinafter provided for the administration and management of all such Gurdwaras or shrines, and such Board of Commissioners (hereinafter referred to as the Board) shall exercise such powers and perform such duties as may be conferred or imposed upon it by this Act.

APPOINTMENT OF COMMISSIONERS.

5. (1) The Board shall be appointed by notification by the Local Government and shall consist of the following:—

i. A non-Sikh to be appointed by the Local Government as President.

ii. A Sikh to be appointed by the Local Government.

iii. Two Sikhs to be selected by the Local Government from a panel of eight to be proposed by a majority of the Sikh Members of the Legislative Council.

(2) Upon any vacancy occurring in the Board by reason of the death, resignation, incapacity or removal of any Commissioner, the Local Government shall, by notification, appoint another person possessing the same qualification as such Commissioner to fill such vacancy.

(3) The President shall in case of an equality of votes have a second or casting vote.

Pay and Duration of office of Commissioners.

6. The Commissioners shall be paid such remuneration and shall hold office for such period not exceeding two years as may be prescribed.

Managers and Committees.

7. Subject to any restrictions that may be prescribed in this behalf, the Board from time to time may appoint a manager or a committee of management for any disputed Gurdwara or shrine and may delegate to such manager or committee all or any of the powers or duties conferred or imposed on the Board by this Act.

Central and Local Establishments.

8. (1) The Board may from time to time appoint such officers and servants as may be necessary for the general administration of all disputed Gurdwaras and shrines.

(2) The Board may from time to time appoint such officers and servants as may be necessary for any disputed Gurdwara or shrine.

SALARIES.

9. (1) The managers and members of any committees of management appointed under Section 7 and the officers and servants appointed under Section 8, shall receive such salaries as the Board, subject to the control of the Local Government, may determine.

(2) Subject to the control of the Local Government, the remuneration of the Commissioners, other than the President, and the salaries of the officers and servants appointed under Section 8 (1) shall be paid by contribution from the funds of disputed Gurdwaras and shrines in such manner and to such extent as the Board may determine.

(3) The salaries of managers and members of committees of management appointed under sections 7 and 8 (2) shall be charged against the funds of the Gurdwara or shrine, for the management or service of which they have been appointed.

TAKING OF POSSESSION.

10. (1) Upon the making of a declaration under Section 3 in respect of any Gurdwara or shrine, the Board shall be entitled to take possession of such Gurdwara or shrine and of all property belonging thereto.

(2) Subject to the provisions of subsection (3), the Board may, when it apprehends any opposition to its taking or retaining possession of any Gurdwara or shrine,

apply to the District Magistrate to be placed or maintained in possession, and the District Magistrate shall thereupon take steps to place or maintain the Board in possession, and shall have all papers necessary for that purpose.

(3) Where any claim is preferred to, or any objection is made to the Board's taking possession of, any property on the ground that such property does not belong to a disputed Gurdwara or shrine, the Board shall proceed to investigate the claim or objection and its decision shall, so long as the declaration made under section 3 in respect of such Gurdwara or shrine remains in force, be final, subject to the result of any suit that may be brought in accordance with the provisions of this Act.

BOARD'S POWERS OF MANAGING PROPERTIES.

11. Subject to any restrictions that may be prescribed in this behalf, the Board shall, for the purpose of providing for the management or administration of any disputed Gurdwara or shrine, have, in addition to the powers conferred by this Act, all the powers which may be conferred on a receiver under the provisions of the Code of Civil Procedure, 1908.

MAINTENANCE OF RELIGIOUS OBSERVANCES.

12. During the period of management of any disputed gurdwara or shrine it shall be

the duty of the Board to provide for the conduct of religious or charitable duties, ceremonies and observances.

APPLICATION OF FUNDS.

13. Save as otherwise provided in this Act, the Board shall apply the proceeds of the rents, profits and other sources of income of any disputed Gurdwara or shrine to the following purposes, and no others, namely :—

(*a*) the provision of reasonable maintenance allowances for the existing mahants, attendants and other persons having a claim to support on the funds of such Gurdwara or shrine;

(*b*) the maintenance of religious worship and the performance and conduct of religious or charitable duties, ceremonies and observances of such Gurdwara or shrine ;

(*c*) the payment of the salaries of officers and servants of such Gurdwara or shrine ;

(*d*) the maintenance and repair of structures connected with such Gurdwara or shrine ; and

(*e*) all other purposes which the Board may consider necessary for the maintenance of such Gurdwara or shrine and for furtherance of the object and intention with which it was founded.

Records and Accounts.

14. The Board shall maintain in such form and manner as may be prescribed a complete record of its proceedings and a full account of all monies which have come into its possession, and such records and accounts shall be published in such manner as may be prescribed and be deemed to be public documents within the meaning of Section 74 of the Indian Evidence Act, 1872.

Settlement of Dispute.

15. (1) Where it shall appear to the Board that persons interested in any disputed Gurdwara or shrine are likely to come to a settlement in regard to any dispute connected therewith, the Board may give public notice in such way as it thinks fit of its intention to hear the parties to such dispute at a time, place and date to be mentioned in such notice, and thereupon any person claiming to be interested in the matter in dispute shall be entitled to appear before the Board.

(2) The Board shall have power to receive any proposal for settlement or adjustment of any such dispute, and whenever any settlement or adjustment is arrived at among the parties appearing, the Board shall cause such settlement or adjustment to be reduced to writing and signed by the parties thereto and by the Board, and such settlement

or adjustment in writing so signed shall be a final bar to all actions, suits, claims and demands by any parties thereto in respect of the matter to which such settlement or adjustment relates.

BAR AGAINST SUITS.

16. (1) So long as a declaration under section 3 remains in force in respect of any disputed Gurdwara or shrine no civil or revenue suit or proceeding in respect to any matter connected with such a Gurdwara or shrine shall be commenced or continued, or entertained by any court, except when such suit or proceeding is lodged or continued by or on behalf of the Board or with the consent of the Local Government;

Provided that notwithstanding anything contained in the Indian Limitation Act, 1908, any person who is hereby prevented from instituting any suit or proceeding shall, when a declaration under section 3 ceases to have force, be entitled to institute any suit or proceeding which would otherwise have become time-barred within one year from the date on which such declaration ceases to have force.

(2) Upon the making of a declaration in respect of a disputed Gurdwara or shrine under section 3 any proceeding pending under Chapter XI or Chapter XII of the Code of Criminal Procedure, 1898, in respect

of such Gurdwara or shrine shall abate, and no subsequent proceeding under either of the said Chapters in respect of such Gurdwara or shrine shall be entertained by any court so long as such declaration remains in force.

BAR AGAINST PROCEEDINGS AGAINST COMMISSIONERS, ETC.

17. No suit or criminal proceeding shall be instituted in any Court against any Commissioner or District Magistrate in respect of anything in good faith done or intended to be done in the exercise of any power or duty conferred or imposed by this Act, without the previous sanction of the Local Government.

INQUIRY BY BOARD.

18. (1) It shall be the duty of the Board to examine and inquire into the following matters in connection with all disputed Gurdwaras and shrines, namely :—

(*a*) the origin, nature and objects of the foundation thereof ;

(*b*) the value, title, conditions, management and application of all estates, funds, property and income pertaining or attached thereto ;

(*c*) the law or custom regulating the succession to any office connected therewith ;

(*d*) the nature and character of any religious or charitable duty, ceremony or observance connected therewith ;

(*e*) the rights of any mahants, granthis, chelas, pujaris or attendants connected therewith ;

(*f*) the general character and management thereof, the conduct of the incumbents thereof, and the performance of any religious or charitable duty, ceremony or observance connected therewith, with special reference to the objects and intentions with which such Gurdwaras and shrines were founded, and to the advancement of the Sikh religion ; and

(*g*) any other matter in connection therewith that may be prescribed.

(2) It shall be the duty of the Board to report to the Local Government the result of such inquiry.

(3) The Board shall have power to make such recommendations in connection with any disputed Gurdwara or shrine as it may think fit and calculated to secure the carrying out of the objects and intentions of the foundation of such Gurdwara or shrine and the advancement of the Sikh religion, and it may propose schemes for the future administration and management of any such Gurdwara or shrine.

(4) The Board shall, for the purposes of any inquiry under the section, have the same powers as are vested in a court under the Code of Civil Procedure, 1908,

when trying a suit, in respect of the following matters :—

(*a*) enforcing the attendance of any person and examining him on oath or affirmation ;

(*b*) compelling the production of documents ; and

(*c*) issuing commissions for the examination of witnesses.

PENALTY FOR RESISTING.

19. Any person resisting or obstructing the Board or any one acting on its behalf or under its instructions in taking possession of a disputed Gurdwara or shrine under this Act and any person interfering with such possession when taken shall, on conviction by a Magistrate of the first class, be liable to a fine not exceeding one thousand rupees, or to rigorous imprisonment for a term not exceeding twelve months, or to both.

RULES.

20. (1) The Local Government may by notification make rules for the purpose of carrying into effect the provisions of this Act.

(2) In particular and without prejudice to the generality of the foregoing power such rules may provide for—

(*a*) the remuneration of the Commissioners and their term of office ;

(*b*) the restrictions on the powers of the Board to appoint a manager or a committee of management and to delegate their function to the same ;

(*c*) the restrictions that may be placed on the powers of the Board under section 11 ;

(*d*) the number required to constitute a quorum of the Board, or the circumstances in which the Board may act in the absence of any member ;

(*e*) the records and accounts to be maintained by the Board and the method of publication thereof ; and

(*f*) the matters in connection with disputed Gurdwaras or shrines into which the Board shall inquire.

Statement of Objects and Reasons.

Recent events have brought into prominence the fact that the management of Sikh Gurdwaras and shrines leaves much to be desired.

The object of this Bill is to obtain by the appointment of a Board of Commissioners information relating to the foundation, past management, rights of succession, titles in property and other necessary matters relating to such institutions so as to enable Government, the legislature and the public to know on what matters legislation is necessary to ensure that in the future these Gurdwaras and shrines shall perform their proper functions, *viz.*, the maintenance and furtherance of the Sikh religion.

The Commissioners who will be appointed under the Bill, besides enquiring and reporting, are, in order to prevent further tension, empowered to take possession of Gurdwaras and shrines which are notified as disputed and to manage them during the period of their office; and at the same time by powers conferred on them to entertain compromises and settlements in respect of particular Gurdwaras entered into by parties disputing.

(Sd.) FAZL-I-HUSSAIN,
Minister for Education.
(Sd.) E. JOSEPH,
Secretary to Government Punjab.

Even the Sikh members of the Select Committee, who did not fully represent Panthic views, were not satisfied with the Bill and recorded the following minute of dissent :—

1. "The Gurdwaras and shrines, as defined in the amended Bill, are obviously the holy places of the Sikhs, and as such they are in theory at least under the control of the Sikh panth. The principle is perfectly sound in law and justice, and there is no reason why

the present Bill should not be based on it. To ignore this fundamental principle at the very outset and to leave the recognition of it to be determined from the Commissioners' report will be to go against the sound canons of such legislation. The Sikhs can in no way feel satisfied with the enquiry, if it is not meant to secure to them the control of their own sacred places of worship. The very object of the Bill is likely to be defeated, because this guiding principle is not incorporated in it.

2. The feelings of the Sikhs, which we ourselves fully share, are very keen, that all members of the Board should be of the Sikh faith elected or selected by the Sikh members of the Legislative Council. But we have agreed as a last resort to the constitution of the Board as given in the Bill as amended, in the hope, that the Sikh member to be nominated by the Government under sub-clause (2) will not be one whose views may be antagonistic to the spirit of religious reform among the Sikhs. We feel bound to express our opinion on this point, because the success or failure of the proposed legislation depends entirely upon the constitution of the Board.

3. We are opposed to the provision in the Bill that the salary of the Commissioners

and their staff should be paid out of the gurdwara funds for the following reasons:—

(*a*) That the money meant for religious and charitable purposes alone should not be spent in any other manner.

(*b*) That no Sikh Commissioner would agree to be paid out of the religious offerings and proceeds of the sacred property.

(Sd.) DASAUNDHA SINGH,
(Sd.) KARTAR SINGH,
(Sd.) HARNAM SINGH,
(Sd.) MEHTAB SINGH."

The consideration of the Bill was postponed to 16th April. Those few days were of the greatest commotion and anxiety for the Sikh community. They were, on the one hand, trying their best to keep themselves calm and pacific in the face of an unprecedented campaign of prosecution and harassment and had, on the other, to meet the mischievous attempts of some people to set the Hindus against the Sikhs. Besides fighting tooth-and-nail against the Sikh interests in the Council, some Hindu gentlemen were trying to raise an artificial opposition outside in the country. The Shromani Committee had made it clear several times in the press and on the platform that it had got nothing to do with the Hindu shrines or those temples which are not historically associated with Sikh Gurus or Sikh saints. And yet the Punjab Hindu Sabha was made to issue a circular letter, dated 4th April, to different orthodox Hindu bodies, emphasising that no changes should be allowed in the system of worship and other conditions prevailing in the Gurdwaras, and that if a Gurdwara Commission be appointed, a sufficient representation should be granted to Hindus. As a result of this some resolutions were passed here and there to oppose the Sikh demands. This unfortunte difference between Hindus and Sikhs was, however, averted by the timely action of other Hindu leaders, like Swami Shankracharya of Sharda Peeth and Lala Lajpat Rai, who came forward to actually sympathise with the movement. The deputation of the Shromani Committee, which toured in the country to remove misunderstandings about the Sikhs, was enthusiastically received everywhere by Sikhs, Hindus and Mohammedans, who passed resolutions of sympathy with the Gurdwara Reform Movement.

On April 11, the Shromani Committee again met at the Akal Takht to consider the situation created by the publication of the Bill and the refusal of the Government to release the Sikh prisoners. The Bill was declared unsatisfactory, as none of the important amendments suggested by the Committee's representatives had been incorporated in the Bill. The Government would not recognise the Shromani Committee, nor would it accept the principle that the Gurdawras belonged to the Panth and that the Mahants were its mere servants to be removed whenever proved unfit in the eyes of the Panth. The principle of heredity with regard to any office in connection with a Gurdwara was diametrically opposed to the spirit and dictates of the Sikh religion and the object of the present reform movement. The creation of Commissioners to enquire into cases of dispute and, if necessary, to take charge of Gurdwaras would have been only a veiled extension of the existing defective law under which the Gurdwaras were being attached and which treats the whole Sikh Panth, the rightful owner, as a mere party against its servants, the Mahants. The effect of such legislation, if passed, would have been that, instead of one Sarbrah whom the Sikhs had with great difficulty ousted, there would have been many Sarbrahs and, instead of controlling one Golden Temple, the Government would have come to control all the Sikh temples. The Committee resolved to reject the Bill on another ground too, that is, the failure of the Government to release the Sikhs arrested in connection with the reform of Gurdwaras.

To decide upon a definite line of action to be taken by the Sikhs in pursuance of the last meeting's decision, a working committee of the following seven gentlemen was appointed :—1. S. Kharak Singh, B.A., L.L.B., of Sialkot; 2. S. Harbans Singh of Atari; 3. Professor Jodh Singh, M.A.; 4. Professor Harkishen Singh, M.A.; 5. Bhai Tara Singh, B.A.; 6. S. Batan Singh, Canadian; and 7. S. Teja Singh of Samundri. This committee issued a manifesto calling upon the Sikhs to enlist in Akali jathas for taking concerted action whenever necessary. The jathas were to be reorganized and measures were taken to see that each man who enlisted was a regular Sikh strictly pledged to purity and non-violence. The Sikhs felt as if they were entering the Valley of the Shadow of Death, where their only source of strength was Almighty God. The 14th of April was fixed as the day of prayer for all Sikhs to seek divine help in the great task of suffering before them. Many Sikhs left off their business and their homes, and came to offer their free services to be employed in any capacity by the Shromani Committee. Many Sikhs serving in the Military and Police Departments asked as to whether they should leave their services, but they were told by the Shromani Committee to continue in the faithful discharge of their duties where they were employed, as the time for giving up Government service had not yet come.

The Bill was presented in the Council on April 16, but in the hope of arriving at some compromise in the meanwhile its consideration was postponed to May 9. On April 23, a conference was arranged by Government between the representatives of the Shromani Committee and of the Mahants, Lala Ganpat Rai and Raja Narendra Nath taking part with the latter. The Councillors and Ministers of the Government and some other Sikh leaders were also present. At first it was tried to bring about reconciliation about certain points which were to form the basis of a permanent legislation. The Sikh leaders were able to argue their opponents into reason, and made them agree to the following three principles :—

(1) That only those Mahants had the right to remain in charge of Gurdwaras, who bore good character ;

(2) that all Gurdwaras belong to the whole Panth and should, therefore, be under Panthic committees ; and

(3) that regular accounts of the income and expenditure of Gurdwaras should be kept and rendered to the public.

The meeting was adjourned for further discussion, and there was every hope of a complete understanding on most of the points at issue. But when the conference met again on April 26, quite a new and irreconcilable attitude was adopted by certain fresh members to the conference on the opposite side. It was insisted in behalf of the Mahants that the question of ritual and ceremony must be decided there and then, and that it should be agreed that no changes would be made in the form of worship that had prevailed up to the year 1920. On the side of the reformers it was suggested that the question, being highly controversial, should be left to be decided in each case by the committees of control which had been agreed upon in the last meeting. But the other side would not consider even the last meeting's decisions finally settled if the new question was not taken up and decided in their favour. They wanted a declaration that the same ritual which was observed a year before should be followed in every case in future. It was most unreasonable to expect the reformers to stop all progress in reform for ever and bind down the future generations to the prevailing customs of a particular time. And why should they go back only one year? Why should they not go back 300 years and revert to the simple beliefs and practices that prevailed in Guru

Arjan's time, when the temples were first organized? The Sikhs as a compromise suggested the formula that the worship held in Sikh temples should be according to the teachings of Guru Granth Sahib. But even this was not acceptable to the champions of the Mahants who were determined not to come to any agreement with the reformers.

Then it was tried to come to some understanding as regards the temporary measure that was before the Council. The controversy raged about the composition of the Board of Commissioners. The Sikhs came down from their original demand, which was to have at least two-thirds of the Commissioners elected by the Shromani Committee, and simply asked that the President of the Board may be nominated by the Government, but must be a Sikh. They were not averse at that time even to the appointment of an official. The Mahants insisted that the President must be a European and not a Sikh. It was futile to argue with them any more, and the conference came to an end.

The Government postponed the meeting of the Legislative Council, which was to have been held on the 9th of May, to some day in June or July. The Sikhs realised that there was no chance of getting a suitable Bill from this Government, as long as it was bent upon attaching too much importance to the views of the Mahants, whose self-interest could never make them agree to any change, and as long as it was allowing certain men of other communities to interfere in this purely Sikh question. The Shromani Committee met on May 10 at the Akal Takht to finally settle their attitude towards the Government in matters religious. The Working Committee, including Sardar Harbans Singh and Professor Jodh Singh, had been asked to prepare a programme according to the policy of passive resistance passed in the Executive Committee on 1st May. But owing to differences about certain terms, that sounded political, no unanimous conclusion had been arrived at. The General Committee postponed their meeting to the next day to allow time to the Working Committee to come to some decision by majority, if not by unanimity. The Working Committee presented their majority report to the General Committee on May 11, and recommended that as the Government, owing to its callous disregard of the Sikh rights about Gurdwaras and kirpans, had forfeited the confidence of the Sikhs, the Committee should call upon the Panth—

(1) to resort to Passive Resistance so far as the possession of the Gurdwaras that had

already come under the Panthic control was concerned ; and—

(2) as a preparation for this to resort to a process of self-purification, otherwise called Non-co-operation, by

(*i*) boycotting the intoxicating liquors,

(*ii*) fostering the use of Swadeshi goods, and

(*iii*) by organizing and availing of Panchayats.

This recommendation, after a hard contest put in by a few members like S. Harbans Singh and Professor Jodh Singh, was adopted by the General Committee. S. Harbans Singh and Professor Jodh Singh put in their resignations. The Committee decided to do without a Bill and make every effort to reform the remaining Gurdwaras by making compromises with the mahants ; but with the existing attitude of the Government towards the reforming party no headway could be made. The resolution of Non-co-operation was purely constructive and did not suggest any boycott of courts, schools or titles. But the Committee in the eyes of the Government began to appear as a political body and incurred an unmerited suspicion of its intentions. Its supporters, who wore black turbans, were suspected of sedition and suffered many indignities at the hands of the police or the departments wherein they served.

The Government, too, dropped the idea of introducing a Bill, and issued a communique in which it advised the Sikhs to carry out reform by persuasion and the legitimate pressure of public opinion, or by resort to law, which was now discovered by Government to contain 'provisions which go a considerable way towards achieving the objects in question'! For the benefit of the Sikhs it also published the main provisions of the law and explained how the expense and delay involved in the Gurdwara cases could be minimised. It was promised that the Deputy Commissioners and the civil courts would be instructed to prevent delay in deciding the Gurdwara suits—which is too evident from the Hafizabad and other cases. The Government also discovered for the Sikhs in July that, in addition to the remedies provided in the substantive law for the explusion of bad Mahants, there also existed a general or special power by *custom* in the Punjab to claim the removal of a Mahant for misconduct.

When the Shromani Committee was re-elected according to the new constitution the situation was still unchanged. The Sikhs arrested in connection with the Gurdwaras were still rotting in jails and the monstrous sentences passed on Bhais Kartar Singh Jhabar, Teja Singh Bhuchar, etc., further intensified the discontent. The Non-co-operation resolution passed in May was confirmed by the new Committee in its meeting of 28th August. There was not one vote against the resolution this time; the moderates, who remained neutral, promised not to stand in the way, but to follow the lead of others. The Sikh members of the Punjab Council were called upon to resign their seats in protest against the Government's policy of repression in regard to the Gurdwara movement; but just as they had gone to the Council, so they chose to remain in the Council against the expressed wishes of the Panth. Sardar Bahadur Mehtab Singh, who had already thrown up the Public Prosecutorship, now resigned the membership and with it his appointment of the Deputy President of the Punjab Council.

In the beginning of September the Government saw reason to release most of the Gurdwara prisoners, including Bhais Kartar Singh Jhabar and Teja Singh Buchar, and the situation became somewhat easier.

The Government officers felt disposed to discuss again the necessity of restoring peace with the Sikhs. It was even given out that the Government was ready to accept a Sikh as President of the Board of Commissioners, which they had refused in the April discussions. On September 13, Mr. Dunnett, the Deputy Commissioner of Amritsar, met some members of the Shromani Committee at the Committee's office to learn what the Sikhs wanted. He alse discussed the affairs of the Darbar Sahib. The difficulty with the Government officers was that they did not want to recognise the Shromani Committee, and so they always suggested committees and conferences. They were told that there was no use wasting time over conferences, as there was no party among the Sikhs in general opposed to reform. Only the Government must change its policy of suspicion, and then everything would go on well. The Mahants would be ready to agree and make compromises with the reformers, if the Government indicated its genuine sympathy for reform. Many Mahants had actually offered to accept the Panthic control, but when they saw that the law was being illegally used in their favour and that the reforming Sikhs were being arrested in hundreds, they put up their backs and turned away from their plighted word. Even documents of agreement duly signed by Mahants in the presence of the most respectable representatives of the people were repudiated. Mr. Dunnett refused to believe that there was no party among the Sikhs opposed to the Shromani Committee. He said, "for instance the Chief Khalsa Diwan might not accept the Shromani Committee's decisions," and suggested that if the Committee took two or three members of the Diwan on its Executive all would be well. This was playing one party against the other. But the Diwan quickly repudiated any intention of hostility on their part. The fact is that there were many members of the Chief Khalsa Diwan on the General Committee, but they themselves had declined to serve on the Executive, when some of other members had offered to vacate their seats for them.*

The things were, however, settling down, and even the resolution of boycott of the Prince of Wales' visit, introduced in September, was postponed for reconsideration to November. But suddenly by a strange freak of unwisdom the Government raised a storm of indignation against it by snatching away the keys of the Golden Temple.

**The Khalsa Advocate* of November 11, 1921.

CHAPTER XIX.

THE KEYS AFFAIR.

On 7th November at 3 P. M. Lala Amar Nath, E.A.C., accompanied by a body of police came to the house of Sardar Sundar Singh Ramgarhia, Vice-President of the Shromani Gurdwara Parbandhak Committee and President of the Local Gurdwara Committee which was in charge of the Golden Temple, Akal Takht, Baba Atal and Tarn Taran. The Sikhs felt it like a bolt from the blue. They could not understand this action of the Government taken after the community had been in possession for full thirteen months. There was no party among the Sikhs that had gone to court against the possession of the Darbar Sahib by the Shromani Committee. The Government issued a communique, two days later, in which it tried to explain its arbitrary action as being due to its desire to divest itself by legal process of the control which by 'long practice' it had exercised over the affairs of the Darbar Sahib of Amritsar. It declared that as a step in that direction, it had formed in November, 1920, "a provisional advisory committee" of 36 members to propose rules for the future management of the shrine. But as that had been absorbed by the

Shromani Committee it now wanted to institute a friendly suit for the settlement of a scheme of management by a civil court. The communique also stated that the Government was compelled to take the keys into its custody, as it was apprehended that the Shromani Committee, which, according to Government, had received no legal authority to control the Golden Temple or its treasure, might bring pressure to bear upon the manager of the Golden Temple to surrender to it the Keys.

The whole position of the Government was untenable. In the first place it appeared that the Government thought that it had still got some control, a legal one, over the affairs of the Darbar Sahib. We have already shown in the account of the Golden Temple how illegally this control had been acquired by the Government. For many years from 1859 the management was in the hands of a Committee of Trustees presided over by a nominee of the Government, but about 1883 the Committee was quietly dropped and the president, called Sarbrah, who should have gone the way of the Committee, came to take all instructions from the Deputy Commissioner of the district. Therefore *long practice*, as admitted in the communique, was the only excuse for the Government to have controlled the Darbar Sahib for so long.

But we had supposed that even of this the Government had divested itself when in November, 1920, it had handed over the management to a committee of 36. According to Government's own Publicity Committee, the then Lieutenant-Governor accepted the following proposal of certain Sikhs, who waited upon him on 13th November, 1920 (only two days before the representative meeting of the Panth was to be held for the purpose of appointing a Managing Committee) :—

"The Government has already expressed its desire of handing over the management to a representative Sikh Committee, so we respectfully propose that the following Provincial [? provisional] Committee may be appointed to prepare rules for the future managemaent of Sri Darbar Sahib and attached Gurdwaras (in a manner acceptable to the Panth), and meanwhile to supervise the management of the institutions."

This does not show that the Committee was merely *advisory*, as was alleged in the Government communique. It also showed that with the formation of this Committee the connection of the Government with the Darbar Sahib and attached shrines ceased altogether, and the new rules were to be presented to the Panth for acceptance and not to the Government. The Lieutenant-

Governor at the same time told S. Sundar Singh Ramgarhia, the Sarbrah, that from that time he was to take his orders from S. Harbans Singh of Atari, President of the Committee, and not from the Deputy Commissioner. And he did so. S. Harbans Singh did sign many papers and money drafts, as presented by S. Sundar Singh Ramgarhia to him, and he continued to do so until the Shromani Gurdwara Parbandhak Committee, which had been elected in the meanwhile, was inaugurated in December, 1920.

With the establishment of the Shromani Committee (in which the members of the Government-appointed Committee had willingly amalgamated themselves and which was accepted by all parties including the Sikh States), Sardar Sundar Singh Ramgarhia took his orders from this new Committee, whose President was Sardar Sundar Singh Majithia and whose Vice-President was Sardar Harbans Singh. S. Sundar Singh Ramgarhia published the proceedings of the Committee as its Secretary, setting forth its claims of final authority over all the aflairs of the Darbar Sahib, as of other Gurdwaras in the country.

That the Government had nothing further to do with the management of the Darbar Sahib was openly assumed all along in the several negotiations between the Government and Shromani Committee' representatives. Sir Edward Maclagan in a speech at an informal meeting of the Council members on November 13, 1920, while mentioning many favours shown to the Sikh community by his Government, said, "It (Government) has arranged for its withdrawal from the control of the Darbar Sahib." In a meeting of the Punjab Council, on March 15, 1921, Sardar Mehtab Singh addressed the Government thus : "Now that the Government has given up control of the Darbar Sahib, will it kindly present the accounts thereof for the period of its stewardship ?" The Government is said to have replied, "we had never anything to do with the accounts. We only appointed the Sarbrah and that we have given up." On March 14, Mr. Fazl-i-Hussain, in his speech on the resolution recommending an Ordinance on the Gurdwara question, used these words : "The Government, realising that public opinion was strong and united, superseded the manager of the Golden Temple at Amritsar, and appointed a representative managing body"; and yet a full year after *superseding* this manager the Government still held that he was a functionary appointed by itself. In a communique published on 20th April, 1921, the Government gave examples of its kindness towards the Sikhs and mentioned "the withdrawal of Government interference in the management of the Golden Temple" as an accomplished fact.

Tarn Taran was also one of the Gurdwaras whose keys were taken away, and yet on July 9, 1921, the possession of the Gurdwara by the Sikh Committee had been left undisturbed by an order of the Additional District Magistrate under Section 145 of the Cr. P. C. In a case filed by Pandit Dharm Sarup about the same Gurdwara, Sardar Sundar Singh Ramgarhia, the Sarbrah, had stated that the suit should have nothing to do with him, as the control rested with the Shromani Committee.

In view of these clear declarations it had come to be regarded as a settled fact that the Government had got nothing more to do with the management of the Darbar Sahib. But when it attempted to reassert its control by snatching away the keys, it simply staggered the Sikhs who were not used to such turning away from the given word. It was ridiculous to say that it was 'apprehended that the Shromani Gurdwara Parbandhak Committee intended to take these keys by force from the manager.' The keys had for a year been at the command of the Committee and the Sarbrah had never demurred in using them at its bidding.

The Sikhs felt extremely disturbed in their minds about the liberty of their Gurdwaras, and resolutions of protest were passed all over the country. The high-handed action of the Government was deeply resented especially in view of the fact that the keys of the Gurdwara treasury being with the Government the *jalau* or exhibition ceremony could not be held on the sacred day of Guru Nanak's birth. A hurried meeting of the Shromani Committee was called at the Akal Takht, where on 12th November it was resolved not to allow Captain Bahadur Singh, the new Sarbrah appointed by the Government, to interfere in the management in any way. The decision was duly communicated to the Deputy Commissioner, who, however, sent Captain Bahadur Singh with the keys to exercise his authority as Sarbrah. When he came to the Temple on the sacred morning of November 15, the day of Guru Nanak's birth, he was asked by the assembled Sikhs why he had come. He said tremblingly that the Government had sent him as Sarbrah. Pointing to Sardar Kharak Singh, the Secretary asked Captain Bahadur Singh to compare his position with that of the venerable Sardar. The Captain was a nominee of a Government officer, while Sardar Kharak Singh derived his position of the President from the whole Panth. The poor Captain was perspiring with shame and perhaps cursing his fate for having been placed in that predicament by an alien Government. He slunk away with the bundle of keys under his arm. He became ill physically and mentally, and in a few days sent word to the Shromani Committee that he felt accursed for his conduct towards the Panth and that he had resigned. He begged the Community to forgive him and pray for him. The whole assembly felt touched at his humiliation and prayed for his recovery. Then another Military Sardar was asked to become Sarbrah and take the keys, but he is said to have died by falling from the roof of his house. After this the Government had much to do to find a man who would accept the keys, but nobody would touch them.

The Deputy Commissioner held frequent meetings at his house to explain his position to those who cared to go to him. And then he adopted another method to allay the growing tension between the Sikhs and the Government. He went round to different villages and held meetings, in which he misrepresented the position of Sikhs. The Sikhs, therefore, felt compelled to hold counter-meetings at the same places to contradict the misstatements of the Government officials. The Deputy Commissioner announced a meeting of his own to be held at Ajnala, a few miles from Amritsar, on the 26th of November. The District Gurdwara Committee also announced a religous Diwan to be held at Ajnala on the same date. The Government applied the Seditious Meetings Act to the districts of Amritsar, Lahore and Sheikhupura, and an order about this was promulgated in Amritsar and Ajnala on the night of the 25th. A copy of it was also served on the Secretary of the *Congress* Committee of the district, which was supposed to be the convener of the Sikh meeting.

The Deputy Commissioner held his meeting on the 26th at noon and explained the Government's position about the Keys affair. S. Dan Singh of Vachhoa and S. Jaswant Singh of Jhabal, two Sikh leaders who were present there, asked the permission of the Deputy Commissioner to express their views, but it was refused. The Sikhs, therefore, held their own diwan. But before they had begun the proceedings the Deputy Commissioner arrived with a few executive and police officers and demanded to know what was going on. S. Dan Singh and S. Jaswant Singh came out of the diwan and told the Deputy Commissioner that the meeting was religious and that they were singing hymns. The Deputy Commissioner asked if there would be any speeches. S. Jaswant Singh replied that there would be no speeches on Swarajya, Swadeshi, or any other political subject. The Deputy Commissioner asked further if there would be any talk about the Keys affair. He was told that undoubtedly there would be. On this, without waiting to see if any speeches were actually made, he ordered the Police Inspector to arrest S. Dan Singh, S. Jaswant Singh, Pandit Dina Nath, S. Teja Singh of Samundri and S. Harnam Singh Zaildar. The last-named gentleman was arrested, according to the Deputy Commissioner's own admission, merely because he had taken part in a meeting at another place and had attended the Deputy Commissioner's meeting "clad from head to foot in Khaddar."

When the news of the arrests was brought the same day to Amritsar, the Shromani Committee was in session at the Akal Takht. The meeting was at once adjourned to Ajnala. The members reached the diwan in motors at 4-30 P. M. and continued its proceedings, which had gone on undisturbed in the meanwhile. After 19 persons had spoken the Superintendent of Police came and called out one by one the names of and arrested Sardars Kharak Singh, President the Shromani Committee, Mehtab Singh, Bar-at-Law, Secretary, Sundar Singh Lyallpuri, Manager of the *Akali*, Bhag Singh and Gurcharan Singh, pleaders, and Hari Singh of Jullundur. The Superintendent of Police then read out a proclamation by the

Deputy Commissioner declaring the diwan to be an unlawful assembly under Seditious Meetings Act. It was pointed out by Professor Jodh Singh, M. A., S. Tara Singh, B. A., and others that it was a religious meeting and, therefore, would continue. The diwan went on for two hours more, and speeches were made by a large number of prominent Sikhs, members of the Gurdwara Committee and non-members. After the close of the diwan with the evening prayer, about 40 members of the Shromani Committee present there met in a separate place and elected S. Amar Singh of Jhabal as President, Captain Ram Singh as Vice-President and Bhai Tara Singh, B. A., as Secretary of the Committee.

The Shromani Committee met at the Akal Takht on 27th November and learnt from a letter of the Deputy Commissioner that even religious meetings were not exempted from the operation of the Seditious Meetings Act. The official attitude had become so prejudiced against the Shromani Committee that a regular embargo was placed on its telegrams, most of which merely announced the arrest of Sikhs without any comment; so that the Committee was obliged to appoint special messengers to convey its news to the press and to the important Sikh centres. The Committee after congratulating those arrested passed the following resolution :

"In order to keep the freedom of our sacred places and to get back the Darbar Sahib Keys and also to assert our liberty of holding religious meetings, the Gurdwara Committee resolves—

(*a*) that in all places, especially in the Districts of Amritsar, Lahore, Sheikhupura and Delhi, religious diwans be held to explain facts about the Keys affair ;

(*b*) that on 4th December, which is the day of Guru Tegh Bahadur's martyrdom, in all places diwans be held and after completing the sacred readings the following additional words be recited in the Prayer, "May God remove the persecutors of religion" ;

(*c*) that every Sikh on that day should recite the Japji five times and then offer the above Prayer ; and

(*d*) that the Gurmukhi communique issued by the Shromani Committee should be read in all such diwans."

A few days later the Committee took up the deferred question of the boycott of the Prince of Wales' visit, and passed that a complete hartal should be observed on the day of His Royal Highness's landing on the Indian shores and that no Sikh should participate in any function connected with the Royal visit. It also passed a resolution on December 6, "that no Sikh should agree to any arrangement about the restoration of the keys of the Golden Temple, unless and until all the Sikhs arrested in connection with the keys are released unconditionally."

Morning and evening diwans, exactly of the type as was held at Ajnala, were held daily in front of the Akal Takht and in the Guru Ka Bagh, where speeches were made to explain the Keys affair and to protest against the high-handed action of the Government. Arrests were made daily from among those who spoke at these meetings. S. Amar Singh of Jhabal, acting President of the Shromani Committee, Master Tara Singh, B. A., Secretary, S. Sarmukh Singh, brother of Sardars Amar Singh and Jaswant Singh of Jhabal and President of the Akali Dal, Dr. Gurbakhsh Singh, who became Secretary after Bhai Tara Singh, and Bhai Kartar Singh Poet were arrested in the Court compound in the presence of thousands of Sikhs. Perfect calm prevailed, inspite of the provoking way of making arrests. The police were asked to send in the names of those whom they wanted to arrest. As soon as the Sikh sangats came to know that one of them was wanted, they went with him to the Kotwali and handed him over to the police. Often the scenes of arrest were most impressive.

The wife or mother of the accused would come forward in the presenee of thousands who showered flowers and coins, and garlanding their hero would bless him on his way to jail. Hundreds of people poured in from different districts and offered themselves in turns for the cause of the Guru. Captain Ram Singh and Risaldar Sundar Singh, two retired Military officers, who would never have thought of displeasing the Government in any other matter, felt so strongly on this question of religious importance that they wrote to the Deputy Commissioner on December 1 that they were going to address the meeting in the Guru Ka Bagh on the Keys affair, and asked him to arrest them if he was so minded.

The movement became more intense when the leaders arrested at Ajnala, who had put in no defence, were convicted and awarded the maximum sentences prescribed by law. Sardars Kharak Singh, Mehtab Singh, Bhag Singh, Gurcharan Singh, Hari Singh and Sundar Singh were sentenced each to six months' rigorous imprisonment and a fine of Rs. 1000 or in default to another six weeks' R. I. Pandit Dina Nath, Sardar Dan Singh, Sardar Jaswant Singh and S. Teja Singh were sentenced to five months' R. I. and a fine of Rs. 1000 or in default to undergo six weeks' further R. I. ; and S. Harnam Singh Zaildar to four months' R. I. and a fine of Rs. 1000 or six weeks more in default. The standard by which religious meetings were adjudged as political will be evident from the following extract from the judgment delivered by the Additional District Judge : "There could be no doubt that in the present political situation of the Amritsar District any public discussion about the keys of the Darbar Sahib is likely to cause public excitement, and no one who stood up to make a speech on the subject could be free from political motive, and such a public meeting could not be obviously classed as a purely religious one." The Sikhs held that a meeting, in which the Holy Book was open, hymns were sung and speeches delivered contending that the Darbar Sahib could remain only under Panthic management and control and that the Government's action in interfering with such control was high-handed—such a meeting could never be conceded to be called other than purely religious. Reference in religious meetings to actions of Government was inevitable, unless the Government ceased to interfere in religious matters. Exactly a similar situation would arise in academic, commercial and other spheres of life, if Government chose to interfere in those matters.

Other leaders arrested in the same connection were similarly sentenced. S. Tara Singh, B. A., who was sentenced to 4 months' R. I. with a fine of Rs. 100, had merely repeated the resolutions of the Gurdwara Committee to the evening diwan. S. Amar Singh of Jhabal, who got 6 months with a fine of Rs. 1,000, had scrupulously avoided speaking in obedience to the orders of S. Kharak Singh, but on November 28 the following words had escaped from his lips in the morning diwan : "Khalsa Ji, what could be expected from you, when many of you cannot have the courage even to put on khaddar and black turbans?" But what could be expected from the court which depended mainly on official witnesses, the most important of whom, the Tehsildar, produced reports which had been written after the meetings from mental notes taken of all the scores of speeches delivered continuously.

As the arrests continued in full vigour, the Sikhs felt as if they were on their last trial for resolution and self-sacrifice. They grimly determined not to give in, but to see it through. Everywhere, in cities and villages, not only in the Punjab but also in Bengal and elsewhere, they held meetings to add their share to the general toll by protesting against the action of the Government. It was a great strain on the suffering capacity of the Sikhs, but they held on with the old tenacious spirit of the Khalsa. When the Sikh prisoners were daily taken to courts, it was a sight for the gods to see them singing hymns stoutly in the midst of the police bayonets and the people repeating solemnly after them. The following hymn was usually sung :—

" No king is like unto the Lord.

These rulers of the earth are only for a few days. They merely make a false show.

A man, who dedicates himself to Thee, never wavers; his influence spreads over the whole universe.

Who can lay his hand on such a man? None can dare to speak before him.

Kabir, my doubts and fears are over now. God did honour thus his Dhruva and Prahalad."

Other communities looked on with satisfaction and blessed the Sikhs for giving a good account of themselves. Beside the Khilafat and Congress associations, even the Sadhus' All-India Rajnik Mahasabha and the Parsi Rajkiya Sabha sent resolutions of sympathy and appreciation. Lala Lajpat Rai felt happy and wrote about the Sikhs: "People had thought that they were lagging behind the struggle for liberty. People had also thought that being a martial race they would be the last to imbibe the doctrine of non-violence. They have given the lie to both these misconceptions. They might have been a little behind others in the preliminary stages, but they made up the leeway rapidly and passed the others by over a length at the crucial moment; while as regards non-violence, with its attendant conception of self-sacrifice, they have given the most amazing proofs by their behaviour at Nankana Sahib on the 15th November and later at Ajnala and Amritsar. They have proved themselves worthy descendants of their Gurus and the example they have set of self-sacrifice, calm courage, devoid of swagger and absolute self-control in the face of provocation, will be hard to beat."

The Government had been trying all along to find out the best way of disposing of the Keys. When it was discovered that no Sikh would become a Sarbrah, it was proposed to form a small committee which would take over the duties of Sarbrah and with them the fatal Keys. The Government would do anything but accept the Shromani Gurdwara Parbandhak Committee, and declared it unrepresentative solely on the alleged ground that it did not include representatives of the Darbars of the Sikh States. The fact was that the Constitution of the Committee provided for representaion through election of all Sikh populations, whether in the British districts or Sikh

States, in the Punjab or outside. The Sikh States had been allotted seats as follows :— Patiala 7, Nabha 5, Jind 2, Faridkot 2, Kalsia 1, Kapurthala 2. The Sikh Maharajas had the right of nominating 4 of the total number of members allotted to their respective States. The elected representatives of these States had been attending the meetings of the Committee. Then, from the attitude of Baba Parduman Singh of Multan and others in the friendly suit, it was thought that perhaps the Babas or descendants of the Gurus might take up courage to stand against the Gurdwara Committee. It was, however, a forlorn hope. The Babas were already represented on the Committee, one of them holding a prominent position even in the Working Committee. They held a meeting of the Executive Committee of the Gurbans Conference at Amritsar on 1st January, 1922, and, inspite of their president Baba Parduman Singh, who resigned, they resolved to support the Shromani Committee. They directed their representatives, who were to appear as defendants in the friendly suit, to put the following plea—"That the Shromani Gurdwara Parbandhak Committee is an elected representative body of the Sikh Panth for the management and control of the Darbar Sahib and connected Gurdwaras, that we have got full confidence in it and that the

Government should not interfere in the Sikh religious matters."

Only two days after this the Government in a communique expressed its wish that the Keys should at once be handed over to the Executive Committee of the Gurdwara Parbandhak Committee for use in the service of the Temple for Guru Gobind Singh's birthday celebration, which was to come off on the 5th January, 1922. It also declared that it had no objection to the Committee's holding the Keys even after that day, pending the decision of the friendly suit, which the Deputy Commissioner had filed under section 92, C. P. C., in the court of the District Judge. Could not the Government have adopted this very attitude from the beginning? While the Keys remained with the Gurdwara Committee, the Government could have pleased itself by carrying on its civil suit, in which, of course, the Gurdwara Committee would have taken no part. Where was the necessity of creating so much heart-burning by taking away the Keys forcibly and arresting hundreds of Sikhs for protesting against the very action, the futility of which the Government now tacitly admitted? How could the Committee now accept the Keys, unless the Government undid the effect of its whole action? In reply to the offer conveyed through the District Judge the

Gurdwara Committee referred to its resolution of 6th December, 1921, and informed the Government officer that it could not avail itself of the proferred temporary and conditional restoration of the Keys, unaccompanied by the unconditional release of the Sikhs arrested in connection with the Keys affair. The sacred day was celebrated without the usual *jalau*.

After this the Government found it hard to find any responsible body of Sikhs that would present the case before it. Everybody said that Sardar Kharak Singh himself would take the Keys and nobody else could. The Deputy Commissioner came to the office of the Shromani Committee to note down the terms on which it would agree to take the Keys. While he was still trying to make up his mind whether the Government should release the prisoners before or after the acceptance of the Keys, Sir John Maynard made the announcement in the Punjab Council that the Sikh prisoners would be released unconditionally. It was also declared in a communique that as far as the Government was concerned it was prepared to leave the administration, as it now stood, in the hands of the Shromani Gurdwara Parbandhak Committee, and to allow the Keys to be given over at once to that Committee.

Out of 193 men arrested, most of whom had been convicted, about 150 were released on 17th January from the jails of Dera Ghazi Khan, Mianwali, Lahore and other places. With its peculiar blundering obstinacy the Government did not release Pandit Dina Nath, inspite of his co-prisoners' protest. The released Sikhs came to Amritsar on the morning of 19th January and were accorded a right royal welcome. The whole city wore a festive look. Triumphal arches, draped in khaddar and Swadeshi silks and with pictures of national heroes, had been erected all over the route. Thousands of people, Hindus, Mussalmans and Sikhs, had come out to greet the leaders with joy. The long procession, which started from the Railway Station, extended over a mile. It was a most orderly piece of exhibition. The tall muscular Akalis, clad in black and wearing kirpans, moved in front in rows of five. They were singing holy songs. Then came the bands of volunteers belonging to different denominations, showing sympathy with the sacred cause of the Sikhs. Next came the turn of ladies, thousands in number, all wearing kirpans and moving four-deep in regular detachments. They, too, were singing hymns. Then followed the carriages of the Sikh leaders, who were profusely garlanded and had at every step to stand up and acknowledge the affectionate showers of rose-petals and greetings offered by the enthusiastic crowds. There was no rush, no confusion. The spectators carefully stood aloof, lining the sides or crowding the roofs. The police were conspicuous by their absence.

At 6 P. M. the leaders reached the Akal Takht, where a big meeting was already waiting for their reception. After they had paid their respects, they were presented with robes of honour for having served the Panth well. It was announced at that time that the Clerk of the Court of the District Judge had come there to hand over the Keys to Sardar Kharak Singh. The venerable Sardar stood up, and with tears in his eyes asked permission from the sangat to take the Keys. When the bunch of Keys wrapped in red cloth was handed over to Sardar Kharak Singh, there arose a general shout of Sat Sri Akal, which rent the skies. All eyes were streaming with tears and throats choking with emotion. Sweet is pleasure after pain.

The court had decided that the Keys should be given over to the Shromani Committee, but the decision about the way in which the Darbar Sahib was to be administered was still held over. The Court formed a sub-committee of four gentlemen, impleaded in the case as defendants, to draw up a scheme of management. The scheme which was drawn up by Professor Jodh Singh, Sodhi Charn Singh, Baba Teja Singh and Professor Arbel Singh, and which is yet pending in the court, is understood to run as follows :—

"1. The Government shall have no connection with the management and control of the Darbar Sahib and connected Gurdwaras (*i. e.*, the Golden Temple, the Akal Takht, Baba Atal, Jhanda Bunga and other shrines situated in their precincts).

2. The Shromani Gurdwara Parbandhak Committee, the elected representative body of the Sikhs, shall be the sole authority for management and control of the Darbar Sahib and connected Gurdwaras, and also for the maintenance of the religious worship therein.

3. All properties (including tha Bungahs), pertaining to the Darbar Sahib and connected Gurdwaras, shall be administered by the Shromani Gurdwara Parbandhak Committee.

4. The Shromani Gurdwara Parbandhak Committee shall have full power to frame or amend rules and regulations for the management, control and maintenance of religious worship in the Darbar Sahib and connected Gurdwaras.

5. The Shromani Gurdwara Parbandhak Committee shall have full power to change the Dastur-al-Amal or make a new one.

6. The Shromani Gurdwara Parbandhak Committee shall have full power to appoint sewadars (*i. e.* Granthis, ragis, pujaris, ardasias and other sewadars).

7. The Shromani Gurdwara Parbandhak Committee shall have full power to remove, suspend, dismiss or replace any sewadar, and to inflict any suitable punishment on any sewadar for misconduct, breach of rules, negligence of duty or for any other sufficient reason. In all such cases the Shromani Gurdwara Parbandhak Committee shall be the ultimate judge, and its decisions will be final.

8. The Shromani Gurdwara Parbandhak Committee may exercise all its powers itself or delegate any or all of its powers to any of its members.

It remains to be added that in the opinion of the Committee the Shromani Gurdwara Parbandhak Committee should have the power of supervision over all other Bungahs and Akharas bordering on these Gurdwaras in order to ensure that these places are not used for a purpose offensive to the Sikh religious practices and are not misused or frequented by undesirable persons."

But as long as Pandit Dina Nath was still kept in jail, the Shromani Committee decided to consider no scheme. The Deputy

Commissioner who had promised the release of Pandit Dina Nath, when asked about it, wrote to the Gurdwara Committee saying "that if Pandit Dina Nath makes a representation to Government as to his release, his petition will be considered." The Keys had been accepted only on the understanding that the Pandit was going to be released forthwith. The Sikhs considered it more incumbent on them to strive for his release than of any Sikh, for he was suffering simply for the Sikhs. On February 8 they began again to hold meetings in contravention of the Seditious Meetings Act to protest against the detention of Pandit Dina Nath, and on the first day the whole Executive Committee made speeches on the subject. Then the gentleman was released;—a fine way of doing things indeed. Thus was the "first decisive battle won", as Mahatma Gandhi put it when he heard the news of the Sikhs' success.

CHAPTER XX.

THE THIRD WAVE OF REPRESSION.

The Government defined its attitude towards the Shromani Gurdwara Parbandhak Committee as that of sympathy, and acknowledged the Committee 'as representing a large section of Sikh religious opinion on the subject of Sikh Gurdwaras.' It also expressed its readiness to take a similar attitude in dealing with questions connected with other shrines as it had done in leaving the administration of the Golden Temple in the hands of the Committee. In dealing with disputes over the management of Gurdwaras, the local officers, while maintaining peace and order, were declared to be at liberty 'to consult the Shromani Gurdwara Parbandhak Committee or its local representatives, and to give to their views on Gurdwara questions the attention due to the representations of a large section of Sikh religious sentiment on the subject.' The Deputy Commissioners were also instructed to try to get the lands and jagirs attached to Gurdwaras entered in the name of the Gurdwaras concerned, or to form committees of management to supervise the control of Mahants. But as both of these alternatives were made subject to the consent of the Mahants, the futility of the new move was evident. Then a satisfactory Gurdwara Bill was announced to be in preparation, and the kirpan question, too, was settled—as it was understood at that time—once for all. The Government took pride in the doubtful fact that for about eight months past no Sikh had been arrested 'for wearing a sword or kirpan,' and it gave a public assurance that 'kirpans or swords worn by Sikhs' would not be interfered with, as long as they were ordinarily worn peacefully by the side and were not unsheathed except for purely religious purposes.

The Shromani Committee on its side adopted a most correct attitude. It issued instructions to Sikhs to work for a calm atmosphere. It reiterated its declaration that it was a purely religious association, and condemned the obnoxious acts perpetrated by certain persons masquerading as Akalis. Everybody thought that the whole trouble was going to be over, and that a permanent peace was in sight.

But the Sikhs were again disappointed, as the Government was trying to use the Homeopathic and the Allopathic methods both at the same time. While it was promising support in settling the Gurdwara and the kirpan questions, it was at the same time issuing orders to its officers in all the 13 districts to break up the Akali bands, who were declared to be disturbing the public tranquility in the central Punjab. The Sikh States of Patiala and Kapurthala also took similar action against the Akalis at the same time. Prosecutions for wearing kirpans were also started with full vigour. Even small axes meant for agricultural or domestic use were treated as offensive arms within the meaning of the Arms Act, if they exceeded any of the measurements laid down below :—

(1) Length of shaft from end to end 2′ 5½.″

(2) Breadth of blade from blunt side to cutting edge 4½″.

(3) Length of cutting edge from top corner to bottom corner 3½.″

Military forces were posted in the central districts in order to support the police in dispersing the Akalis and effecting their arrests. Lists were prepared of all the black-turbaned Sikhs, and their leaders were marked out for arrest or harassment by the police. The campaign of arrests began from Hoshiarpur, and spread in a short time all over the province. We can only mention a few cases that produced some stir at the time.

At Sabraon 9 Sikhs were arrested on the charge of resisting the demand made by authorities to pay the cost of the punitive police, and 8 of them were sentenced each to rigorous imprisonment for two years under Section 145 and for six months under Sec. 151 of the I. P. C., the sentences to run concurrently. What troubled the people most was not the sentences so much as the way in which the collections were forcibly made. The people had organized a Panchayat in order to effectively stamp out crime and thereby to minimise the chances of police interference. They were remarkably successful in doing this ; but the police, instead of appreciating their work, were distinctly opposed to it. The people urged their inability to pay for the punitive post on account of their poverty, but nobody would listen to them. On 7th March their village was surrounded, and after the arrest of leaders the people were subjected to beating and humiliation. Next day leaving their homes to the mercy of the police they came out, and sitting down in a retired place began to sing hymns and offer prayers. The assembly was declared unlawful and the people were dispersed, after being dragged by the *keshas* and assaulted. The police dues were then realized. The non-violence of the Sikhs in the face of great provocation was praised by all.

In Orara, another village where a Panchayat had been established, similar assaults were made on the peaceful villagers. Mr. Prance, Assistant Snperintendent of Police, admitted in court that he had pulled an Akali by the beard, but said that he did not regard it as an act of sacrilege*. Twelve Sikhs were convicted in a case arising out of a Panchayat's decision.

In several other places Sikhs came to trouble for having taken part in deciding cases in Panchayats with the full consent of the parties appearing before them. A typical case was reported from Buchhoke in Kasur Tehsil. A man had been punished by the local Panchayat for the offence of damaging crops, and he had willingly accepted the punishment. But nine men were hauled up under Sec. 342, I. P. C., before Mr. Keough.

Akalis were arrested at Amritsar, Sialkot, Lyallpur, Bughiana, Samundri, Sarhali, Sukar Chak, Verka, Fatehgarh, Marhana, Chabba, Ghawind, Hudiara, and hundreds of other places, mostly from religious diwans.

---

* In answer to a question about this put in the Legislative Council Sir John Maynard gave the following reply: "The officer referred to, who is young and inexperienced, did not intend to injure or insult the Sikh in question; he has since been informed of the respect attached to beard and hair by a Sikh, and warned that for the future he should avoid touching them."

About 15 most respectable Sikhs were arrested at Sialkot. Three first-class Magistrates, with a moving column of military police went round in three different directions in the district of Sialkot to make arrests of Akalis. From Narowal, Daska, and other villages about 80 men were hauled up. The total number of arrests in this district, according to Government's own computation, was 253, of whom 103 were discharged after some time without being even sent up for trial. The Government itself admitted in this case that the arrests had been made on a scale which suggested a lack of careful discrimination. The arrests that attracted the greatest attention were those made from the Gurdwara of Nonar in the same district.

NONAR.

The Gurdwara of Nonar is an historical place, to which 750 bighas of land, belonging to Nonar, were attached by a Sikh baron named Nahar Singh, who ruled there before the time of Maharaja Ranjit Singh. He had also endowed considerable land out of other villages, but that seems to have been confiscated after the Sikh rule. The income used to be spent on missionary work and on a free kitchen kept at the temple. The present income is about Rs. 3000 per annum.

There were many complaints about the youthful Mahant, named Harcharan Das. There is a judgment, passed on 10th July, 1916, by Lala Kesho Das, a first-class Magistrate of Sialkot, in which his findings were that Mahant Harcharan Das was of bad character, had an evil connection with a widow, named Maya Devi, and was associating with badmashes, whom he brought to the temple. It also appears that he had sold up some Gurdwara property and had alienated waqf land. He was squandering the income of the temple on Maya Devi and her relations. Although a high priest in charge of a Gurdwara, he did not know how to read Guru Granth Sahib. All day long he gambled or remained busy with his pigeons, parrots, quails, and monkeys, with which he had made the Gurdwara a regular zoo. He was under the influence of his creditors who often brought their marriage and other joy parties to the temple and desecrated it with huqqas.

The Sikh population of the place being negligibly small, the whole onus of effecting reform fell on the people of the neighbouring towns and villages. They held a big meeting at Nonar on 15th February, 1922, and appealed to the Mahant to remove the abuses. The Mahant agreed and stood up to announce that he was no master of the

Gurdwara, but a servant left there in behalf of the Sangat. He consented to work under a committee. Satisfaction was expressed by everybody, including the zemindars, who spoke through their representative, Bhai Mangal Singh, to give their approval. Two days later the Mahant willingly gave up the keys, and a list of property was prepared. On 19th February Bawa Jhanda Singh, Sub-Judge, accompanied by the Tehsildar and a Thanedar, came to Nonar to settle the case on behalf of the Government. After much discussion it was agreed that the Mahant should consent to work under the Shromani Committee and should improve his character. In the presence of the above officers and other important people of the locality, the Mahant agreed to these conditions in consideration of a suitable maintenance to be granted by the Shromani Committee. An agreement was drafted with his approval, and he declared that he would sign it after it was announced to the Sangat waiting below. When all came down, however, the Mahant absconded. The Sub-judge sent a Zaildar with Munshi Nathe Khan, a friend of the Mahant, to find him out, but they came back disappointed. By this time many respectable people, Khatris, Zemindars and others, had come to the meeting, and it was unanimously resolved by those present that the Mahant, who was a notorious bad character, should be removed. A committee of 17 members, approved by the Shromani Committee, was appointed to control the Gurdwara and its property.

A month passed and no interference was offered in the work of this committee. Rather on one or two occasions certain Government officials visited the temple and assured the Sikhs of Government support. But when the campaign of arrests began in the whole province, those Sikhs, about 40, who had taken part in the above proceedings, were arrested, some on 24th and others on 27th March, 1922, from the Gurdwara. The sacred flag was taken down and shoe-beaten by certain Kashmiris. The police, who did not prevent this desecration, were themselves seen sitting with huqqas in the temple. The Mahant was reinstated and a committee of seven (one Mohammedan, four Hindus, and two Sikhs) was appointed to help him.

Among those arrested were S. Gurcharan Singh Vakil and his old father, who is a great landlord and is looked upon in the locality as a most respectable gentleman. The charge on the latter was that he had committed dacoity and illegal interference in the temple and that he had taken away a brass-kettle, a dhotie, and a pillow from there. The case never came up for hearing, but they and others were kept in Sialkot jail for a month, during which time Mr. Fyson tried to negotiate about the appointment of a committee for Nonar. His proposal was that he would release them, if they agreed to the above mentioned committee of seven members. The Sikhs refused. They were, however, released on April 23, the Deputy Commissioner informing them that the Mahant had accepted a committee of six genuine Sikhs. Four of the so-called genuine Sikhs refused to accept membership, and the Akalis again took charge of the temple on May 3, restoring the original committee of 17 appointed by the sangat on February 20.

The Deputy Commissioner sent alarming reports to the Government and the Sikhs were blamed for ousting his second committee, which, as we have seen, never came into being. Mr. Tollinton, the Commissioner of Lahore, suggested that the Shromani Committee's representatives should meet the new Deputy Commissioner, Mr. Talbot, to settle the matter amicably. On June 7, S. Teja Singh of Samundri, Risaldar Sundar Singh and S. Gurcharan Singh met Mr. Talbot, who had also summoned the Mahant and his friends to the conference. The Deputy Commissioner enquired if the Shromani Committee was ready to give maintenance to the Mahant.

'Yes' was the reply. Bawa Jhanda Singh said that when he had first gone to make a settlement, the Akalis had consented to grant him Rs. 550 yearly, but the Mahant had asked Rs. 800. Let the Mahant come down by Rs. 150 and let the Akalis increase their offer by Rs. 150; that is, the Mahant should get Rs. 650 yearly or Rs. 55 per mensem. Then followed discussion about the formation of a committee of management. It was agreed that two members should be supplied by Akalis and two by the Mahant. The Mahant nominated Sardars Nand Singh and Sher Singh, and the Akalis named S. Harcharan Singh and S. Sher Singh Ghiaspuria. On the Mahant objecting to S. Harcharan Singh, the Sikhs accepted S. B. Varyam Singh, Hony. Captain, whose name was suggested by the Deputy Commissioner. The Mahant agreed to the settlement and a document began to be drawn up. When they had gone half-way through, the Mahant went out to take water. When he came back he was entirely changed. He would not agree to any settlement with the Shromani Committee. A Mohammedan E. A. C., who had been taking the Mahant's side, suggested that the Mahant should be given ⅓rd of the income, which he said, was fixed by him when he had recently made a committee for the Gurdwara. The Shromani Committee people agreed on the understanding that the Mahant would keep good character and that the land would be entered in the name of the Gurdwara. But the Mahant would not agree. The Deputy Commissioner asked the Shromani Committee's representatives to write down the above terms and offer them to the Mahant. They did so, and took a copy of it attested by Bawa Jhanda Singh. It was provided in the document that if the Mahant did not accept the terms, the offer would be considered withdrawn. Narowal was fixed by the Deputy Commissioner for another meeting with the Mahant, but the infatuated priest declared that he would have nothing to do with the Shromani Committee. The terms were, therefore, withdrawn with the consent of the Deputy Commissioner, and the Akali Committee remained in possession.

Heran.

In village Heran, District Ludhiana, there is a Gurdwara where Guru Hargobind had spent some time with a Sikh saint named Bhai Hamira. The couch on which the Guru had sat and the hearth where Guru's food used to be prepared are still preserved. From the days of Mahant Kirpal Das, who had fought for Guru Gobind Singh at Bhangani, the temple had been a great meeting place for the Sikhs. The Mahant of the place named Har Prasad, like his predecessor, was living with a woman of loose character, whom he kept in the upper storey of the Gurdwara. The worship in the temple was neglected. Property was being misused or alienated, and the income was being squandered on illegitimate and frivolous pleasures. The Mahant spent most of his time with his mistress or his pigeons, of which he had a large stock in the temple.

He was clearly breaking the condition of good character which had been entered in a stamped deed executed by him at the time of his appointment by the Malwa Sangat. On February 16, the same Sangat, consisting of Lambardars and other respectable people of Heran and other villages, came together and removed Har Prasad from the gaddi. He appealed to the authorities, and Mr. Hilton, the Deputy Commissioner, went there with British and Gurkha military forces with guns and a large number of police from several districts. After some days of military show it was found necessary to arrange matters amicably, especially when the Mahant openly admitted the truth of the Sangat's allegations against him. Mr. Hari Kishen Kaul, the Commissioner of Jullundur, accompanied by the representatives of the Shromani Committee, reached the spot and five Sikhs were nominated by consent of both parties to take charge of the Gurdwara, until the passage of the proposed Gurdwara Bill, or, failing that, until the case was adjudicated upon by a competent civil court. Mr. Hilton clearly declared that, the matter having been settled by mutual agreement, he would not prosecute the Sikhs who had removed the Mahant unless asked by the Government to do so. On this the Commissioner remarked that Mr. Hilton had gone further than he himself (the Commissioner) would have done; but that the District Magistrate could drop the police investigation, which was still pending, at any time, and that there was very little likelihood of his discretion being interfered with. After this regular lists were made of the Gurdwara property and the offerings and rations collected by the Sangat during its occupancy, and formally charge of everything was made over to the new committee in writing. The Commissioner and the Shromani Committee both issued communiques about the above arrangement, pending "the final settlement of the dispute by competent authority." But a little before the end of March, without the knowledge of the Shromani Committee, the committee of management was turned out and the Mahant was put in possession of the temple. The prosecution of the Sikhs who had taken part in the affair was also ordered.

The wholesale arrests of Sikhs included not only of those who had taken part in the Gurdwara reform, but of those also who were found baptizing Akalis or wearing and manufacturing kirpans. At Varyam Nangal, District Amritsar, while the Sikhs were performing the ceremony of Sikh initiation, a body of armed police appeared on the scene and began to interfere in the religious observance. They threatened that all those who would take part in the ceremony and become Akalis would be arrested. With great difficulty were they persuaded to wait until the ceremony was over, when 17 Sikhs were arrested. It was said to them at the Thana at Kathu Nangal, that those who would put off their black turbans and apologise would be let off. One man of Rasulpur agreed to this and was released. The remaining 16 having stoutly refused were taken away. On 26th March two jathas of Akalis, numbering about 70, who were coming to attend a diwan at Dosanjh in Phillour Tehsil, were arrested while only singing hymns, and were sentenced to various terms of imprisonment on the spot. In order to avoid any cause of excitement during the prevailing repression the Shromani Committee discouraged the Sikh public from holding even religious diwans. But this was misinterpreted as a weakness. In Lyallpur a Magistrate, Tikka

Rajendra Pal passed an order*, forbidding Akalis from gathering even in religious meetings in a Gurdwara.

Although the Government had declared the kirpan to be synonymous with the sword, many confiscations and arrests were being made in that connection too. Mr. E. M. Jenkins, Assistant Commissioner of Amritsar, on March 28 convicted two Sikhs, Bhais Ram Singh and Makhan Singh, for possessing kirpans and sentenced each of them to one year's R. I. About 750 kirpans were taken away by the police from the Kirpan Factories of Sardar Kharak Singh and Sardar Khazan Singh of Sialkot. The police raided a kirpan factory of Tobateksingh and arrested four Sikhs. Kirpans were also removed from a shop and two Sikhs arrested therefrom were sentenced to one year's R. I. Bhai Ajit Singh was arrested at Abbottabed for wearing a kirpan. The score of arrests reached 844 even before the end of March.

The Shromani Committee summoned an urgent meeting of its members to consider

---

* The original copy of the order which is in the Shromani Committee's possession included these words:—"I declare hereby that their assembling even in the Gurdwara is clearly for political purposes and not for religious or devotional purpose at all. As required by them I hereby again order them to go away even from this place, otherwise they will be proceeded against according to law."

the situation into which the whole movement had been thrown by the ill-considered action of the Government. On 28th March, when the repression was at its full swing, the Government sent a letter to the Secretary of the Shromani Committee to send a deputation on April 5 to discuss with the Government the draft Bill for legislation regarding Gurdwaras. The Shromani Committee met on 30th March and, in answer to the invitation, passed the following resolution :—

" While the Government and the Shromani Committee's representatives were negotiating about the Gurdwara Bill, it was agreed by both parties on 8th March, 1922, that in order to produce the requisite atmosphere nothing should be done by either party to prejudice the chances of conciliation. In pursuance of this purpose simultaneous communiques were issued. The Government made an announcement about its recognition of the Shromani Gurdwara Parbandhak Committee as representative of the Sikh religious opinion and about the freedom of the kirpan or sword. The Shromani Gurdwara Parbandhak Committee advised all Sikhs to refrain from doing anything calculated to disturb the calm atmosphere.

" The Shromani Committee is satisfied that the Sikhs have scrupulously adhered to the understanding and that the Government, in absolute disregard of its obligations, has launched forth a campaign of widespread, indiscriminate and intensive repression of the Sikhs participating in the Gurdwara reform movement under all sorts of pretexts.

"Inspite of its plighted word about the kirpan, the Government is arresting Sikhs for carrying or manufacturing kirpans, and is confiscating hundreds of kirpans from factories.

"Unmindful of the breach of faith involved, the Government has dispossessed the Sikhs of the Gurdwaras of Heran and Nonar and has made over the Gurdwaras to the sacrilegious Mahants condemned by the sangats.

"The Government is arresting and prosecuting the Sikhs peacefully worshipping in Gurdwaras.

"Hundreds of Sikhs are being indiscriminately arrested and mercilessly beaten for no obvious fault but that of wearing black turbans and kirpans.

"Even women have been molested by the police; *keshas* of Sikhs have been pulled and filthy language has been used, in the presence of Sikhs, for the Sikh Gurus.

"All this and much more, coming on the top of the High Court judgment in the Nankana Sahib case and the final refusal by the authorities to take action against the police official who made a sacrilegious attack on Guru Granth Sahib and assaulted an old Sikh lady near Sri Darbar Sahib, has shattered the belief of Sikhs in the pledges of Government, however solemnly made, and has dissipated the hope of an amicable settlement.

"Therefore the Shromani Committee feels compelled to resolve that all negotiations with the Government be broken off, until the Government gives up its unholy attempt to kill the Gurdwara Reform Movement by crushing the Akalis."

The police went on making arrests, and in a few days hundreds of more Sikhs, including 30 members with four successive Presidents and 3 Secretaries of the Shromani Committee, were hauled up. Sardar Kharak Singh, President of the Committee, was arrested on April 4 under Section 107, Cr. P. C., but two days later he was charged under Section 5 of the Arms Act for manufacturing kirpans and sentenced to one year's rigorous imprisonment. Then he was tried under another Section, the famous 124A, I.P.C., and was sentenced to three years' R.I. S. Khazan Singh, a retired E. A. C., was also arrested for manufacturing kirpans, but he threatened to start a case against the Deputy Commissioner for the latter's illegal action and was released after being kept for a few weeks in prison. Master Tara Singh,

B. A., a prominent member of the Working Committee, was arrested under Section 108, Cr. P. C., but was released soon after.

On 31st March a warrant under Sec. 107, Cr. P. C., had been issued against Sodhi Pritam Singh, who belongs to the most revered family of Anandpur. On 4th April the customary notice was issued to him to present himself within 30 days, otherwise his property would be attached. On April 16, long before the expiry of the month, when Sodhi Pritam Singh and his father Sodhi Moti Singh, called Bari Sarkar, were absent from Anandpur, a body of police surrounded the house and locked it up after turning out the *parda nashin* ladies, one of whom was pregnant. After much ado Sodhi Moti Singh was able to persuade the authorities to release his house, which was done on April 22. It was on the same day that the pregnant lady gave birth to a child. On April 26, when Sodhi Moti Singh was away, a burglary was committed at his house and his property worth Rs. 80,000 was taken away by thieves. Both father and son suffered enormously. They were hard pressed to dissociate themselves from the Gurdwara movement, but they manfully stuck to the Guru's cause.

S. Raghbir Singh, Reis of Sarhali, was asked by the Tehsildar to put off his black turban and kirpan, and was threatened with the confiscation of his jagir if he did not do so.

Bhai Ajit Singh, a cloth merchant of Pahla (district Jullundur) alighted at Ludhiana Railway Station on April 5, and was proceeding to the city to buy yarn, when he was detained by some military men near the Clock Tower and taken to their officer. His name and address were taken down and he was sent under escort to the Kotwali, where the Subdear told the Sub-Inspector of Police that the man was to be challaned under Section 109, as the order of the Deputy Commissioner was that all Akalis coming from outside districts should be challaned. The police told the Subedar to give the report and bring written orders from the Deputy Commissioner. While the report was being written, two more Akalis were brought in. They had been detained on the Railway Station, when they had alighted to change their train. Bhai Ajit Singh was then asked to get his bona-fides attested by his *arhti*, or commission agent. This was done, and yet he was pressed to give a personal security. He refused and offered to go to jail. After great trouble and delay he was released on supplying chits from certain shop-keepers from the city. Similar demand was made from the other two Akalis, but being utter strangers they could not comply. This is a typical case of trouble incurred by Sikhs for wearing black turbans and kirpans. S. Harbans Singh, a very respectable and well-known merchant of Seistan, was detained at the Railway Station of Duzdab and was told that he could not proceed any further pending further orders. He, however, communicated directly by wire with His Majesty's Consul and got permission. Other Sikhs who were not so influential suffered much in Baluchistan for no other fault than that of wearing black turbans and kirpans. On May 15, Bhai Avtar Singh, a blind musician, who belongs to the Gujranwala Sikh Orphanage, while going with his music party for preaching work, was arrested on the Railway Station Mandhra under Section 19 of the Arms Act. His fault was that he was not wearing the kirpan by his side, but was keeping it loose with him, as his shoulder-belt was broken and the sheath of the kirpan was also out of order. The Shromani Committee's deputation, consisting of Giani Sher Singh, Sardar Labh Singh, Bar-at-Law, and Sardar Dalip Singh, Bar-at-Law, was subjected to the same harassment at Ludhiana. While going from the Railway Station to the City their carriage was stopped, and they were asked to give up their kirpans. After some altercation with the police they were allowed to proceed; but they were not gone far when they saw that a jatha of Akalis was stopped by the police who forbade them to sing the sacred songs. The police men, when questioned, replied that they had orders to disperse more than two Akalis and to take away the long kirpans from them. At this the members of the deputation went to join the jatha and challenged the police to come and stop them singing hymns. They were forced to remain where they were, but they continued singing. At last a constable came and released them. The police were asked to show the order by which they were stopping people and interfering with their liberty, but they would show no order. They simply said : "Our word is the order."

Several Sikhs serving in the Army were awarded heavy punishments for wearing black turbans and kirpans. According to a report supplied to the Shromani Committee two Sikh soldiers belonging to Regiment No. 45 stationed at Jhelum were sentenced, one to 18 years' and the other to 8½ years' R. I. for insisting to wear black turbans inspite of orders to the contrary. Fifteen soldiers of the 57th Rifles stationed at Piaza Ragza were reported to have been sentenced to various terms of imprisonment ranging from 10 to 4 years for insisting to wear kirpans. Similar reports came from Mesopotamia. In answer to an allegation about certain Sikh soldier of 4th Cavalry being punished for wearing a black turban and kirpan, the Government itself admitted in a communique dated August 2, 1922, that "one man in the regiment put on a black turban and that suitable disciplinary action was taken against him." In a letter dated 27th October 1922, the Adjutant General in India mentions a Sikh sepoy being punished for wearing a black turban in a regimental Gurdwara, and orders a regimental pattern of *pagri* to be worn even in mufti to be fixed. Any contravention of this order would be punished as disobedience of orders. The whole number of arrests may be approximately put at 2000.

On several villages, which were predominately Sikh, punitive police posts were imposed and the Akalis were made to pay the same tax as badmashes. At village Hudiara in Lahore District, the punitive tax was to be realised at the rate of Re. 1 per village menial, Rs. 2 per tenant, Rs. 3 per land-holder, Rs. 30 from previous convicts or persons entered in the Register No. 9, and Rs. 40 from badmashes of the register No. 10, members of the Akali, Congress and Panchayat organizations and persons convicted under the Seditious Meetings Act, most of whom were Sikhs punished in connection with the Keys affair. At Ghawind, in the same district, a punitive police post was placed, although according to all Moderate and Congress leaders, who personally made enquirie on the spot, there was no valid reason for the location of the police. In the matter of collecting the punitive tax the Akalis were placed on the same footing as badmashes and convicts.

Although the Government had alienated the sympathy of the reforming Sikhs by carrying on a vigorous campaign of arrests against them, it still flourished before them the hope of getting a satisfactory Gurdwara Bill. It looked almost ironical. And yet the Government persistently invited the Sikhs to come and tell them what they wanted. The Sikhs insisted that they could not talk about a Bill as long as their brethren were rotting in jail. On 1st May a few Sikhs had an informal talk with Mr. Tollinton, Commissioner of Lahore, and Mr. Wilson Johnston, Home Secretary. The Government officers, when reminded of the repression of the Akalis, tried to throw the whole blame on the subordinate Magistrates and Police officers, and offered to appoint a High Court Judge to look into the Akali cases. The Sikh leaders, on the other hand, pressed for a mixed Committee of Enquiry. As there was no agreement reached on this essential point the Sikh leaders refused to talk of the Bill. Mr. W. Johnston, however, by way of a parting shot, which sounded like a threat, told them that the Bill would be carried through with the help of the Sikh members of the Council and the public outside it. The Sikh leaders retorted that if the Bill was passed inspite of the expressed wishes of the Panth, it would fail as the Rowlett Bill had failed.

The Government, however, went on with the draft, announcing now and then in the press how deliciously it was progressing under the nominal blessings of the Sikh members. The Gurdwara Committee in the meanwhile had enjoined on all Sikhs, including those in the Council, not to have anything to do with the Bill. A deputation was also sent out in the country to explain the necessity of rejecting the Bill as long as the Government pursued its aggressive policy. The Sikh opinion became unanimous in condemning the Bill and even the Sikh Councillors declared in July that they would have none of it, unless the prisoners were released and the Bill was substantially altered.

To refute this unanimity, deputations of Nirmalas and Udasis, mostly from outside the Punjab, began to appear before Sir John Maynard to oppose the claims of Akalis, who, they declared, were in a hopeless minority. The Shromani Committee, which believed itself to be the most representative body of the Sikhs, declared in answer : " Let there be a number of Commissioners freely elected by Sikh voters on the official lists prepared for the Provincial Legislative Council, and let the settlement of the Gurdwara Reform question be left entirely in their hands." Feeling that there was no hope of getting a solution of the problem from the Government, the Shromani Committee passed the following resolution on July 16, 1922 :

"As, judging from the experience of the past full year, there is no hope of getting the Gurdwara question settled through the Government, which has been trying in every way to suppress the Gurdwara Reform Movement, the only course left open to the Sikhs now is to get the service and the administration of the Gurdwaras into their own hands. Therefore this meeting of the General Committee, after full deliberation, feels itself compelled to authorise the Executive Committee to take proper action, whenever necessary, in regard to any Gurdwara which has to be brought under the Panthic control."

On 31st July, 1922, Sir John Maynard announced to the newly-assembled Punjab Council that the Government had abandoned the Gurdwara Legislation, resting contented with the fact that in about 40 cases of Sikh shrines the entries regarding property and assignments of revenue were already in the name of the institutions and that in about 15 other cases entries had now been made in the names of the shrines through the influence of Deputy Commissioners.

CHAPTER XXI.

GURU KA BAGH.

At a distance of about 12 miles from Amritsar there is a place called Guru ka Bagh, where there are two Gurdwaras, one sacred to Guru Arjan and the other to Guru Tegh Bahadur. Both of these Gurus were martyrs, who had passively suffered all the insults and tortures that the rulers of the time could inflict on them. The Gurdwara of Guru Arjan was founded in honour of the Guru's visit by Baba Ghuka, after whom is named the neighbouring village of Ghukewali. After Ghuka his descendants continued in charge of the place, which was called Guru-ka-Raur, until Guru Tegh Bahadur came to visit it; and then its name was changed into Guru-ka Bagh, as a garden was planted on the bare, desolate land and its whole outlook was made beautiful. Guru Tegh Bahadur stayed here for some time, and Baba Lall Chand, a descendant of Baba Ghuka, and other Sikhs of the neighbourhood built a nine-storeyed house for the Guru at a little distance from the Gurdwara of Guru Arjan. The tall house, however, was demolished the enemies of Sikhism in the days persecution, and later on Sardar Nahar Singh Randhawa of Chamiari built the present Gurdwara. The Gurdwara of Guru Arjan, as it stands, was built by S. Punjab Singh, an officer of Maharaja Ranjit Singh. It was also about that time that an Udasi Sadhu was appointed by the neighbouring Sangat to take care of the Gurdwara. The Sikh Maharajas, Sirdars and Zemindars granted lands for the upkeep of the Gurdwara and its free kitchen, but many lands were resumed by the British Government.

Mahant Sundar Das, in charge of the Gurdwaras, was reported to be keeping mistresses, and the Sikhs of the neighbourhood had been complaining for a long time about his character. On 31st January, 1921, some Sikhs under the leadership of S. Dan Singh went to the spot to see if they could bring the Mahant to reason. The Mahant, when he saw that the Sikhs were not after ousting him, submitted at once and signed an agreement* to the effect

* The following is an extract from the printed report of Hakim Iqram-ul-Haq, Deputy Superintendent of Police, C. I. D., produced as part of his evidence in the Nankana Sahib Massacre Case :—

"On the 31st January (1921) a party of forty men and five women of the Akali Dal under Dan Singh Jathedar of Wachhoa arrived at the Guru ka that he would marry one of his mistresses and would work under a committee of 11 Sikhs to be appointed by the Shromani Committee. The document was read out by himself in the presence of the villagers assembled. He also declared that he would get himself baptised as a regular Sikh. Five men with his consent were left to help him without expecting any remuneration, and then the Jatha withdrew. On February 8, 1921, the Mahant took Sikh baptism at the Akal Takht and was renamed Joginder Singh. His mistress Ishri also took *amrit* and was renamed Gian Kaur. On the same day she was married to the Mahant at the Akal Takht according to the Sikh rites.

An account of all these proceedings was published in the press.

Bagh Gurdwara, Sansra, from Amritsar. The Mahant, Sundar Dass, was aware of their intention and had collected fifty or sixty men to meet them. There were also about three hundred villagers present. Terms on which the Mahant might remain in possession of the Gurdwara were announced to him. These were that he should take Amrit, work in consultation with a Committee and marry his paramour. He agreed to these terms. A number of persons were appointed as members of the Committee and a day was fixed for the Amrit ceremony.......It is true that many Mahants are very bad characters and are generally most unpopular with the people in the neighbourhood of their Gurdwaras."

After the Nankana Sahib tragedy, when Sikhs began to be arrested in large numbers, this Mahant, like so many others, went back on his pledges and adopted his old ways. On August 23, 1921, the Shromani Committee was obliged to take charge of the institution in its own hands. The rejected Mahant sought the help of the authorities, but when Mr. Macpherson, Superintendent of Police, went to the spot with a force of police and studied the facts, he confirmed the possession of Sikhs and left a body of police to protect the Akalis in charge of the place. After some time when the danger of an attack from the Mahant's party was over, the Superintendent of Police wrote to the Gurdwara Committee that he wanted to remove the police guard, unless the Gurdwara Committee wished to retain it at its own cost. Tbe Gurdwara Committee consented to the withdrawal of the police.

In February, 1922, the Mahant agreed to abide by the decision of three arbitrators, S. Teja Singh of Samundri, S. Gurcharan Singh and S. Bal Singh, about his maintenance. They decided to offer him Rs. 120 p. m. and a house at Amritsar, and he accepted this offer ; but, encouraged by the repressive policy of the Government towards the Akalis in March and April, he went back again on his word.

Ever since the Gurdwara had come under the Committee's control the fire-wood required for the free kitchen attached to the Gurdwara had always been taken, as of right, from a portion of the land which is entered in the name of the Gurdwara and which is not, and has never been, "valuable agricultural land" as has been alleged, but a mere grove of *kikar* trees for which no land revenue had ever been paid. It was from the same place that on August 8, 1922, five Akalis, who were admittedly in charge of the Gurdwara, cut wood from a dry kikar tree for use in the Gurdwara kitchen. They were arrested on August 9, not on the complaint of the Mahant, but by the orders of Mr. Dunnett, the Deputy Commissioner, on the basis of a confidential diary of Bedi Brijlal Singh. It was on August 10, after Mr. Beaty and other officers and policemen had reached the spot, that the complaint of Mahant Sundar Das was obtained in support of the step which had already been decided upon. On August 10 the arrested Sikhs were hurriedly convicted of theft and sentenced to six months' rigorous imprisonment with a fine of Rs. 50 each. The Sikhs had got the same right to cut wood from the Gurdwara land as to control the Gurdwara itself. Both go together. The property of a Gurdwara is a trust meant only for the maintenance of the Gurdwara and its institutions, like the free kitchen, and it cannot be used for any other purpose. It was, therefore, unjustifiable on the part of Government to start criminal proceedings against the Sikhs at Guru ka Bagh in aid of a Mahant who, having now no Gurdwara to support, was still trying to use the trust property for his own private and illegitimate purposes.

The Sikhs did not cease to exercise their right of cutting wood for the Guru's kitchen. The police, which had remained inactive in the meanwhile, became suddenly active on 22nd August and began to carry out wholesale arrests of Sikhs. By 24th August, 180 arrests had been made and on the 25th the total reached 210. With the return of the Deputy Commissioner from Simla the policy of beating under Section 127 and 128 of the Cr. P. C. began in order to overawe the Sikhs. On the very first day of his arrival about 100 Akalis were severely beaten with fists, kicks and the butt-ends of guns. The next day about 40 Akalis, left in the garden in charge of Guru Granth Sahib, were beaten with lathis and dragged by the hair, simply because they had dared to remove the Holy Book from the sun and brought it under shade. On the 26th the following office-bearers and workers of the Shromani Committee were arrested for abetting theft.

and the holding of unlawful assemblies :— Sardar Mehtab Singh, Bar-at-Law, President; Bhai Jaswant Singh, B. A., General Secretary; Sardar Narain Singh, Bar-at-Law, Secretary; Bhai Sahib Singh, B. A., Assistant Secretary; Master Tara Singh, B. A., Member of the Working Committee; Sardar Sarmukh Singh of Jhabal, Member of the Working Committee and President of the Shromani Akali Dal; Sardar Teja Singh of Chuharkana, Member of the Executive Committee and Vice-President of the Shromani Akali Dal; and Sardar Ravel Singh, Member of the Shromani Committee and Secretary, District Gurdwara Committee, Amritsar.

On the 26th Baba Kehar Singh, the great peace-maker, had brought round the Mahant to acknowledge his guilt and agree to an understanding with the Panth. Mr. Beaty and the Tehsildar were pleased with the prospect of a settlement, and the former gave his car to Baba Kehar Singh and the Tehsildar to take the Mahant to Amritsar and make peace with the Shromani Committee.

Before sitting in the car, however, Baba Kehar Singh said that he would like to cut wood from the land in dispute, as he had pledged to do so. Mr. Beaty said that when a compromise was going to be made any number of trees might be cut. The Baba Sahib cut some wood from the grove and brought it to the Gurdwara. Then they started for Amritsar. Before entering the city, however, the Tehsildar took them to the bungalow of the Deputy Commissioner, who expressed his satisfaction when he heard from the Mahant that he had made a compromise with the Shromani Committee. As soon as Baba Kehar Singh had gone out of his room, the Deputy Commissioner called in the Tehsildar and then again Baba Kehar Singh, whom he told that warrants had been issued for his arrest. This startled even the Tehsildar, who had hoped for a better appreciation of the situation by the Deputy Commissioner. The Deputy Commissioner asked Babaji to go back to Guru ka Bagh and get himself arrested there, for his arrest in Amritsar would have brought discredit upon the Tehsildar The Baba Sahib did so and was arrested. On 27th the batch of Sikhs who went to cut wood at Guru ka Bagh were beaten and ducked. About 96 who had been kept under arrest in the Garden were asked to march towards Amritsar. When they did so they were belaboured with lathis and left unconscious on the ground.

From that time onward the policy of beating the Sikhs in Guru ka Bagh or on the road leading thereto was followed most vigorously. The Sikhs, too, began to pour in from all directions to put in their share of sacrifice at the altar of the Guru. All approaches to Guru ka Bagh were stopped and no means were left to the blockaded Sikhs for receiving provisions or any other kind of help. Those who were suspected of preparing or taking provisions for them were beaten and the rations seized. A professor of the Khalsa College, Amritsar, who was going with his family towards Guru ka Bagh, was severely assaulted in the presence of his ladies. All pilgrims proceeding to Amritsar were detrained at Lahore and other stations in the neighbourhood of Amritsar, and were sent back or arrested. The roads, bridges and ferries were also picketted.

Inspite of these restrictions, however, Sikhs were able, somehow or other, to reach Amritsar. Every day at the Akal Takht a party of Sikhs took a solemn vow to go for sacrifice, and under all circumstances to remain non-violent in word and deed. Another jatha, of a smaller size, would go every day from the Gurdwara of Guru ka Bagh to assert their right of chopping wood for the Guru's kitchen. Both the jathas were beaten invariably in a most heartless manner until all the Akalis became senseless.

In the beginning no medical relief was allowed to be sent to the injured, and a small party of doctors and scouts was actually driven out unceremoniously from Guru ka Bagh, even though they had a permit from the Deputy Commissioner. But afterwards it was allowed, and a regular service of doctors and assistants was arranged by the Committee in Amritsar. There were three big well-equipped hospitals maintained at the cost of about Rs. 2,000 a day, and a set of ablest doctors belonging to different communities offered themselves to attend to the wounded.

From 31st August onward everyday a jatha of about 100 Akalis, after taking the vow of non-violence at the Akal Takht, would start from Amritsar with a train of ambulance cars and take the road to Guru ka Bagh. It was invariably stopped in the way, and beaten mercilessly with lathis until all its members became unconscious. When the police had done their work, they would drag the prostrate and wounded Sikhs by their sacred hair and throw them into muddy ditches or leave them in the fields. Then the forces of mercy, the medical relief party supplied by the Shromani Committee, would begin their work. They would bring the wounded in ambulance lorries to Amritsar and put them in the Committee's hospitals.

The beating was mostly directed at the joints or the private parts, so that the Akalis might be soon disabled or made unconscious. It was declared to be most cowardly and inhuman by all the great leaders like Pandit Malaviyaji, Hakim Ajmal Khan and Mr. C. F. Andrews. The whole affair is full of harrowing details, but we will give here a few impressions of what went on for about a month. The following joint report was issued by a few most prominent journalists :—

As is well known, every day a jatha generally composed of about 100 men started from Amritsar to Guru-ka-Bagh after taking the vow of non-violence before *Akal Takht.* Their immediate objective for the day was the Gurdwara at Guru-ka-Bagh, though it was understood that, on some other day, they might be allowed to go forward to the disputed land in small batches of three, four or five. The jathas were stopped at some point *en route* to Guru-ka-Bagh by a body of policemen armed with regulation lathis, and dealt with in the manner described below. Policemen on horseback were sometimes added, while on two occasions the police were supported by cavalry also.

We should like to add here that the vow of non-violence taken by the bigger jathas before *Akal Takht* at Amritsar, or by the smaller batches of three, four or five men before the Darbar Sahib at Guru-ka-Bagh, was kept by all the Akalis to the letter. Not a single individual, out of the hundreds of men whom we saw being severely beaten with lathis and kicked and in several cases having their beards and sacred hair pulled, etc., etc., *raised even his little finger by way of resistance or retaliation.* Let any responsible officer of Government come forward and deny this fact. Every day, both at Guru-ka-Bagh itself and at one point or another on the road leading to it, the beating was carried on under the immediate orders and supervision of, and often led by, one or more British Police Officers (Superintendent, Additional Superintendent and Assistant Superintendent of Police) and, on certain occasions, high Police and Civil Officers like the Inspector-General, and the Deputy Inspector-General, and the Deputy Commissioner, Amritsar, and the Commissioner, Lahore Division, were present at the scene.

It may be a marvel or even a miracle of human endurance and patient, resigned, prayerful suffering which the Akalis have shown, but it is a miracle which thousands of persons saw with their own eyes, and which we witnessed with admiration and reverence on a dozen occasions or more.

The Police excesses were most in evidence in three separate areas, *viz.* (1) at three specific points on the road leading from Amritsar to Guru-ka-Bagh Gurdwara, a distance of 12 miles, *viz.*, Gumtala, Raja Sansi and Chhinna bridge, (2) at Guru-ka-Bagh itself, specially on the boundary line between the premises of the Gurdwara and the attached land which is the subject of dispute, and (3) the villages surrounding it. We consider it convenient to give a general idea of the excesses in each of these areas and then leave it to others to judge for themselves how far the Home Member's statement does justice to the terrible realities of the situation as we witnessed it from day to day.

I.—(*a*) GUMTALA BRIDGE.

September 1. On this date, the Jatha was stopped on the road by the Police armed with lathis, not *batons*. Out of a dozen occasions not once have we witnessed the Police even carrying batons. The lathis were about 5 feet long, iron-bound at one end to a length o about 5 to 6 inches, and brass-bound to the same length at the other end. There was also, in some cases, a round metal knob at the thicker end. The lathis were about 1½ inches thick, and they were plied mercilessly on the backs, heads and other parts of the person including the private parts. Professor Jodh Singh, M. A., lately Principal, Guru Nanak Khalsa College, Gujranwala, (a Moderate gentleman) also witnessed the beating on this occasion, and he says in his Daily Gurmukhi paper, the *Khalsa* (September 4): "It lasted for about twenty minutes and, on a signal being given with a flag, the cavalry was ordered to advance forward. The whole column came up close to the Jatha, but only three horsemen advanced and passed over the Akalis, and hurt some of them with the hoofs of their horses. Many spectators were weeping and crying aloud and were shocked." He further writes, on the strength of the Doctor's report, that out of those wounded at Gumtala Bridge, there was one serious case. He was probably hit on the private parts and, as he could not pass urine for a considerable time, his bladder had to be evacuated by artificial means. In two cases, wounds were produced probably by the hoofs of horses. There were several cases in which the injuries were inflicted on the private parts.

(*b*) Raja Sansi.

The next day the scene of beating was shifted to Raja Sansi, six miles from Amritsar, on the road to Guru-ka-Bagh. Pandit Madan Mohan Malaviya came upon the spot immediately after the beating had taken place, and while most of the men were still lying in an unconscious or disabled condition, on either side of the road, like so many corpses, as he himself described the sight. The Senior Superintendent of Police and two other European Officers were present. The representative of the Associated Press and one other European were also there. As soon as the Jatha reachcd a point on the road close to the village of Raja Sansi, a body of lathi police led by two European officers rushed on them from the side and after asking them to disperse, which they refused to do, charged them. The sight was one of the most frightful witnessed in connection with the Guru-ka-Bagh. The Sikhs stood with folded hands singing hymns. As soon as the Policemen came near, they sat down on the ground with their heads bending forward, still singing, "Wahiguru, Wahiguru, Wahiguru Ji, Satnam, Satnam, Satnam Ji." This they continued till they all became unconscious or exhausted by severe beating. A shower of lathis and kicks fell on them to the accompaniment of a drum, which the police had brought with them and which now began to beat. It was a frightful sight and was witnessed by several thousand persons who also uttered prayerfully "Wahiguru, Wahiguru, Wahiguru Ji." Soon some of the Akalis lay prostrate. The lathi blows continued descending vigorously and quickly on those still sitting, till all lay down stretched on the ground. Those that lifted up their heads received blows individually. They were then dragged and kicked, a few were lifted up by two or more Policemen and thrown from a height of at least three feet into pits on either side of the road. Here they received first-aid treatment from doctors and boy-scouts, who had volunteered their services, before they were carried on stretchers into motor-lorries which had been provided by the public and the Gurdwara Parbandhak Committee. The Police force on this occasion was partly composed of Gurkhas and partly of Mussalmans from Sone Ilaqa of the Shahpur District. Subsequently Pathans were also added. A lady was abused and roughly treated while attending to the wounded. Some on-lookers were also beaten, but none received severe injuries.

(c) Chhinna Bridge.

On the following day, the police moved a mile and a half further up the road before blocking the way for the Jatha. This point is situated only a short distance from Chhinna bridge. The police had pitched their camp here, and up to the 9th September when the Jatha was allowed for the first time to pass on without obstruction, this point was, day after day, the scene of police excesses practised on a Jatha of about 100 Akalis. Here the beating (on the 3rd) was even severe than that on the previoue day, and it was carried on till late after nightfall. Pandit Madan Mohan Malaviyaji, Sirdar Jogender Singh, Member, Council of State, and some twenty other leading Sikh gentlemen, including several members of the local Legislative Council and the Chief Khalsa Diwan, were present in the evening, but being assured by one of the officers present that no beating would be given to the Jatha during the night they returned at about 8-30 p. m. As soon as the police came to know that Pandit Malaviyaji had gone away, they rushed forward and charged the Akalis, who were at this moment squatting on the ground singing hymns. No warning was given and both the Akalis and on-lookers were rushed upon and beaten. The Akalis went on chanting *Wahi-Guru* and *Satnam*, while blow after blow descended upon them. They were then dragged and kicked. Some of the wounded men were thrown into a shallow running water-channel on one side, and afterwards they were dragged far into the field and left there. Some were thrown on the low lying ground off the road. They were struck with lathis and kicked in all parts of the body. On this, as well as on other occasions, we noticed kicks being given on private parts of the Akalis. Some of the officers not only took part in the beating but very often they led the way. The drum wa used on the 3rd September as on the previous day.

The scene on the following five days, when the Jathas were stopped at this point on the road, was equally heart-rending. On the 4th a novel method was tried. We saw the crowds of on-lookers being chased into the fields, and there some of them were robbed. Numerous complaints were brought to our notice there and then, including some from very respectable gentlemen. Some of us brought a few specific cases to the notice of the Superintendent of Police and the Naib-Tehsildar. Certain Policemen were pointed out and the officers were requested to have them searched in our presence, but not only was no heed paid to this request, but one of the officers gave a threatening reply, saying: "Go and report at the *Thana* and see the result."

On this occasion, the officer in charge delayed the beating till late at night and then told Pandit Madan Mohan Malaviya that he was not going to administer any beating, adding that if every body left the place, the Akalis would disperse to their homes. The officer solemnly assured Pandit Madan Mohan Malaviya and others, again and again, that there would be no beating that night, and that the men would not be molested during the night. He further said that the Akalis had no heart in the movement, and that, if they were left to themselves, they would slip away, one by one, during the night. At his request the ambulance cars, doctors, boy-scouts and even the reporters were sent back half a mile from the scene of action. Only three press representatives were allowed to lie down un-observed at a point off the road some little distance behind the Akali Jatha, which was squatting on one side of the road leaving about half the road free for traffic. One doctor was also allowed to be close at hand to send for his assistants in case of need. The three press representatives first noticed two white-turbaned men being led away by the Policemen, then an old man with a black turban, then another white-turbaned man, and after this several men being dragged, carried, beaten and kicked. The men were loudly protesting against the "Zulum," saying they would rather die than go back. Several of these men, who were able to walk, actually returned and rejoined the Jatha. After this there was a lull for a short time and every one thought there would be no more beating. At about 10-15 p. m. Pandit Madan Mohan Malaviyaji, who was meanwhile waiting at a distance along with some members of the Chief Khalsa Dewan, left the place at our request and only a couple of minutes after his departure, general beating began as on the previous days. The beating, kicking, dragging, ducking and throwing into the fields went on as usual, only the beating was much severer, probably because of exaspertion at the failure of the "experiment", or the late hour. This latter part of beating was witnessed by many of us, though earlier in the night, while the officers' experiment of testing the faithfulness of the Akalis was in progress, only three reporters were present. Owing to the great distance to which the wounded Akalis had been dragged or carried into the fields on this day, it took the doctors and the boy-scouts a couple of hours to search for the men and carry them to the ambulance cars. They were afraid lest some one should remain unattended to during the night.

On the 9th September, the Government came to the conclusion that there was no hope of its successfully coercing the Sikhs into submission and that the public indignation, which was becoming more articulate, was doing irreparable harm to its reputation. The police post on the road to the Gurdwara was, therefore, withdrawn and the Jatha of that day, the Daljit Jatha, as it was appropriately called, was the first to proceed to Guru-ka-Bagh without molestation on the way.

II.—At Guru-ka-Bagh.

Here four or five small batches, generally of three, four or five men, proceeded from the Gurdwara to the " Garden " day after day for about a fortnight to assert their religious right to cut fuel for the Gurdwara's free kitchen and were dealt with by the Police with *lathi* blows, kicks, etc. In some cases the beard was pulled, and at least in one case a Gurkha Policeman put his heavily booted foot right across the neck of a fallen man and kept the man down in that condition for about a minute. A little while after the foot was removed, the man got up and faced the Gurkha Policeman again, only to be thrown and beaten and kicked more severely than before, till he became quite unconscious. Almost all the men were either disabled or became unconscious before they were finally removed on stretchers from the scene of action. This was the usual practice day after day. Kicks in private parts and other delicate parts were not infrequent, and not much care was taken as to where the *lathi* blows fell. Men were pulled by their hair or the beard. In several cases the face was covered with blood by cuts on the head or the face. During the last four or five days the method of using the *lathi* was varied, but the results, so far as serious injuries are concerned, were but a little better, while the kicks were continued as before. In certain cases strangulation was also adopted. Hakim Ajamal Khan himself noticed one such case.

III.—Beating and extortion by the police in the villages surrounding Guru-ka-Bagh.

We have no personal knowledge of these excesses, though several of us have seen some men, who stated that they had been severely beaten and fleeced by bands of policemen, who visited the villages all round Guru-ka-Bagh and, according to our information, terrorised the villagers. In some villages a good many men were beaten on suspicion of sending supplies or articles of food to the Gurdwara, which was blockaded by a cordon of police pickets. One man of Sansara Kalan had 24 clear marks of what were apparently *lathi* blows on his back, some faint ones on his chest, and four marks on his loins near the private parts. These last were examined by a Vakil friend at our request in a secluded spot. Another man showed us 18 marks, while a third bore 21 marks. It is useless to go into all the stories that we heard. If these stories are to be believed, and we say again that we met so many persons, off and on, from different villages who deposed to having suffered at the hands of the Police that we do not see any reason to disbelieve them—a regular reign of terror existed in this area for about a week. The death of two persons, Bhai Bhagat Singh and Bhai Tara Singh (father and son) in the fields near the village Tera, the details of which have been published in the papers, is part of this story.

Before closing this statement we would like to give a brief analysis of the wounded persons who were admitted into the hospitals after receiving the beating, to show, at a glance, the nature of the injuries inflicted by the Police in "dispersing" the Akali Jathas by the use, as the Government claims, of the 'minimum force' necessary for the purpose. Out of about 1300 persons, more or less, who received the beating, 269 cases of injuries above the trunk have been reported by Col. Gulab Singh, the medical officer in charge of the hospitals, 300 cases of injuries on the frontal part of the body and 60 cases of injuries to testicles. There are 79 cases of brain injuries, 19 cases of injuries to prenium and 7 to teeth. There were 158 contused wounds, 40 cases of urine trouble, 8 of incised wounds, 2 of punctured wounds, 9 of fractures, and 2 of dislocations, an alarming total of 953 cases! It addition to these, there were 120 men who received a beating at Guru-ka-Bagh and are not taken into account in the figures given above. Mr. C. F. Andrews visited the main hospital at Amritsar, provided by the Gurdwara Parbandhak Committee, several times and saw serious cases of various kinds.

A word may also be said about the snapshot photographs that were taken on the various occasions. Owing to the special conditions prevailing on these occasions, the photographs do not show—indeed, even in the best circumstances, they could not show all that took place; but there is enough in them to support our statement, if any support were needed, of the facts witnessed by thousands of persons. It is a pity that we have to controvert statements made in a document of the weight and importance like the one which has been issued by the Home Member; but it will, we hope, be recognised that we are not only privileged to defend our honour and that of our profession against undeserved aspersions cast on us in the official statement, but that we owe a duty to the public at large and, above all, to Truth. This duty became all the more pressing and imperative, when we found that S. Man Singh's motion in the Legislative Assembly asking for an adjournment of the House in order to consider the grave Akali situation was disallowed by the President on a technical ground, and thus a valuable and much needed opportunity for an open discussion of the happenings connected with Guru-ka-Bagh was denied to the public.

(Sd.) RUCHI RAM SAHNI, M. A.,
Trustee and Representative of the *Tribune*, (Lahore).

(Sd.) GIAN CHAND RAMPAL,
Joint Editor, *Bande Matram*, Lahore.

(Sd.) G. A. SUNDRAM, B. A., B. L;
Assistant Editor, *Independent*, Allahabad.

(Sd.) BALMOKAND VARMA,
Representative, *Swarajya*, Madras.

(Sd.) MILKHI RAM.
Representative, *Bande Matram*, Lahore.

(Sd.) SHAFAAT ULLAH,
Manager, *Zamindar*, Lahore.

(Sd.) ABDUL MAJID ATIQI,
Representative, *Zamindar*, Lahore.

(Sd.) UTTAM SINGH, GYANI.
Representative, *Akali-te-Pardesi*, Amritsar.

(Sd.) ANAND NARAIN SEWAL, B.A. LL.B.
Assistant Editor, the *Tribune*, Lahore.

Lahore, 26th Sept., 1922.

In order to show how the jathas proceeded to Guru-ka-Bagh and how the beating was delivered, we cannot do better than quote in full the description given by Mr. C. F. Andrews of what he saw on September 12 :—

"At 1 p.m. on that day I started for Guru-ka-Bagh, and after leaving the main road proceeded along the bank of a canal. There were three tongas in all. When we had gone some distance along the bank of the canal, we saw two Sikhs in black turbans on the opposite bank waving their hands to us and pointing to the sky, where a great bird was circling in its flight towards Amritsar. Immediately all those who were in the tongas got down and eagerly pointed out the bird to me and told me that every day, as soon as the beating at Guru-ka-Bagh began, the golden hawk rose from the Guru's garden and took its flight to Amritsar to tell those who were serving at the Golden Temple what was taking place. They asked me if I had seen the bird, and I answered that I had seen in the distance the great bird which they had pointed out, but that I could not say whether it was a golden hawk or not. They said to me, "*That* was the bird. It *was* the golden hawk. It has gone to tell at the Durbar Sahib about the sufferings of the people." There *was* a light in their faces as they spoke to me, which betokened joy. I was especially struck by the look of devotion in the face of a Sikh lady of middle age who accompanied us. I can only describe it by saying that she looked, in her quiet devotion, like a picture of the "Madonna." The whole scene—the intense faith of my companions, the look of reverence in their faces, the solemn awe mingled with joy, moved me very deeply. It was the first event which really gave me the religious atmosphere of all that I was afterwards to experience in the later scenes. It put me in touch with the Akali reform movement in its spiritual aspect as perhaps nothing else could have done.

After leaving the bank of the canal we had to pass across open ground for a long distance which was covered with water in certain places. Our progress was naturally slow in the tongas. We met on the route a band of hundred Akalis in black turbans, who had marched that morning from Amritsar after having taken the vow at the Golden Temple that they would not commit one single act of violence, either by word or deed. I was to see, later on, how faithfully they kept that vow. On subsequent days I had opportunities of witnessing the scene at the Golden Temple itself, as they came out with religious joy written on their faces and a tiny wreath of white flowers placed on their black turbans which dedicated them to the sacrifice. I was able to see also, in the city, the crowds of spectators, Hindus, Musalmans, and those of every religion, welcoming and encouraging them, as they marched solemnly and joyfully forward calling upon the name of God as their protector and saviour. There, in the city, they were at the very beginning of their pilgrimage. Mile after mile of mud-stained, water-logged road lay before them. When I saw them on this first day of my visit, as they drew near to the end of their march, they were bespattered with mud and dirt and perspiration was streaming from them; but their garlands of white flowers were still encircling their black turbans, they were still uttering with triumphant voices their prayer to God for protection, and the light of religion was still bright upon their faces. There were some who were young lads among them, and a very few old men with grey beards who had insisted on being taken and would not be denied; but the great majority were of military age and it was easy to guess that out of these stalward bearded men there had been many who had served in the army. I had an opportunity later of getting accurate statistics, and it would appear that at least one in three of the Sikhs in these Akali Jathas (as they are called) had been a soldier and had served during the Great War.

We got down from the tongas and went along with them for some distance. I was dressed in my English dress, with a sun helmet on my head, but even before they knew my name they returned my greeting without the slightest trace of bitterness in their faces. There was a halt to drink water and they got to know who I was and came forward. Then one who was serving water with a brass vessel came to me and offered the water to me also to drink. I put my hand forward to receive it, but he said to me, 'Please take the vessel itself,' and I took it in my hands and drank from it. The act had a strongly religious aspect to me. It was as if I was sharing in a sacrament of consecration before the suffering was to begin.

At any place where water could be received along the road there were villagers, both men and women, who waited eagerly each day to fulfil this small act of service by giving water to the Akali Jathas. Again, I noticed the extraordinary devotion of the women. Their faces were full of motherly tenderness towards those who were going forward, in the name of their religion, to receive suffering without retaliation.

After very great difficulty and many halts at impassable places we reached Guru-ka-Bagh at last. The first sight that met our gaze was that of eight motor lorries, such as usually carry passengers for hire which were now being used as a substitute for ambulance wagons. When I looked at them, I could picture vividly the acute suffering to those who would be carried in them for more than fourteen miles to the base hospital in the city. Here and there the motors would almost certainly get stuck in the deep mud. The jolting in other places would be difficult to bear even for a man who was quite well. What must it have been to men who were suffering from many contusions and wounds?

There was one act of humanity which might at once have been thought of on the part of the officials, but no one among them seemed to have noticed it or suggested it. The public road along the canal was almost worse, from the point of view of jolting, than the open track beyond. But on the other side of the canal was a private road, kept for officials, along which the motor lorries with the wounded persons might have passed smoothly and quickly. It would have been an inexpressible relief to them on that terrible journey back from Guru-ka-Bagh, if the lorries had been allowed to use it. But the subordinate Government officials who were approached time after time by the doctors and attendants refused altogether to allow them. I am quite certain that if the higher officials had been approached they would not have refused. But one of the greatest hardships in India at the present time is the tension which exists on both sides, the open gulf which grows day by day wider and wider, the almost complete distrust with which Indians have learnt, by bitter experience, to regard the official world.

When I reached the Gurdwara itself, I was struck at once by the absence of excitement such as I had expected to find among so great a crowd of people. Close to the entrance there was a reader of the Scriptures who was holding a very large congregation of worshippers silent as they were seated on the ground before him. In another quarter there were attendants who were preparing the simple evening meal for the Gurdwara guests by grinding the flour between two large stones. There was no sign that the actual beating had just begun and that the sufferers had already endured the shower of blows. But when I asked one of the passers-by, he told me that the beating was now taking place. On hearing this news I at once went forward. There were some hundreds present seated on an open piece of ground watching what was going on in front, their faces strained with agony. I watched their faces first of all, before I turned the corner of a building and reached a spot where I could see the beating itself. There was not a cry raised from the spectators, but the lips of very many of them were moving in prayer. It was clear that they had been taught to repeat the name of God and to call on God for deliverance. I can only describe the silence and the worship and the pain upon the faces of these people, who were seated in prayer, as reminding me of the shadow of the Cross. What was happening to them was truly, in some dim way, a crucifixion. The Akalis were undergoing their baptism of fire, and they cried to God for help out of the depth of their agony of spirit.

Up till now I had not seen the suffering itself except as it was reflected in the faces of the spectators. But when I passed beyond a projecting wall and stood face to face with the ultimate moral contest, I could understand the strained looks and the lips that silently prayed. It was a sight which I never wish to see again, a sight incredible to an Englishman. There were four Akali Sikhs with their black turbans facing a band of about a dozen police, including two English officers. They had walked slowly up to the line of the police just before I had arrived and they were standing silently in front of them at about a yard's distance. They were perfectly still and did not move further forward. Their hands were placed together in prayer and it was clear that they were praying. Then, without the slightest provocation on their part, an Englishman lunged forward the head of his lathi which was bound with brass. He lunged it forward in such a way that his fist which held the staff struck the Akali Sikh, who was praying, just at the collar bone with great force. It looked the most cowardly blow as I saw it struck and I had the greatest difficulty in keeping myself under control. But beforehand I had determined that I must, on no account, interfere by word or deed, but simply watch ; for the vow, which had been taken by the sufferers, must be sacred to me also. Therefore passive silence on my part was imperative, but it is difficult to describe to those who have not seen the sight with their own eyes how difficult such a passive attitude was.

The blow which I saw was sufficient to fell the Akali Sikh and send him to the ground. He rolled over, and slowly got up once more, and faced the same punishment over again. Time after time one of the four who had gone forward was laid prostrate by repeated blows, now from the English officer and now from the police who were under his control. The others were knocked out more quickly. On this and on subsequent occasions the police committed certain acts which were brutal in the extreme. I saw with my own eyes one of these police kick in the stomach a Sikh who stood helplessly before him. It was a blow so foul that I could hardly restrain myself from crying out loud and rushing forward. But later on I was to see another act which was, if anything, even fouler still. For, when one of the Akali Sikhs had been hurled to the ground and was lying prostrate, a police sepoy stamped with his foot upon him, using his full weight ; the foot struck the prostrate man between the neck and the shoulder. A third blow, almost equally foul, was struck at an Akali when he was standing at the side of his fallen companion. This blow hurled him across the body of the fallen man who was unconscious at the very time when he was being taken up by two ambulance workers. The intention of such a blow was so brutally insolent, that I watched for the Englishman in command, in this as also in other cases, to rebuke the police sepoy who did the deed, but as far as I could see he did nothing to check or to rebuke his men. I told all these things that I had seen to the Governor and every officer whom I met the next day.

The brutality and inhumanity of the whole scene was indescribably increased by the fact that the men who were hit were praying to God and had already taken a vow that they would remain silent and peaceful in word and deed. The Akali Sikhs who had taken this vow, both at the Golden Temple before starting and also at the shrine of Guru-ka-Bagh, were, as I have already stated, largely from the army. They had served in many campaigns in Flanders, in France, in Mesopotamia and in East Africa. Some of them at the risk of their own safety may have saved the lives of Englishmen who had been wounded. Now they were felled to the ground at the hands of English officials serving in the same Government which they themselves had served. They were obliged to bear the brunt of blows, each of which was an insult and humiliation, but each was turned into a triumph by the spirit with which it was endured.

It was a strangely new experience to these men, to receive blows dealt against them with such force as to fell them to the ground, and yet never to utter a word or strike a blow in return. The vow they had made to God was kept to the letter. I saw no act, no look, of defiance. It was a true martyrdom for them as they went forward, a true act of faith, a true deed of devotion to God. They remembered their Gurus how they suffered, and they rejoiced to add their own sufferings to the treasury of their wonderful faith. The onlookers, too, who were Sikhs, were praying with them and praying for them, and the inspiration of their noble religion, with its joy in suffering innocently borne, could alone keep them from rushing forward to retaliate for the wrong which they felt was being done.

There has been something far greater in this event than a mere dispute about land and property. It has gone far beyond the technical questions of legal possession or distraint. A new heroism, learnt through suffering, has arisen in the land. A new lesson in moral warfare has been taught to the world. This fact, in the ultimate issue, is independent of the mere legal question of trespass decided for or against the Akali Sikhs. They believe intensely that their right to cut wood in the garden of the Guru was an immemoral religious right, and this faith of theirs is surely to be counted for righteousness, whatever a defective and obsolete law may determine or fail to determine concerning legality.

One thing I have not mentioned which was significant of all that I have written concerning the spirit of the suffering endured. It was very rarely that I witnessed any Akali Sikh, who went forward to suffer, flinch from a blow when it was struck. Apart from the instinctive and involuntary reaction of the muscles that has the appearance of a slight shrinking back, there was nothing, so far as I can remember, that could be called a deliberate avoidance of the blows struck. The blows were received one by one without resistance and without a sign of fear."

After 13th September, when the Governor paid a visit to Amritsar and was deeply impressed with what he had heard from Mr. C. F. Andrews, the beating of jathas was stopped and arrests began again.

The police, however, continued in other ways to take exercises in the use of lathi, which Mr. Macpherson, Superintendent of Police, by writing a booklet on the subject has reduced to a regular science. In it we find laid down how the lathi is to be struck into the opponent's face. his belly, his throat and even his 'fork.' The stray Sikhs found outside the Gurdwara Guru-ka-Bagh, or on the roads leading to it, were set upon, beaten and robbed. The robbing, as the beating,was carried on most publicly in the presence of hundreds, who can testify to these acts done by the forces of peace and order.

For a few days only 20 Sikhs offered themselves daily for arrest at Guru-ka-Bagh, but from 24th September the number was raised to 30 per day, then to 40 and then to 60. On the 28th it became 80 and then after a few days it was raised to 100. From 10th October one hundred Sikhs went regularly in batches of four to chop wood for the Guru's kitchen from the Guru's land, and were arrested without fail. Seeing the Sikhs coming in large numbers to court arrest, the Government gave out by way of warning that it was making accommodation for ten thousand Akalis in Jails. The whole Sikh community felt it like a challenge, and prepared to make every sacrifice for the vindication of its rights. Military pensioners, graduates, villagers and townspeople, all heard the call and made themselves ready. It was the sowing time, but the agriculturists, leaving their ploughs and the seeds with the younger brothers or the old parents, came away to Amritsar to march to Guru-ka-Bagh. The military Sikhs, who had grown grey in the service of the Sirkar and had retired in their old age to live on their hard-earned pensions, felt themselves constrained to sacrifice their all and lay their old bones at the altar of the Guru. They formed a jatha of hundred and marched with a band playing before them to get themselves arrested at Guru-ka-Bagh. They were arrested on 25th October. On being tried and convicted 74 of them, including their jathadar Sardar Amar Singh who had 23 years' service to his credit, were awarded 2 years' rigorous imprisonment with a fine of Rs. 100 each or in default another 6 months' hard labour. The remaining 26, classed as old, were given 6 months' simple imprisonment with a fine of Rs. 100 each or in default another 3 months. The following written statement was put in by Subadar Amar Singh on behalf of the whole Military Pensioners' Jatha :—

We avail of this opportunity to make it clear to the Government how the Sikh mind feels in regard to the Gurdwara Reform Movement generally and the Guru-ka-Bagh affair especially. The members of this Jatha are glad that they rendered services to the Crown of which no loyal heart need feel ashamed. We fought on the battle-fields of Tirah, Chitral, Afghanistan, Burma, China, East Africa, the Sudan, Egypt, Persia, Mesopotamia, Palestine, Gallipoli, Russia, France, and innumerable other fields less worthy of note. This service was done in the extremes of climate. While in France thousands of Sikh soldiers stood entrenched for days together in icy water. They also saw service at Rumadee, in Mesopotamia, where the thermometer stood at 135°; and there were no fewer than 190 deaths from thirst in one single day. The world seriously doubts if the on-rushing tide of victorious German hordes would have been stemmed but for the hand-to-hand bayonet fight by the Sikhs at Neu Chapelle and Ypres. At Kut-ul-Amara we held out when all chances of help became entirely remote; when all communications were cut off and we had no provisions save the flesh of horses and mules to feed on. Twenty-four of us were wounded in action, and, having been incapacitated for further military service, retired on pension, while one lost his leg and two got their eyesight injured by gas. Almost all of us possess medals of one distinction or another, in addition to two I. O. M.'s, one D. S. M. and one M. S. M.

Most of us belong to families whose blood has seen continuous military service since the unhappy times of the Indian Mutiny when the British flag stood tottering on the soil of India. We did nothing more than what our duty to the Crown demanded, and that we did to the utmost of our ability and strength. But since the Gurdwara Reform Movement began, the official attitude towards it has given rise to painful misgivings in our mind which, as the days passed, have acted severely on our feelings. We have witnessed the Nankana Sahib massacre, the official sympathy for the aggrieved party in the form of jails and blots on unsullied lives, and the justice of a High Court in an unparalleled case of most barbarous and cold-blooded massacre. We have seen the Government's solicitude for the inviolability of their solemn pledges not to interfere in the religious liberties of their subjects, in the matter of Kirpan, black turbans and the Golden Temple keys affair. All this we have seen, heard and felt; felt like a Sikh, felt like a friend rudely disillusioned from his loving and blind faith in the honesty of others. On top of all comes the Guru-ka-Bagh affair. During the two months or so, since this struggle began, we have seen our brothers beaten most brutally and illegally, we have seen their beards and *keshas* pulled by sacrilegious hands, heard our holy Gurus spoken of in terms most insulting and provoking, seen things done by the police in the name of law, in a manner most lawless, and all this anxious concern for law and order having no real basis for it. Our patience having thus been tried to the utmost, we have come forward to prove our devotion to the Guru and the Panth. As if to give us a true idea of the humiliation to which our brothers are subjected, the police was good enough to give us a taste of it. We were first searched naked like the meanest criminals, then kept under such severe and close guard as not to allow us to answer the call of nature or pass water from 11 p. m. to 6 a. m. the next day. We shall now be pleased to see hand-cuffs fastened on our wrists by those whom we have been considering our friends, for so long and in whose service we have been so little calculating of our own interests. We deem ourselves all the more fortunate that, in attempting to chop wood from land belonging to Guru-ka-Bagh for the Guru's free kitchen, we have been arrested and are to-day being sent to jail—which we have come to regard as paradise—for the sake of freeing our temples from vice and corruption."

On November 12, another jatha of a hundred grey-bearded military pensioners marched to Guru-ka-Bagh and was arrested.

After a few days a jatha of Nirmala Sikhs also proceeded to Guru-ka-Bagh.

Beside those arrested at Guru-ka-Bagh scores of people were being arrested in the same connection in other parts of the country, so that by 17th November the total number of arrests made amounted to 5605. Out of these about 35 were members of the Shromani Gurdwara Parbandhak Committee.

The Akalis, when arrested, were kept for the night at Guru-ka-Bagh in an exposed place where there was no cover, and made to sleep on bare ground without blankets in the cold of the Punjab nights. Consequently many caught chill and one actually died of the effects in the Amritsar jail.

Four more deaths have occurred since as the result of the rigours of jail.

The courts dealing with the arrested Akalis did not bother themselves with the usual legalities of procedure. Although the Akalis were arrested and convicted for the same acts, the terms of imprisonment assigned to them vary widely different, ranging from simple imprisonment for one day to rigorous imprisonment for two years. All convictions were based upon the evidence of the same few tutored official witnesses, zaildars, lambardars and men of the Mahant, most of whom had not been even present at the time of arrests. In consequence of this, many blunders were committed by the courts. One such blunder was the double conviction of a jatha on 12th October. The Government has admitted this, but has not proceeded against the witnesses in the second trial for giving false evidence. The courts generally would not supply certified copies of prosecution evidence, even when the accused applied for them. The usual plea for this refusal was that the accused wanted to prolong their cases unnecessarily. In the case of the Military Pensioners' 2nd Jatha, who wanted to defend themselves, the magistrate did not stop to allow the defence or even to admit their written statement, and hastened to convict them.

The anxiety of the Government to respect the law is perhaps best displayed in the methods employed to realize the fines imposed on the convicted Akalis. Those entrusted with the realization cared very little to arm themselves with correct information as to the particulars of the persons convicted. If an Akali happened to be absent from his village for a few days, he was taken by the village patwari, or other informers of the same sort, to have gone to Guru-ka-Bagh, been arrested and convicted. The report is made to the authorities and the suspected person is proceeded against. His property or that of some relative of his is immediately attached.

In this connection the following typical cases will be read with interest :—

a) Munshi Sadhu Singh issued a warrant to attach the property of Akali Gurbachan Singh s/o Ruldu Ram, (caste Arora, residence Tarn Taran), to realize the amount of fine due from him. Great was the dismay and surprise of the boy's father when the bailiff was proceeding to attach his (father's) property in lieu of his 7 years old son, who had never gone to Guru-ka-Bagh or been arrested, challaned, convicted or fined. The bailiff was confounded to see the child playing before his father and had to go away disappointed. It is noteworthy that no Gurbachan Singh was convicted on the date mentioned in the warrant. The particulars in the warrant were :— No. of warrant 55; Name, Gurbachan Singh, s/o Ruldu Ram Arora; residence Tarn Taran; date of conviction, 25th October, 1922; date of issue, 9th November, 1922.

(b) Bhai Randhir Singh of village Burj Raika is a nephew of the well-known Baba Kehar Singh, arrested in connection with the Guru-ka-

Bagh affair. It is two years since he went to America to prosecute his studies there, and has not yet returned. But all the same, his house was visited by the bailiff on 15th November, with a warrant of attachment. This was issued by Magistrate Banwari Lal on 8th November.

(*c*) Tahl Singh zaildar and Boota Singh lambardar went with the bailiff to the house of Bhai Sunder Singh, village Wegewala, on 16th November, 1922, and forcibly attached his buffalo. The poor fellow protested that he had never been arrested, convicted or fined; but the bailiff replied that according to the court files he was supposed to be in prison and fined, and that was enough for his purpose. So the buffalo was taken away. This warrant again was issued by Munshi Sadhu Singh and bore the date of 9th November, 1922.

(*d*) On the same date, Munshi Sadhu Singh had issued another warrant for the realization of fine from Bhai Jagat Singh of Tarn Taran. His mother had gone to Jandiala

Guru, locking her house. The lock was broken open by the bailiff in her absence and whatever he could lay his hands on was attached.

(e) On 19th November, a bailiff from Tarn Taran Tahsil Head Quarters visited Naurangabad and for some time went about the village in search of the house of Parsa Singh who, arcording to the information emanating from the Amritsar judiciary with which he was armed, had been sentenced to 9 months' imprisonment and a fine of Rs. 200 in connection with Guru-ka-Bagh. The house was found out, and the bailiff found himself face to face with none else but Bhai Parsa Singh himself who, if the Government agent were to be believed, should have been either in Attock or Ambala jail. The bailiff informed Bhai Parsa Singh in all seriousness that a fine of Rs. 200 (beside imprisonment) had been imposed on him in connection with Guru-ka-Bagh and that he had been ordered by *Sarkar* to realise the amount. Bhai Parsa Singh urged that, as he himself was a free man talking to the bailiff, a fact than which there was nothing easier of verification, there was evidently some mistake somewhere. The bailiff did not, as he could not, deny that he was talking to Parsa Singh of Naurangabad and that the latter was thus not a convict in some frontier fort but a free man; but said, nothing daunted, that he could not have been sent by *Sarkar* for nothing. He had been sent to realise a fine of Rs. 200 by whatever means he could, and he had not got the face to go back and confess before his superiors that he had failed to do it. Accordingly, having been reinforced by a few village sweepers, the redoubtable bailiff took possession of 4 heads of Parsa Singh's cattle, one bullock and 3 buffaloes and quietly made for Tarn Taran. Subsequent fate of the cattle is not known upto the moment of writing.

These are but a few out of many similar cases. There are also instances where property has been attached of persons related to the supposed convicts and where objections urged in courts were not even entertained.

At last when the position of the Government became utterly untenable, a 'kind-hearted' gentleman came forward to rescue the Government. On November 17, Sir Ganga Ram, C. I. E., a retired engineer, took the land of the Gurdwara of Guru-ka-Bagh on lease from the Mahant and wrote to the Government that he did not require the protection of the police. The arrests ceased on the same day and 170 men who were on trial were released. The remaining thousands are still rotting in jail.

CHAPTER XXII.

THE AKALIS.

The term 'Akali', meaning immortal, has been used, ever since the days of Guru Gobind Singh, for those Sikhs who dedicate themselves to the protection of temples and the preservation of pure ceremonial in them. They are no sect, for they do not differ from other Sikhs in any respect about doctrines.

They first appeared as the army of Baba Fateh Singh, one of the two sons of Guru Gobind Singh, who were bricked up alive at Sirhind. Baba Fateh Singh was so young that once at Anandpur before sending him out his father had to size him up by tying a tall conical turban on his head. His army put on the same uniform, with quoits and double-edged swords worn on the head, and the top of the turban having a piece of cloth sticking out to serve as a plume or a flag. These people fought most zealously and came to be called Nihangs or dragons. As they never cared for death, they were also called Akalis or deathless. As a sign of this determination they wore dark blue clothes. They were noted for the purity of character. Their chief work was to protect temples and keep the ceremony pure. With the aggressive attitude of the rulers and with the Sikhs being always in a minority, the Nihangs had no easy time in discharging the duties assigned to them. They, however, bore all difficulties with a spirit ever cheerful and airy. They developed a peculiar slang among themselves which denotes an unparalleled humour coupled with a determination that knows no bending. A single Sikh was called a lakh-and-a-quarter, that is a host in himself. When provisions ran short the kitchen was said to be 'tipsy with joy'. The parched grams were almonds, the onion shreds were silver pieces, and the wild berries were apples. A mud hut was called a crystal palace, the shade of a tree a green temple, and a coarse blanket a shawl. The big stick was called a lawyer or a store of wisdom. A blind man was called sun-eyed, and a deaf man was said to be in the upper storey. Even to take food or bathe was called carrying a position in the battle-field.

They were respected most highly for their sincerity of conviction and the purity of character. Even Maharaja Ranjit Singh allowed himself to be hauled up by Akali Phula Singh at the Akal Takht for having done a forbidden thing. Baba Kehar Singh Akali corrected Maharaja Narindar Singh of Patiala in 1859. He would not see the Maharaja who had come to him at Anandpur, and ordered him to go first to the Takht at Kesgarh and get pardon for his remissness in Sikhism. The Maharaja did so, and after confessing and doing penance he was baptised.

With the establishment of the Sikh rule, when there was not much need for defending the temples, the Nihangs like the Templars of the West began to deteriorate in character. The Maharaja tried to keep them busy by giving them a chance to fight, but they were not always amenable to discipline, except when they were led by such heroes as Baba Phula Singh. After the Maharaja, most of them, who were not incharge of temples, became like guns without ammunition. They kept up the forms and the peculiar vocabuliary, but the spirit had undergone a great change. They did not drink and in this they kept up the old tradition, but they took to the use of *bhang*, which was equally intoxicating. They were forbidden to beg, and their tradition was to work for their living, but many of them in the days of idleness did indulge in begging under a disguise. A Nihang stopped at the shop of a confectioner and asked him pre-emptorily to give him something. The shop-keeper, who understood the meaning of the order, smilingly laid some sweet balls before the poor man. But the Nihang would not have them that way. He asked the confectioner to place them on the road, and, when it was done, he "bullied" over them with his stick and then carried them away saying as he ran: "The Khalsa does not beg, but conquers."

When the reform of temples began in the twentieth century, a new order of Akalis arose, which was quite distinct from the old order. The new edition, if we may use the figure, had nothing in common with the old one except the title page and the table of contents. All the Sikhs, who were in favour of Gurdwara reform and were resolved to suffer any hardships in the course of it, came to be called Akalis. Their method was distinctly non-violent and their instrument personal purity and pressure of the public opinion. The title 'Akali' was adopted slowly as the Sikhs showed signs of the old spirit. The Panch Khalsa Diwan and the Central Majha Diwan, with their unflinching zeal for the upkeep of the baptismal vows, had infused a determination in the masses that would brook no opposition to a genuine reform. These associations had been in the field for a number of years and had done much to revive the old spirit. The fight for kirpan and Rikab Ganj had rallied the scattered forces of the Panth and created a readiness to make sacrifices. The services of the Central Majha Diwan in connection with the release of Babe-di-Ber at Sialkot, the Akal Takht at Amritsar and Panja Sahib at Hasan Abdal, revealed to the Sikhs the capabilities of a jatha. The leaders of this Diwan were clad in black and looked very imposing. They had not yet adopted the title Akali. The word had already appeared on the title page of the strong newspaper *Akali* at Lahore. In general talk the word Akali came to be applied to anything high and noble. The word of the Scripture and the message of the Guru would be called Akali. Gradually the members of the Majha Diwan in charge of the Akal Takht, for their excellent conduct, came to be called Akalis, especially when the old Akalis or Nihangs by committing assault on the Akal Takht had forfeited the confidence of the people.

When Gurdwara after Gurdwara came into the possession of the Panth it was felt that the bodies of Sikhs who took part in the reform might be demoralised by the addition of irresponsible and mischievous persons. It was considered advisable to organize a central body to which all the scattered jathas should be affiliated. The Shromani Akali Dal was founded at Amritsar on 14th December, 1920, and the first jathas to be affiliated were : the Central Khalsa Diwan, the Bar Akali Jatha, and the Malwa Khalsa Diwan of Dhuri. After the Nankana Sahib massacre other jathas were formed and the whole organization was based on a division by districts. The Akali jathas of the following districts have been affiliated so far :—Amritsar, Lahore, Skeikhupura, Lyallpur, Sialkot, Gujranwala, Gujrat, Jhelum, Shahpur, Abbottabad, Montgomery, Ferozepore, Gurdaspur, Jullundur, Hoshiarpur, Ludhiana, Ambala, Kapurthala State, Nabha State and Nahan State. Their object is to serve the Panth and reform the temples in accordance with the wishes of the Shromani Gurdwara Parbandhak Committee. The Shromani Akali Dal consists of delegates drawn from all the affiliated jathas, each of which is entitled to send 5 representatives for every 100 members. It has got an Executive Committee of 41 members, including five office-bearers, who have also to serve as Five Piaras. There are two sources of income : (1) donations from the public, and (2) contributions of *daswandh* or 1-10th part of every jatha's income. The members who attend the meetings are paid their railway expenses.

In the beginning only a few people wore black turbans, but afterwards when a Government officer was said to have remarked that the black-turbaned Sikhs should be especially cared for, the movement became general, and the Nankana tragedy followed by the wholesale arrests of Sikhs literally dyed the Sikhs in black. In May, 1921, the Shromani Gurdwara Parbandhak Committee passed a resolution enjoining on all Sikhs to wear black turbans up to 15th November, 1921, the day of Guru Nanak's birth. But, as the sufferings of Sikhs did not cease, the order was extended indefinitely. The black turban is not a sign of mourning, for the Khalsa never mourns, but a grim sign of resolution to suffer all difficulties and sacrifices in the way of religion.

The Akalis are no sect, for they do not differ in belief from other initiated Sikhs. Any baptized Sikh, who believes in the injunctions of the ten Gurus and is ready to suffer in the Panthic cause, especially in the matter of Gurdwara reform, can be called an Akali. There is no ceremony to be gone through for this purpose, neither is there any distinctive mark to be adopted except the black turban, which also may be abandoned any moment when the Shromani Committee so decides.

The Akalis in the present movement have vowed to remain non-violent under all circumstances. In this they are not inconsistent with their past history. Their Gurus were perfectly non-violent as long as they believed that by suffering passively they could soften the callousness of their oppressors and shame them into reason. The sufferings borne by the first five Gurus did stir up conscience in their opponents, and the rulers always tried to befriend them. But when a saint like Guru Arjan was roasted alive on heated plates, the Sikhs came to reconsider their policy in the face of the brute force run amok. It is perfectly reasonable to expect a hard-hearted man to get his soul awakened by witnessing the enormities produced by his brutal nature. But when by the constant practice of cruelty his nature is completely brutalised and the human element in him is dead, it is quite futile to present to him a sight of suffering. We do not willingly offer ourselves to be gored by a horned beast. The Sikhs, therefore, after the death of Guru Arjan took up the sword to defend themselves. After some time they again put by the sword and gave a chance to the rulers to recover their lost soul. The seventh Guru kept with him armies and wore arms, but he had resolved never to use hem. He, however, ceased to co-operat with the Government—, and refused even to see the face of the Emperor. His son, who succeeded him, did likewise. The ninth Guru suffered passively, as did so many of his Sikhs like Bhai Mati Das, who allowed himself to be sawn alive without uttering even a sigh of bitterness. Under Guru Gobind Singh the policy of passive suffering was again reconsidered.

The Sikhs of the present day are, therefore, quite consistent with the policy of their fore-fathers in deciding to remain non-violent under all provocations. It is a compliment to the British Government that it is believed to possess a soul, or have the fear of public opinion, which the Sikhs along with their other countrymen are trying to awaken. The advancement of the times and the fear of the world opinion has made it practically impossible for the modern governments to indulge in those barbarities which were possible in the dark ages.

How far the Sikhs have been successful in carrying out the policy of non-violence will be evident from their behaviour at Tarn Taran, Nankana Sahib and Guru-ka-Bagh. The Government has, however, persistently maintained that the Akali jathas are nothing but violent, a danger to the peace and order of the country. The *Civil and Military Gazette* and the Associated Press have lent themselves freely to depict the Akalis in as black colours as possible. All the violent crimes committed in the central districts are attributed to the Akali movement. It is not recognised that crime has increased as a result of the lack of proper surveillance on the part of police, which is too much pre-occupied with the harassment of Akalis or with the reporting of crime more than its suppression.

An oft-repeated charge against the Akalis is that they march in 'military formation.' The Sikhs do walk in orderly fashion, and when they wear kirpans they present to the eyes of the Government officials a spectacle of 'armed bands'. The Sikhs from the days of Guru Nanak have been in the habit of moving to their diwans in parties called sangats, singing hymns in chorus; and when they do so their robust and disciplinary instinct makes them fall into step. Such a party of nearly forty Sikhs, while proceeding to a diwan in Jullundur district, was arrested and sentenced there and then. What does the Government want? Does it think that loyalty consists in walking in a shuffling, slouching manner? Does it like that mobs should not be arranged in rows of four or five, and that they should always be huddling and scampering through the streets for the police to use their batons?

An instance or two will show to what lengths the police would go to connect crimes with the Akali movement. A Government communique was issued in May, 1922, alleging that a double-barrelled breech-loading gun, some cartridges, melted silver and other stolen property were found from the house-search of the Secretary of the Akali Jatha of Chuhar Kana, near Atari Station in Montgomery District. There was only one Akali

Jatha in the whole Montgomery District, and its Secretary was Bhai Narindar Singh, who knew nothing of the search or the seizure of arms. The fact was that a Sohan Singh was arrested in Chuhar Kana in the Sheikhupura District and the objectionable articles were found in his house by the police. But this Sohan Singh had got nothing to do with any Akali Jatha. He was neither an Akali nor a member of any jatha. There was, however, another Sohan Singh who was Secretary of the Akali Jatha of Chuhar Kana, District Sheikhupura, and the police in their anxiety to condemn the Akali movement supplied his name to the Government. This allegation was withdrawn by Government many months later, but not before the report had done much mischief. In September, 1922, it was reported that nineteen Akalis had committed a dacoity in Sheikhupura District in March, 1922 ; while the fact was that these nineteen men had gone under instructions to plough the land belonging to Nankana Sahib, which was in possession of the Sikhs. It was also complained that the Akalis at Rajajang did not allow the Mohammedans to call the Azan. The quarrel was a long-standing one and belonged to the time before the Akali movement had begun. It had got nothing to do with the Akali movement. The Sikhs of this place, who were old-fashioned bigots, had never allowed the Azan, which according to the Government's own admission, was "only a recent innovation in this village." This prejudice of the Sikhs, who were not touched by the Akali movement and had rather been praised and rewarded for their aloofness, was a relic of old bigotry which is happily passing away. Led by the same spirit the Mohammedans of many villages do not allow their Sikh fellow-villagers to do *jhatka* ; but the Government has never issued a communique to air this grievance of the Sikhs. We do not want that it should. The Shromani Committee placed the matter in the hands of the Sikh League and the Khilafat Committee to make a settlement.

Even Hon'ble Lala Harkishan Lal, who should have known better, took some share in spreading misrepresentations about the Akalis. In an interview given by him in April, 1922, to a representative of the 'Statesman' of Calcutta, he is reported to have said : "With regard to the Akali movement, the Akalis have worked up a desire to control the destinies of the Punjab over the heads of other communities." From the frequent talks he had with the representatives of the Gurdwara Committee, he must have known that it was untrue. The Akalis have never demanded a Raj for themselves. Rather the Government has been taunting them with playing into the hands of Congress men. There is, however, one verse coming down from olden days, which is recited by Sikhs after the morning and evening prayers and which is often misunderstood. It is "Raj karega Khalsa", the Pure One shall rule. It does not mean that the Sikhs will rule. It is not an innovation, but has been constantly sung after prayers. It was freely sung in the Khalsa College of Amritsar, even in those days when the Government had got full control over it. When so many Sikhs had been butchered at Nankana Sahib and their bodies lay mangled and burnt in the temple, the Sikhs still sang, "the Pure One shall rule." When hundreds of Sikhs were arrested and brought in batches to court, they still sang at the gate of the court that "the Pure One shall rule." The Khalsa beaten and wounded and thrown in the dust still rises and sings that "the Pure One shall triumph." It is like Job crying out from ashes that the Redeemer liveth.

It cannot be asserted that the Akali movement has stamped out all crime and that there are no thieves and robbers among the Sikhs. But it is quite unfair to foist the stray crimes of villagers on the Akali movement, which has done so much to reduce crime. In most cases the defaulters are not members of any Jatha, but irresponsible individuals masquerading as Akalis, which is as unavoidable as the misuse of any other uniform, such as the European hat or the Khaddar cap. The Shromani Committee has always condemned any dishonourable behavior on the part of Sikhs, as it did when some Sikhs were reported to have joined with Hindus and Muslims at Tarkhaniwala Bungalow in harassing the Deputy Commissioner of Lyallpur. Everybody knows that on account of great congestion and mismanagement on railways some people cannot secure tickets. There are cheats too, who purposely travel without tickets, but they are not confined to the Sikh community alone. When, however, once a few Sikhs were found to have travelled without tickets, the Secretary of the Shromani Committee paid out their fare on the spot. The behaviour of these Sikhs created a great sensation in the Community and was condemned by everybody including the Shromani Committee. When a few Sikhs, without the knowledge of the Shromani Committee, took possession of the Gurdwaras at Anandpur and Kiratpur, they were at once called off and friendly relations were restored soon after with the priests. The Shromani Committee has always condemned the misuse of kirpan, and once actually helped the police in discovering a Sikh who had made an attack with it on a Mohammedan at Amritsar. Whenever a member of a recognized Jatha is suspected of having taken part in any discreditable occurrence, an enquiry is held by his Jatha and, if anything is proved against him, he is given a suitable religious punishment. In serious cases the offender is turned cut of the Jatha.

The Jathas on the whole have shown a wonderful spirit of discipline, gallantry and non-violence. Wherever their organization is allowed to bę strong and is not interfered with, they have practically stamped out robbery and theft. Their gallantry reminds one of the days when the Khalsa existed solely for the purpose of defending the honour of men and women. A grown up daughter of a Sindhi widow was forcibly taken away by a Mohammedan from one of the densely populated quarters of Amritsar. The widow ran about for help, but nobody would dare to come. She came to the Akalis, who held a hasty council of war and decided to send seven of themselves to rescue the abducted girl. They came upon a body of Mohammedans who were going to give the girl in marriage to her abductor, but seeing the Sikhs they ran away with her to a house and shut themselves up there. The Sikhs jumped after them into the house and a hand-to-hand fight began. They received severe injuries but they succeeded in bringing away the girl, whom they restored to the bereaved mother.

On April 17, 1921, fifteen dacoits armed with guns and pistols entered the village of Kallar, District Rawalpindi, at 11 p. m. and began to loot the shops. The villagers came out when they heard the noise, but retired soon after when the dacoits began to fire on them. Only the Akalis were left on the spot to face the robbers. They shouted Sat Sri Akal, and rallied each other to save the village at any cost. The dacoits also challenged the Akalis to come forward at the peril of their lives. The Akalis continued to advance, showering stones on their enemies and receiving bullets in return. The fight went on for about an hour. When the Akalis got near enough to use their lathis the dacoits ran away. The all-vigilant police reached the spot after the dacoits had made good their escape, although the whole place had been ringing for an hour with the shouts of Sat Sri Akal and the sounds of bullets at the dead of night. It is worthy of note that the police station is just outside the village. Twelve Akalis received bullet wounds, some of them getting two or three each.

The following letter, dated 11th March, 1922, sent by Mr. C. A. Macpherson, Superintendent of Police, Amritsar, to the Shromani Committee, will speak for itself :—

" Dear Sir,—A number of men said to be Akali Sikhs working at the Darbar Sahib tank performed a very gallant and meritorious act last evening. They rescued Lala Ishar Das and his family from the hands of armed robbers. I have not been able to ascertain their names, and am thus unable to convey to them any appreciation of their conduct. If your Committee can very kindly help me in this matter, I should be most grateful. I would also like to draw the attention of the Shromani Gurdwara Parbandhak Committee to the action of one Banta Singh of Dhotian who boldly tackled a man armed with a revolver, a truly lion-hearted and altruistic act. His services will be duly acknowledged, but I feel that his name and fame cannot be too widely known.

With greetings.

Yours sincerely,

(Sd.) C. A. Macpherson, Supdt., Police."

In regard to the temperance reform, the Akali movement has done in a short time what hundreds of societies founded for that purpose could not do in fifty years. Drunkenness has been practically stamped out from all villages where the Akalis are strong.

It is impossible for an Akali to drink. For effecting this and other social reforms the Akalis have organized Panchayats, in which they co-operate with Non-Akalis, whether Sikh, Hindu or Mohammedan. For some time they left off taking even tea, lest it should become a craving and take the place of wine or *bhang*. They have removed other evils too, like the holding of nautch parties with prostitutes. They have made life quite simple. An Akali would be rarely seen in anything but Khaddar. The Akalis are doing their utmost to get rid of the curse of untouchability. Rather their whole movement, as we have seen, began with a contest on this point with the old priests.

All these reforms have been made possible by the remarkable awakening among the Sikh women. They are working shoulder to shoulder with their husbands and brothers to justify Guru Gobind Singh's baptism, which they receive along with men. In the beginning of the present movement an old-fashioned Sikh happened to remark, before an assembly of Sikhs at the Akal Takht, that women should not be allowed to come upon the sacred Takht, as they did not show the same force of character as men. As soon as these words were uttered, a host of women, old and young, wearing kirpans, came forward and demanded of the Sikh to tell them what the men could do which they, the women, who had received Guru Gobind Singh's *Amrit*, could not do. They carried children in their arms, and were not ashamed of being mothers. Some of them, in their zeal to work along with men, have taken to tying turbans. The Akali Jathas of Amritsar, Lahore, Ludhiana, Ambala and Nabha are in favour of this practice.

CHAPTER XXIII.

THE KIRPAN.

The Kirpan or sword is one of the five symbols of the Sikh faith, whose names begin with the same letter. The other four are: Kesh (long hair), Kanga (comb), Kara (iron bracelet), and Kachh (drawers). When a Sikh is baptised, it is enjoined on him not to part with any of these. The Kirpan is a symbol of Power and Dignity *, both of which India had lost and which Guru Gobind Singh wanted to restore.

None of these symbols was invented by Guru Gobind Singh. They were already in vogue and had been separately used with much the same significance. The word 'Kirpan' was used for a sword. Long before it became a religious symbol with the Sikhs, its name had been applied to different kinds of the sword. In the old Sanskrit dictionaries, like the *Amarkosh* and the *Shabdkalpadrumkosh*, it is used as a synonym for *kharag*, *karwar*, *asi*, *chandarhas*, and *rishti*. Guru Gobind Singh himself in his Book of Instruments, called *Shastar-nam-mala*, says :—

" Kari, Karantac (elephant-killer), Kasht-rip (enemy-tormentor), Kalayudh (war-instrument), Karwar (talwar), Kara and

---

*" Charity and Kirpan are symbolic of self-respect."—*Pakhiano Charitra*, 322.

Chol are different names of the Kirpan." (11. 41).

In another book, called *Pakhiano Charitra*, he uses *Bhagauti* and *Kharag* indifferently for the Kirpan :

" She took Bhagauti in her hand,
And with all her might she struck it at his head.
As the Raja cried out, hai ! hai ! !,
She struck the *Kirpan* again and again." (302.9).

Here Kirpan and Bhagauti are used synonymously.

Again : " When the attack on the fort began, she took out her *Kirpan* and, coming to close quarters, plied the *Kharag* and with one stroke finished off the enemy." (199.26)

In these verses the Kirpan is synonymous with the Kharag. We have seen that in the old Sanskrit dictionaries, too, it is described as the same thing as the Kharag.

Guru Gobind Singh did not fix the size of the Kirpan. It depended on the weilding power of the Sikhs. But from the samples preserved at the Akal Takht and other Gurdwaras we can get an idea of what a Kharag or Kirpan was. According to old Hindu books the maximum size of a Kharag was 50 anguls or about 3·12 feet ; and the minimum size was 25 anguls or about 1·56 ft. "A Kharag of 50 anguls is excellent and of half that size is inferior. Shorter than that should not be worn at all."—*Agni Puran.*

"The best Kharag is 50 anguls long; and an inferior one is 25."—*Varah Samhita.*

The same size is given in the *Devi Puran.*

Why did the Guru call the sword Kirpan? Because it alliterates with the names of the other four symbols, is a classic and poetical name, and can be applied to all kinds of swords. The Kirpan is called a symbol from the view-point of the religious art or æsthetics. In order that the symbols might serve their real purpose as a help in the performance of religion and might not become a dead weight on religion, the Guru also emphasized the view-point of utility. The Kirpan, is, therefore, an active symbol, an instrument of offence and defence, and uot a charm to be tied along with the turban-ends or stowed away in the back of the comb, as it came to be done in the British days. It is to be kept in a sheath and worn in a belt (*Pakhiano Charitra,* 52.18). It can cut through armour (*Shastar-nam-mala,* 11.28), through men, horses, even elephants. It is superior to all other instruments (*ibid,* 11.34).

As long as the Sikhs were free, they were able to keep their religious liberty intact and did not part with their Kirpan or sword. They kept it by their side in the day, and took it to their bed at night. When they lost their liberty with the destruction of their empire, the Kirpan was also taken away from them. What a scene, that, at the famous monument of Mankiala, when the day of the Khalsa was over, and the old Sikh veterans were ordered to pile their arms at the feet of Sir Walter Guilbert. How reluctantly each soldier came forward and, embracing his sword, uttered a groan, deep and long, and placed it on the pile in tears.* Thus was lost one of the five symbols of the Sikh faith. In jails even other symbols, like the comb and the bracelet, were not allowed. And the Sikhs had to struggle hard and long to get a concession even in regard to these symbols for their brethren in jail.

We must admit that by the Army Regulations, which emphasize the initiation of a Sikh recruit in Guru Gobind Singh's baptism, the old tradition of the Khalsa was kept up to some extent. But in other ways, as we have seen, the liberty of the Sikhs was controlled. The Sikhs founded Sabhas and Diwans, purely religious bodies, whose object was to restore Sikhism to its pristine glory. They emphasized the carrying out of the baptismal vows, and among other things laid stress on the wearing of the Kirpan. But the law of the country stood in their way.

---

*See *Leaves from the Journal of a Subaltern*, p. 189.

In 1913, one Baba Nihal Singh Nihang was arrested for wearing a Kirpan. The different Sikh bodies passed resolutions of protest and there began a strong agitation, in response to which the gentleman was released. The Ramgarhia Sabha sent a deputation to Sir O'Moore Creagh, the Commander-in-Chief at Simla, who took a sympathetic view. The Chief Khalsa Diwan, whose Secretary was Sardar Sundar Singh Majithia, interviewed several officers in this connection. The Sikhs of Rawalpindi, through their Sabha, showed special activity in moving the Takhts and the general Sikh public; and on June 25, 1914, the possessing and wearing of the Kirpan was allowed by law in the Punjab. After a month it was allowed in Delhi. Then after some months' agitation, and after some Sikhs had suffered arrests, it was allowed in Burma. But whenever a Sikh was found with a Kirpan in U. P. or Bengal he was arrested. It is true that law did not allow it in other provinces, but it was not the fault of Sikhs. It was an anomaly, which the Government unreasonably kept up. Why should a Sikh be required to part with his religious symbol when stepping out of Delhi and put it on when landing at Rangoon. In February, 1917, after Chaudhri Shamsher Singh, Secretary of the Singh Sabha of Sitapur, had been punished for wearing a Kirpan, it was allowed in U. P., and then in the N. W. Frontier Province. In other provinces it was still forbidden. The Sikhs have got their sacred places in U. P., Behar, Bengal, Deccan, etc., and are found travelling in batches to visit these places. One can imagine what trouble they must have undergone in prison and at the hands of the police, which is none too tender in India. On May 19, 1917, it was allowed throughout India. In 1918 the exemption was extended to British Baluchistan and the Residency Bazars and the Railway lands in Hyderabad State. But still cases were not rare when, inspite of this sanction, the police of different provinces were found arresting and troubling the inncent Sikhs for wearing Kirpans.

The representative bodies of the Sikhs went on agitating, for the Kirpan was still not allowed in the Army. Look at the wonder of it! Those who used the sword, those whose profession it was to wear arms, were not allowed to wear the Kirpan. Three soldiers at Roorkee were punished and dismissed for wearing it. The whole Sikh community cried hoarse over the affair, but they were not taken back. Bhai Mangal Singh of 34th Sikhs, who was afterwards martyred at Nankana Sahib, was dismissed and sentenced to one year's R. I. for the same fault. His sentence was later reduced. It was in September, 1920, that "in recognition of the loyal and distinguished services rendered by the Sikhs in the Great War," the Government "was pleased to sanction the wearing of the Kirpans by Sikh soldiers both in uniform and plain clothes while serving on the active list."*

The law, while exempting the Kirpan from all restrictions, did not fix its size, for the Sikhs who had applied for it had stated that its size could be fixed only by Guru Gobind Singh. Nor was its manufacture forbidden. In Schedule II of the Arms Act, which provides for exemptions from the operation of the Act, the Kirpan is declared to be free from *all* prohibitions including its manufacture and sale. For some time the Sikhs freely enjoyed the right of manufacturing, selling and possessing the Kirpan. But when the repression of Sikhs in connection

*This right was, however, curtailed later on, as would appear from the following words in the 'correction' which was made in the Army Regulations on May 27, 1922 :—

"In Units which elect to adopt the wearing of the Kirpan by Sikhs it should be worn on all ceremonial occasions; the other occasions on which it will or will not be worn are left to the discretion of officers commanding units. Uniformity within the unit as regards the method of wearing the Kirpan in uniform and in plain clothes must be insisted on."

with the Gurdwara reform began, those who wore Kirpans also came in for it. In February, 1921, the Deputy Commissioner of Jullundur issued an order requiring the local manufacturers not to manufacture Kirpans of greater length than nine inches. A First Class Magistrate in Lahore pssed an order on the application of a Kirpan manufaturer for license that no license was needed for manufacturing Kirpans. But when in March, 1921, S. Mehtab Singh referred to it in the Council, S. Sundar Singh Majithia replied on behalf of the Government that although the Sikhs had been permitted to wear Kirpan, Section 5 of the Arms Act did not allow them to manufacture it without license. He also declared that the Kirpans were in no case to exceed nine inches in length. Consequent upon this Sikhs began to be arrested everywhere for wearing Kirpans which exceeded the length of nine inches, although there was no specific law or notification issued on that point. The Maharaja of Patiala was, however, more explicit. He ordered on 19th March, 1921, that Kirpans must be bought from the Arms Manufacturers of the State, who were instructed to prepare Kirpans of a fixed size and shape. All other Kirpans possessed or carried were liable to confiscation. This order created much heart-burning among the Sikhs and was withdrawn on October 5, 1921. The prosecution of Sikhs for wearing Kirpans went on in the British Districts. Nobody could understand on what principle the police or the courts proceeded. Some people were arrested for possessing Kirpans, while others were not arrested, even though they carried as long Kirpans as they could. In the case of one Hazara Singh, who was tried in April, 1921, the following great moderate leaders were cited as defence witnesses:—Sardar Bahadur Mehtab Singh, Bar-at-Law; Sardar Trilochan Singh, M.A., LL.B.; Sardar Sundar Singh Ramgarhia, President of the Shromani Committee and ex-Manager of the Golden Temple; Sardar Harbans Singh, Secretary of the Chief Khalsa Diwan, and Vice-President of the Shromani Committee; Professor Jodh Singh, M.A., Principal, Guru Nanak College, Gujranwala; Bhai Takht Singh, Manager, Sikh Girls' School, Ferozepore; and Sardar Shivdev Singh Uberoi, Honorary Magistrate of Sialkot. They declared that the instrument, for carrying which Bhai Hazara Singh was being prosecuted, was a Kirpan, and that Kirpan was another name for the sword. They themselves had with them similar Kirpans. And yet the man was convicted under Section 19 of the Act and sentenced to 6 months' R.I. Bhai Bachittar Singh, Jathadar of the Akal Takht, who had been picked out of so many Kirpan-carrying Sikhs, was sentenced to 2 years' imprisonment, which was, however, reduced to 6 months later on. He appealed to the High Court, which could not come to any decision as to what a Kirpan was, and his petition was rejected. After proceeding in this uncertain way for a few months, the Government in July relaxed its policy of prosecutions, declaring complacently that "the practice of wearing large weapons or ordinary swords appears to have now much diminished." The Sikhs in reality had never given up their practice of wearing the so-called long Kirpans.

In March, 1922, the Government and the Shromani Committee came to an understanding about the Kirpan. It was agreed that the Government would not interfere with the Sikhs for wearing "Kirpans or swords" as long as they ordinarily wore them by the side and did not unsheath them except for purely religious purposes. When listening to the terms of agreement the Sikh representatives had expressed a fear that the Government might take advantage of the words "by the side" and unnecessarily harass the Sikhs. The Government representative had laughed out the objection, saying that the Sikhs should trust the Government, which wanted to finish the Kirpan trouble once for all. It was, however, destined to be used, like so many other previous agreements, as a mere stalking horse.

The ink was not yet dry on the document when a fresh campaign was started for prosecuting Sikhs for wearing Kirpans. The Burma Government even in February had issued a notification fixing the size of the Kirpan to 9 inches. We have seen how Sardar Kharak Singh and others were arrested and sentenced heavily. The ludicrous way in which advantage was taken of the words "by the side" will appear from the following cases. A Sikh boy in Hoshiarpur district was going running to his school to avoid being late. As his Kirpan was hanging down his body, he could not run freely. So he took the Kirpan in his hand, though the belt was on his body. The Commissioner of the Division who saw this ordered the boy to be disarmed. On the boy refusing to give up his Kirpan, he was arrested and, being put before a Magistrate, was tried and sentenced to pay Rs. 55 as fine, or to go to jail for one month and a half in default. The brave boy preferred the latter, and was sent to jail. In a diwan at Samundri the Superintendent of Police snatched away the Kirpan from a Sikh while he was leaning on it. In another place a Sikh was deprived of his Kirpan while he was cleaning it. Sardar Ram Singh of Mandi Dabwali (Hissar District), who was found sleeping with his Kirpan, was arrested and sent to jail. A blind musician was arrested at Mandhra, because his cross-belt having broken in the way he was obliged to put his Kirpan in his bed. In a communique, dated 19th September, 1922, the Government declared that one "Anup Singh was present at a meeting and was arrested there for carrying his Kirpan in contravention to the orders on the subject. He was not wearing a belt and stated that he would never wear one." Sometimes Sikhs were arrested for possessing two Kirpans. As a Sikh is bound to keep his Kirpan always with him, it becomes sometimes inevitable that he should have two Kirpans with him. As for axample, when he buys a new Kirpan to replace an old one, which he already possesses, he will necessarily have two in his possession when he walks away from the Kirpan shop; or sometimes when he comes from his village to a city and buys a Kirpan for his wife or child. The prosecutions in connection with the Kirpan were so manifestly illegal that all disinterested newspapers and associations in India strongly disapproved of the policy of the Government, and the Punjab Provincial Congress Committee in a general meeting condemned "the action of the Punjab Government in prosecuting Sikhs for wearing Kirpans beyond certain length which is not provided in law." Even a Sessions Judge was found to hold that the manufacture of Kirpans was no offence. The following judgment was delivered by Mr. A. H. Parker, Sessions Judge of Ambala Division on 17th June, 1922:—

"In this case Ganesha Singh, who is admittedly a Sikh Lohar of the Ambala District, has been convicted under Section 19 of the Arms Act for manufacturing Kirpans. The Magistrate has sentenced him to one year's rigorous imprisonment with fine. He appeals.

It is admitted on his behalf that he did, in fact, manufacture Kirpans ; and the only question which I have to decide is whether the manufacture of Kirpans by a Sikh is an offence under the Arms Act. The Arms Rules of 1920, schedule 2, shows that within the Punjab the arms, *viz.*, "Kirpans possessed or carried by Sikhs" are excluded from the operations of all prohibitions and directions contained in the Arms Act. These Kirpans, manufactured by Appellant are clearly, while in his possession, Kirpans possessed by a Sikh, and I hold that they are excluded from all prohibitions under the Act. In section 5 of the Act there is a prohibition against the manufacture of Arms, but these Kirpans are not subject to that prohibition. I, therefore, consider and hold that Ganesha

Singh by manufacturing these Kirpans has committed no offence.

The learned Public Prosecutor, while arguing the case before me, laid stress on the words 'possessed or carried by a Sikh,' and argues that the prohibition against manufacturing is not excluded, since the Kirpans have to be possessed or carried by Sikhs. I cannot agree with the argument, since the schedule shows that all prohibitions under the Act are excluded.

For the above reasons this appeal is accepted, and Ganesha Singh is acquitted and released. Fine, if recovered, will be refunded. The Kirpans, etc., confiscated by the Magistrate, will be returned to Ganesha Singh on the expiry of the term of appeal or the decision of appeal, if any be made against this judgment."

In fact the Government does not know its own case about the Kirpan question. The Government is yet undecided as to whether the manufacture of Kirpans is an offence or not. In answer to a question in the Punjab Council the Hon'ble Sardar Sundar Singh Majithia said on 31st July, 1922: "The manufacture of Kirpans has been treated as subject to the provisions of the law applicable to swords, but doubt has been raised as to the applicability of these provisions to *Kirpans* and the Government is taking steps to obtain a judicial decision on the point." In the meanwhile Sikhs, like Sardar Kharak Singh, have to rot in jail. The same member also stated that upto the beginning of June, 1922, " there had been 68 persons arrested, 66 brought to trial and 40 convicted during the previous twelve months for keeping, selling or manufacturing kirpans or weapons passing as such. Eighteen persons were still under trial." Read with this the statement of Government made in the beginning of March, 1922, that " for about 8 months past no Sikh has been arrested for wearing a sword or Kirpan," and then say how many have been punished in this connection and in how many months.

CHAPTER XXIV.

CONCLUSION.

We are not yet out of the wood. The Lathi having failed, the Government has brought forward a Bill again, and this time has passed it, too, through the Legislative Council, inspite of the fact that the whole Sikh Community with one voice opposed it and all the Hindu and Sikh Members, supported by the only Indian Christian and the most enlightened Mohammedans in the Council, voted against it. Even half the Government—one Executive Councillor and one Minister—remained neutral. This was the only form, short of resignation, that opposition could take in their case. The Bill is substantially the same as the first one, published in this book, with this difference that the Board of Commissioners will now consist of three Sikhs to be nominated, one each, by Government, the Shromani Gurdwara Parbandhak Committee and Sikh Members of the Punjab Council. On its merits the Bill could not be accepted by the Sikhs, because it does not meet the requirements of reform. But the Government has made it impossible for the Sikh Community to consider any Bill at present by keeping in jail thousands of Sikhs including almost all the great leaders of the Panth. The Sikhs do want a legislation, but such as will fulfil the purpose of reform and is given in a manner honourable for acceptance.

The defeat of Sikhs over the Bill and their sufferings at Guru-ka-Bagh mean a great moral gain for the movement. The whole Community has been united, and all concerned have been deeply impressed by the earnestness of the reformers. The Nirmala Sikhs have fallen in line with the rest of the Sikhs ; and the Mahants, too, are rapidly coming to realise that their right place is by the side of the Panth. Since the stoppage of arrests at Guru-ka-Bagh on 17th November, 1922, the custodians of the following Gurdwaras have put themselves under the control of the Shromani Committee : –

1. Ramdas (Amritsar), 2. Kot Naina (Gurdaspore), 3. Naurangabad (Amritsar), 4. Mahal (Amritsar), 5. Dehra Sahib Batala (Gurdaspore), 6. Bir Sahib (Amritsar), 7. Babek Sar (Amritsar), 8. Garna Sahib (Hoshiarpore), 9. Bari Lehli (Hoshiarpore), 10. Zahira Zahur (Hoshiarpore), 11. Tahli Sahib (Hoshiarpore), 12. Damdama Sahib (Gurdaspore), 13. Gurusar Kaonke (Ludhiana), 14. Tapiana Sahib (Amritsar), 15. Dehra Sahib of Bughiana (Lahore), 16. Baba

Vir Singh Shahid (Lahore), 17. Tham Sahib of Uddoke (Amritsar).

We may not have gained all the Gurdwaras as yet; but the movement is steadily progressing, and every check only accelerates it. It is one of the greatest successes that the Panth has ever achieved. The Sikhs have obtained experience in organization and administration, which will prove a great national asset. Under the most trying circumstances they have been able to do the Kar Service and carry on the administration of so many temples. They have organized Panchayats, Jathas and Committees, and the experience gained in them has trained them how to work together. What is most important, by the removal of drunkenness, untouchability and other social evils they have gained an awakening and an uplift which have changed the whole outlook of the nation.

This success may be attributed to the following four causes: –

(1) The aim in this movement has been quite definite and every average Sikh can see what his nation is struggling for.

(2) The cause is so just that there has never been any doubt about its success. Only it involved sacrifice for which, thanks to the Sikh tradition not far distant from the present time, the Sikh nation made itself ready in a very short time.

(3) Coming after a period of diffusion of knowledge and expansion of energy it has provided an occasion for a stout-hearted engagement. The Sikhs had tried to reform their religion, to free their education, tried as British Subjects to get free access to British Dominions, and tried even to reform their temples, but they had failed. Now the whole awakening got from the different failures was utilized in effecting one purpose. The whole attention and endeavour of the Community came to be concentrated on the solution of one question; and the whole Community rang with one voice.

(4) This movement has called forth all the united strength of the Community. Men and women, old and young, co-operators and non-co-operators, are joined in furthering one national object.

Further success is in the hands of God.